Understanding Judaism and the Jews in the Gospel of John

Understanding Judaism and the Jews in the Gospel of John

Polemic, Tradition, and Johannine Self-Identity

Nathan Thiel

LEXINGTON BOOKS/FORTRESS ACADEMIC
Lanham • Boulder • New York • London

Published by Lexington Books/Fortress Academic
Lexington Books is an imprint of The Rowman & Littlefield Publishing Group, Inc.
4501 Forbes Boulevard, Suite 200, Lanham, Maryland 20706
www.rowman.com

86-90 Paul Street, London EC2A 4NE, United Kingdom

Copyright © 2024 by The Rowman & Littlefield Publishing Group, Inc.

All rights reserved. No part of this book may be reproduced in any form or by any electronic or mechanical means, including information storage and retrieval systems, without written permission from the publisher, except by a reviewer who may quote passages in a review.

British Library Cataloguing in Publication Information Available

Library of Congress Cataloging-in-Publication Data

Names: Thiel, Nathan, 1986- author.
Title: Understanding Judaism and the Jews in the Gospel of John : polemic, tradition, and Johannine self-identity / Nathan Thiel.
Description: Lanham : Lexington Books/Fortress Academic, [2024] | Includes bibliographical references and index. | Summary: "This book shows how the Fourth Gospel's language about "the Jews" is profoundly shaped by its scriptural imagination. It is the product of a self-consciously Jewish author who saw himself as living and writing from within the Jewish tradition"—Provided by publisher.
Identifiers: LCCN 2024030312 (print) | LCCN 2024030313 (ebook) | ISBN 9781978717466 (cloth) | ISBN 9781978717473 (epub)
Subjects: LCSH: Bible. John—Criticism, interpretation, etc. | Jews in the New Testament. | Christianity and other religions—Judaism.
Classification: LCC BS2615.6.J44 T55 2024 (print) | LCC BS2615.6.J44 (ebook) | DDC 226.5/06—dc23/eng/20240823
LC record available at https://lccn.loc.gov/2024030312
LC ebook record available at https://lccn.loc.gov/2024030313

♾️™ The paper used in this publication meets the minimum requirements of American National Standard for Information Sciences—Permanence of Paper for Printed Library Materials, ANSI/NISO Z39.48-1992.

Contents

Acknowledgments	vii
Introduction: To Build Up or to Destroy (or Something in between)? Johannine "Anti-Judaism" in Perspective	1
1 The Johannine Christians and Their Jewish Neighbors: A Tale of Two Religions?	25
2 Referents and Roles: The Johannine Jews as Microcosm	63
3 Mistaking the Word's Own for an Alien People: The Gospel's Dialectic of Division and Jewish Otherness	85
4 Why "the Jews"? Considerations of Setting and Audience	109
5 Like (Fore)fathers Like Sons: The Wandering Israelites and the Johannine Jews	127
Conclusion: John and the Jews in Retrospect	151
Bibliography	157
Index	183
About the Author	187

Acknowledgments

The present book has, in its own way, matured with the growth of my children. Its initial stirrings came nearly two decades ago, when I was an undergraduate student at the University of Wisconsin-Madison. I want to acknowledge Ronald Troxel for introducing me to the world of biblical studies and for his investment in my scholarship when it was still in its infancy.

I have incurred many debts since that time. I want to thank Julian V. Hills, Joshua Ezra Burns, and Deirdre Dempsey for their untiring support and guidance. They have helped shape this work and my own thinking in many ways, both tangible and intangible. As members of a weekly dissertation writing group, Nathan Lunsford, Samantha Miller, and Tim Gabrielson provided invaluable criticism, encouragement, and friendship. I am grateful for colleagues at Marquette, Carroll, and Pepperdine Universities as I continued to refine this project in the intervening years. Special thanks are due to Laura Locke Estes for our many conversations as we passed through Malibu Canyon.

Though my parents and siblings are strangers to the world of academic biblical studies, this book would not have come to fruition without their love and support. Finally, I would like to thank Megan White and the editorial team at Lexington Books for their warm and generous help in preparing the manuscript for publication. I dedicate this book to my wife Kellie and my children Noah, Sylvia, Jubilee, Mercy, and Felix. Much study may weary the mind, and of the making of books there may be no end, but all these and many others to whom I am no less grateful have helped make this project a labor of love.

Introduction

To Build Up or to Destroy (or Something in between)? Johannine "Anti-Judaism" in Perspective

The Gospel of John has many biting things to say about those named "the Jews" (οἱ Ἰουδαῖοι), who appear some seventy times throughout the course of the narrative. As the Gospel's plot unfolds, Jewish hostility steadily rises. Already by John 5, "the Jews" are ready to take Jesus's life. On two occasions, they unsuccessfully attempt to stone him (8:59; 10:31). Jesus, for his part, rebukes the Ἰουδαῖοι for failing to hear his word (8:43), censures them for seeking human praise rather than the approval of God (5:44; 12:43), and, most startling of all, alleges that the devil himself is their father (8:44). The stridency of the Gospel's criticism and its general depiction of the Jews as Jesus's opponents have laid it bare to charges of anti-Jewish bias. Over a century ago, the Jewish scholar Kaufmann Kohler described the Gospel of John as a "gospel of Christian love and Jew hatred."[1] With its piercing concision, Kohler's epigram typifies a line of interpretation that remains strong within Johannine scholarship today.[2] The Gospel has been branded as "trenchantly anti-Jewish," containing an "anti-Jewish polemic of extreme ferocity" that is inherent to the text itself and "not attributable solely to the interpretive tradition."[3]

And yet there is a peculiar ambivalence about the Jews in the Fourth Gospel, so much so that C. K. Barrett could pointedly describe John as "both Jewish and anti-Jewish."[4] Alongside the more infamous utterances, Jesus tells the Samaritan woman in John 4:22 that "salvation is from the Jews" (NRSV), an odd admission from someone who despised the Jewish people.[5] Nowhere does the evangelist hide the tradition that Jesus himself is a Jew who dies as king of the Jews, nor are all Jewish figures in the narrative painted with the same broad, dark brush. Moreover, when the Gospel speaks of hatred, it is all one-directional. The world hates and persecutes Jesus and the disciples. They are never exhorted to hate the world in return.[6] The Gospel gives no counsel to violence or revenge, no glorying in the prospect of others' destruction (as in some of the Dead Sea Scrolls, or even in the Psalms), no hope for enemies' demise. And Jesus does not come to condemn the world but to save it, the sentence of death being the logical consequence of refusing life. In the wider scope of Johannine theology, there is a fundamental incongruity between God's self-offer to humanity and humanity's response. Jesus's command to love one's enemies is not recorded in the Gospel of John; some have thought it alien to its ethics.[7] Yet although never commanded, this is precisely what God does. He loves the people he has created, all the while they reject him out of a love for human glory and fear that their sin will be exposed.[8]

Barrett's paradox draws out the difficulty of making good literary and historical sense of the Gospel's disparate statements about the Jews. At the same time, it pushes us to think more precisely about what we are asking. In what sense is the Fourth Gospel Jewish or anti-Jewish? What, concretely, do we mean by those terms? As in political discourse, labels may both reveal and conceal. They help orient us, but in using them, we also risk flattening out complex realities. When we try to evaluate the Johannine stance toward Jews and Judaism, it is therefore prudent to consider the matter from multiple angles.

A model from the sociology of religion may help us think through this methodological problem and at least some of the angles from which it could be approached. In their work on the formation of sects and cults, Rodney Stark and William Sims Bainbridge devise a system of classification based upon the measurement of social deviance and its expression as tension between a group and the dominant society. They chart social tension along three axes: antagonism, difference, and separation.[9] The index of antagonism measures the attitudes and feelings of a group toward outsiders, including an assessment of their particularism—the conviction that they alone possess the truth. The category of difference signifies tension in behavioral norms between the subculture and the dominant culture. Separation concerns the retreat of the subculture from its social environment and the manifestation of such distance in patterns of social relations. The three dimensions are naturally related. Groups that hold radically different beliefs and engage in practices that depart significantly from societal norms do often self-segregate, encouraging solidarity between members and restricted interaction with outsiders. These measures of social tension, however, do not always coincide. A group that exhibits marked particularism, for example, could conceivably maintain cordial relations with those not belonging to their association. Similarly, while subcultures that score high on the scale of difference would likely also show some measure of separation, the degree and manner of separation may vary, as we see, for example, between Orthodox and (in common parlance) ultra-Orthodox

Jews. What Stark and Bainbridge capture through their model—and what we can confirm through observation—is the complex interaction between belief, practice, and social interaction.[10] If we hope to avoid caricature and distortion, we cannot collapse the dimensions, moving from one to the other without control.

With respect to the Gospel of John, it would be hard to deny that the individual or community responsible for its composition and generative ideas stood in high tension with the surrounding social environment. But what did that tension look like when we view it through a model like Stark and Bainbridge's? If we could measure the evangelist's beliefs through a survey or similar sociological instrument, they would likely rate high on the index of antagonism. The author of the Gospel is, by all appearances, a religious exclusivist.[11] John 3:16 famously declares that God so loved the world that he sent his Son so that whoever believes in him will not perish but have eternal life. Not as famous is the corollary in 3:18 that those who do not believe stand condemned already, the objects of God's wrath (3:36). If Jesus is the source of true life, the alternatives, whatever shape they take, necessarily result in death. For the evangelist, then, Judaism, insofar as it excludes the confession that Jesus is the Messiah and Son of God, must be rejected as a path to salvation. By that measure, the Gospel is also anti-Islamic, anti-Buddhist, anti-atheistic, anti-agnostic; in short, anti-anything that does not share its Christological profession. For some, this very fact will prove a stumbling block. It violates the spirit of inclusiveness and religious pluralism that is so valued today. John, I think, would not have minded. The Jesus he proclaims has no equal. To put matters this way, however, borders on tautology. It amounts to saying that the evangelist took a stand on the exclusivity of Christ. The Gospel is anti-Jewish in the same sense that Judaism is anti-Christian.[12] That it espouses religious exclusivism, while not insignificant, tells us much less than we would like to know.

Indeed, even at the level of attitudes, a marked particularism could carry with it a wide range of emotive and mental states. For example, while the Gospel often speaks against those called "the Jews," is it right to call this hatred? In the first place, we ought to note that many of the so-called negative references do not directly impugn the Jews or their character but rather narrate their opposition to Jesus (5:16; 6:41; 7:1, 13; 8:59; 9:18, among many others). In the second place, although Jesus's words are often confrontational, we must still determine where criticism ends and hatred begins. As a matter of general experience, the two sometimes overlap, or what begins as an attempt at correction shades into outright anger, but they remain conceptually distinct. It matters not only what people say but whether we receive it as criticism from the inside—from those we number as our own—or as attacks from the outside.[13]

It might be promptly countered that the Fourth Gospel's rhetoric is too severe for any distinction between criticism and hatred.[14] After all, how is it possible to charge people with diabolical origins (John 8:44) and not hate them? A full exegesis of this passage must wait until ch. 2, and it should be observed at the outset that Jesus is addressing a particular group of Jews, not indicting the whole nation. But even here, where the verbal fire blazes hottest, at least two possibilities confront us. To the statement, "You are of your father the devil," the intended readers could have subjoined something like the grim petition of Ps 69: "Pour out your wrath on them; let your fierce anger overtake them." Or they could have echoed the sentiment of Ezek 18:32: "For I [God] take no pleasure in the death of anyone . . . Repent and live!"[15] It is hard to describe the first hypothetical response as anything but hatred. The second will strike some as patronizing, but its tenor comes closer to pained lament than to fervent loathing. So, are Jesus's words in John 8 meant to shake his opponents out of their intended course of action—a drastic warning for a drastic situation—or are they meant to incite anger through a pronouncement of condemnation?[16]

Attitudes and convictions, to be sure, are sustained in practice and group interaction, so we must also consider the social implications of the Johannine insistence on Jesus's unique role as revealer and mediator of salvation. What were relations like on the ground? It has been argued, and for a while was almost regarded in Johannine studies as axiomatic, that those behind the production of this enigmatic text formed a closed conventicle, that the incomprehension Jesus meets in the Gospel mirrors the Johannine community's sense of alienation from the surrounding society.[17] Indeed, we might imagine that Jesus's strong words to the Jews could not but manifest themselves as (or reflect) disdain of and separation from contemporary Jews on the part of the evangelist or his intended audience, a straight line running from there to the nightmarish mistreatment of Jews by Christian hands that was to plague later ages.[18] And yet there are currents within the Gospel that suggest a more open stance to the larger society. If God so loved the world to send his own Son, then did he not love the Jewish people to whom the Word made flesh was first sent? And if, in the Gospel, Jesus himself continues to minister among the Jews up to his final days, even dying on their behalf, should it be assumed that the evangelist encourages a sharp break with the Jews of his own place and time? Both the past and present know all too well of Christian agitators against Jews. On the other hand, even today, many Christians who cherish this Gospel and for whom its vision of a world in darkness is very real harbor no animosity toward the Jewish people. They co-exist with them peacefully. They are co-workers, colleagues, and friends.

The question of John and the Jews, then, is more like a bundle of questions, or rather a deeply entangled knot. They are interrelated, but we must try, as much as we are able, to pull on one string at a time.

THE EVANGELIST'S SELF-UNDERSTANDING

No single study could hope to address all of the questions that have been raised thus far, and because we are dealing with the interpretation of ancient texts, not measurable data in a scientific sense, many of those questions elude a confident answer. But the fact that the Gospel, as an act of communication, serves as a medium to encode meaning also makes it, if nothing else, a window onto the beliefs, values, and religious mindset of the author(s). While some may cavil at any instantiation of authorial intention, it remains indispensable for an emic analysis of ancient societies and thus indispensable to the historian of antiquity. If we are to "engage the mindset, values, and category formation of the ancients," and if we are to ask how they understood the world and their place in it, we must accept that the textual artifacts which have been transmitted to us give us some kind of access to their authors, that they mediate meaning which does not spring *ex nihilo* but from human minds.[19]

I do not subscribe, then, to the school of thought that regards the determination of authorial intention as a fallacy, provided that we supply the concept of intention itself with proper nuance. John Farrell, for example, distinguishes between communicative, artistic, and practical intentions.[20] It is one thing to say, as Wimsatt and Beardsley do, that a literary work's artistic merit should be considered apart from the artist's intentions. It is quite another to say that the determination of authorial meaning is irrelevant or a hindrance to the reading of a text.[21] As Farrell states:

> If the words are not chosen, words that convey an intention, then we simply have no reason to see them as having significance or being subject to interpretation. We have no motive for treating them as anything more than physical phenomena, no motive to resolve their ambiguities, for in fact they have none, being mere sounds or marks on paper.[22]

Farrell clarifies, however, that this "does not mean that evidence about intentions outside the text of an utterance must play a key epistemic role in literary interpretation." Rather, the intended meaning is intrinsic to the text as the author's symbolic encoding of his or her communicative intentions.[23]

This study, then, seeks to enter into the evangelist's world of discourse. When he wrote about "the Jews," what did he imagine himself to be doing? What were his operative social and religious categories? What was the evangelist's self-understanding? The argument has long been that the Gospel of John bears the character of an external assault, written in the heat of battle against the synagogue—that the Fourth Gospel witnesses to a community's burgeoning sense of distinctiveness in which belief in Jesus and Jewish identity push against each other. I will argue, in contrast, that the text reflects a different kind of socio-religious tension: that of someone who numbered himself among the Jewish people but who saw faith in Jesus as the necessary expression of faithfulness to the God of Israel. This model of the author's ethno-religious self-conception becomes increasingly intelligible when we observe how the evangelist patterns Jesus's ministry and its reception after narratives in Israel's Scriptures. The evangelist sees himself as living and writing within the Israelite tradition and thus lies closer in *intent* to the prophetic critique of the Hebrew prophets than to the patristic-era denouncement of Jews and Judaism from an ascendant, and predominantly Gentile, church.[24]

This is not to say that the evangelist's self-ascription would have been readily accepted in antiquity. Self-claims about one's identity, then as now, may be accepted or contested by other parties, and that is precisely what we encounter in the narrative of the Fourth Gospel and likely in the author's own experience. If the fourth evangelist did not envision the birth of a new religion in contrast to the Jewish faith, that does not mean his Jewish contemporaries saw matters equally. But the aim of this study is to *understand* the Fourth Gospel and its author and situate them historically, not to adjudicate self-ascriptions that were in dispute in antiquity and the implications of that controversy for Jewish-Christian relations today. It is not to say what the boundaries of Jewish identity or Judaism should have been in the ancient world or whether it is appropriate to say that the Gospel of John stands within or outside of first-century Judaism. It is to say how the relevant ancient actors positioned themselves with respect to Jewish belonging, belief, practice, and identity.[25]

With that caveat in mind, it is nonetheless true that the contours of the present study most closely resemble what has recently been described as the "John within Judaism" stream in Johannine studies. It builds upon the work of James D. G. Dunn, Stephen Motyer, Craig S. Keener, and Wally Cirafesi, among others, who interpret the Fourth Gospel not as an author or community's attempt to distance themselves from Jewish identity itself but as their negotiation with and reinterpretation of what that identity means.[26] As Cirafesi says:

> There is certainly conflict built into John's composition, perhaps even some type of separation at work, but . . . this conflict and separation can be read as occurring between different modes of interpreting Jewishness. In other words, John does not envision a parting of the ways between Jews and those who consider themselves Jews no longer.[27]

In several important ways, then, the argument of this book resides on the opposite end of the spectrum from Adele Reinhartz's thesis in *Cast*

Out of the Covenant.[28] According to Reinhartz, the Gospel of John creates a chasm between belief in Jesus and Jewishness. The Gospel's rhetoric is meant to disaffiliate Christians from the Jewish people by demonizing the Jews as children of the devil. And its indebtedness to Israel's Scriptures and Jewish tradition marks not an admiration for the symbols of Judaism but their expropriation, rhetorically deployed to show that the Jews had been rejected as God's covenant people and that believers in Jesus had now taken their place in God's economy of salvation. The fourth evangelist, says Reinhartz, was not far in perspective from church fathers like Cyril of Alexandria, who were convinced that God's favor had turned away from the Jews to the Gentiles. While I do not think that Reinhartz's framing of the Fourth Gospel's rhetorical program corresponds to its own conception, it helps to set in relief the sweep of interpretive possibilities and their historical analogues. Did the evangelist level his critique of the Jews as someone who had an abiding commitment to them as his own people, or did he fire arrows from the outside, to harm and not build up? Was he a Paul lamenting the fate of his own people, a self-assured church father boasting about their replacement by the Gentiles, a Martin Luther outrageously clamoring for the burning of synagogues and Torah scrolls, or perhaps something else entirely?[29]

THE EVANGELIST'S ETHNIC IDENTITY AS A MATTER OF INFERENCE

It should be acknowledged at this stage that we cannot hope to *prove* the fourth evangelist's ethnic affiliation. Absent the author's disclosure about his ethnic self-concept, we must infer it from the constellation of features in the Gospel. It is by its nature a matter of plausibility, though the same could be said about most results in the field of biblical studies. There are several critical issues, moreover, that we must adequately account for in the process of inference.

First, we must account for the composite nature of the biblical texts. That is, the evangelists had at their disposal a variety of sources and traditions, whether written or oral, which they appropriated and transformed in their own gospels. Source-critical theories of the Fourth Gospel, once a mainstay of Johannine scholarship, are legion. Some of them are relatively reserved. Others are quite complex, hypothesizing multiple layers of editorial activity and textual rearrangement.[30] In the heyday of source criticism, it became common to speak of an anonymous collective responsible for the Gospel's literary development, authors viewed more as compilers of tradition than creative artists in their own right.[31]

But the barriers to speaking in terms of an individual author in a meaningful sense have largely been removed as the popularity of source criticism of the Fourth Gospel has waned. The advent of narrative criticism in Johannine studies facilitated this sea change, along with a string of studies that thoroughly established the Gospel's stylistic unity.[32] The most meticulous of these, and still unsurpassed, is the monograph of Eugen Ruckstuhl and Peter Dschulnigg.[33] Having identified 153 characteristics of the Gospel's style, Ruckstuhl and Dschulnigg group them according to their distinctiveness against other NT and Greco-Roman literature and track their distribution and interrelation from John 1 to 21. The result is a dense network of linguistic features suggestive of a unifying hand.[34] Whatever oral or written sources were at the evangelist's disposal, they were reworked and stamped with his own voice.

The efforts of Ruckstuhl and Dschulnigg, and before them Eduard Schweizer, Joachim Jeremias, and Philippe-H. Menoud, confirm in some measure what D. F. Strauss felt to be true intuitively, that the Gospel is like that seamless garment of which it speaks.[35] Or rather, they show that it is necessary to speak of an evangelist who, if he received into his hands various pieces of cloth, has sewed them together carefully enough that it is now exceedingly difficult to tear them apart and analyze them in their pre-Johannine form. There are, of course literary trouble spots in the Gospel, *aporiae* as they have come to be known in the field.[36] But whatever we make of these disjunctures, they no longer present a compelling argument against a strong individual hand in the Gospel's production. It is not unreasonable to think that an otherwise great storyteller had occasional trouble crafting seamless transitions. Nor is there any inherent improbability that the author came back to his *magnum opus* over a protracted period of time, as Martin Hengel and John Ashton posit.[37]

A second and related issue is that even given a bona fide author responsible for the shape of the text, we must still determine what stems from memory, what from tradition, and what from invention.[38] Let us suppose, for the sake of example, that the evangelist invented Jesus's speeches out of whole cloth.[39] Since many of these discourses presume a good knowledge of contemporary Jewish practice and exegetical technique, it would seem likely that the author was a Jew or had lived in Judea long enough to know the lay of the social land. On the other hand, if the evangelist received these as already formed traditions and put them into his own words, that inference becomes less certain.[40] Yet in the case of the Fourth Gospel, its engagement with Jewish scripture, tradition, and custom extends throughout the text and through its subgenres. It is apparent in both direct discourse and third-person narrative, as well as in the Gospel's many narrative asides. It is again apparent in units of tradition that have parallels in the Synoptic Gospels and in uniquely

Johannine material that bears all of the marks of the evangelist's style and theology. The separation of memory, tradition, and invention, therefore, becomes less pressing for the question at hand.

The Gospel in its various layers and types of material shows familiarity with the people and places of Palestine.[41] It reflects Jewish liturgical and festal traditions that could not simply be inferred from the Scriptures.[42] Its exegetical techniques conform to known Jewish practices and methods.[43] Its use of Scripture is deep, sustained, and multi-faceted.[44] It is why John has sometimes been described as being the most Jewish of the Gospels even as it is, in the judgment of some, the most anti-Jewish.[45] So, if we are to take the evidence on balance, it seems more probable that the author of the Fourth Gospel was born to Jewish parents and had been immersed in Jewish tradition and Scripture than the alternative: that a Gentile author had attained native fluency in the religion and culture of the Jewish people and wrote about Jesus with acute awareness of that context. Few scholars today, then, would contest that the author of the Gospel of John was most likely an ethnic Jew who had been educated in the Jewish Scriptures and way of life.[46] At the very least, since the discovery of the Dead Sea Scrolls and the publication of J. L. Martyn's *History and Theology in the Fourth Gospel,* the burden of proof has shifted to those who would argue otherwise. To what extent John valued or retained that identity as a believer in Jesus, however, constitutes an important locus of the ongoing debate.

METHODOLOGY AND PLAN OF THE WORK

Those attempting to place what Adolf Schlatter once called a "homeless" Gospel in its historical setting have often looked toward a burgeoning conflict between church and synagogue.[47] From the 1970s onward, under the influence of J. Louis Martyn's slim but monumental *History and Theology in the Fourth Gospel,* the model of a conflict between the Johannine community and the synagogue in which they had once been members has become a standard feature of accounts of the Gospel's distinctive ideas, community history, and combative tone.[48] I will explore the synagogue-expulsion theory and Martyn's two-level reading strategy in the next chapter. For reasons that will become clear, I will not take it as a starting point, nor do I assume any specific communal situation in which the Gospel was written or to which it speaks except in general terms. That does not mean the Gospel is left to "timeless, placeless interpretation," only that the time and place to which it belongs fall within a range that is difficult to narrow down with certainty.[49] The story, of course, is set in the late 20s and early 30s in Palestine, even as the prologue stretches back into eternity. The Gospel's destination, on the other hand, is open to informed speculation: written sometime in the first century in the Greek-speaking world, probably in the first place for the benefit of persons who were already believers in Jesus. The argument of this study neither depends upon nor directly refutes the many competing theories that attempt to reconstruct the Johannine community and its history in detail, even as it questions aspects of the synagogue-expulsion hypothesis.

The method I will pursue is primarily historical-critical, though it is informed by other disciplines. It is in part philological, insofar as the appellation οἱ Ἰουδαῖοι in the Fourth Gospel cannot be isolated from its history and usage, despite the occasional insistence that the identity of the Jews in the Gospel of John is best determined by the Gospel alone.[50] It is in part narrative-critical, to the extent that a proper evaluation of the Johannine attitude toward the Jews must begin with a close reading of the Gospel as we have received it. Above all, however, I am interested in the author's socio-historical context and self-understanding within that context. From what we know of other groups of ethnically Jewish believers in Jesus and from the evidence of the Gospel itself, how might a community facing persecution or imagined threat from fellow Jews have responded? And what resources were available to them to make sense of the fact that most Jews of Jesus's time and their own were not of the same mind as they?

I will begin not with a wholesale rejection of the synagogue-expulsion theory but by scrutinizing the corollary that this event triggered onetime Jewish believers in Jesus to relinquish their own identity as Jews. Chapters 2 and 3 will undertake a reevaluation of the identity of the Johannine Jews and their overall image within the Gospel's narrative framework. I will argue that although the fourth evangelist is in no way sanguine about the Jewish response to Jesus, the criticism is not meant to alienate Jesus from "the Jews" or to pit faith in Jesus and Jewish identity against each other as mutually exclusive categories.

Chapters 4 and 5 form the constructive portion of the book, tackling its central question: Is it intelligible for an author who self-identified as a Jew to write about the Jews as the evangelist does, and if so, how? Why does the author of John speak of "the Jews" instead of opting for terms familiar from the Synoptic tradition (Pharisees, scribes, elders, teachers of the law, chief priests)? Chapter 4 considers how the setting and audience of the Gospel may have influenced the evangelist's choice of terminology. The final chapter sets the Gospel's language about the Jews against the backdrop of Israel's Scriptures. John, I suggest, appropriates the desert wandering traditions to frame Jesus's ministry and the controversy it occasioned, imitating the accounts of the Israelites' rebelliousness in order to weave the story of Jesus and his own into the scriptural drama of faith and unbelief. The evangelist, like the tradents of Exodus-2 Kings, is a relentless critic, or nearly so. But such cutting theological assessment had long been part of Israel's counterintuitive way of telling its own history. The evangelist views himself as operating from within that tradition. The Fourth Gospel's criticism of the Jews, therefore, potent as it is, does not compel us to attribute it to an embattled and embittered author (or community) that had disowned the Jewish people.

A NOTE ON THE TRANSLATION OF ἸΟΥΔΑΙΟΣ

Before proceeding to the first chapter, I must take up one more preliminary matter. Any sustained investigation into the Johannine Jews must sooner or later tackle the question of translation, as this is part and parcel of the set of problems that lie before us.[51] For the time being, I will leave the Fourth Gospel to the side, both because its usage is often seen as idiosyncratic and therefore an outlier, and because the translation of the Greek Ἰουδαῖος has become precarious enough even apart from it.[52] The principal question, as the debate has crystallized, is whether to translate Ἰουδαῖος in ancient texts as "Jew" or "Judean," or perhaps transliterate it as *Ioudaios* and so (ostensibly) evade any prejudicial rendering.[53]

The tussle might seem arcane outside the academy, but it is driven by issues of some substance. It is probably no coincidence that the question of translation has come to the fore at this stage in history, as Christians have become more aware of and more sensitive to the dangers of anti-Judaism/anti-Semitism.[54] Indeed, much of the impetus for "Judean" has come on ethical grounds. So, for example, the latest edition of the Bauer-Danker Greek lexicon prefers "Judean" on the rationale that "Jew" is ethically suspect:

> Incalculable harm has been caused by simply glossing I. with "Jew," for many readers or auditors of the Bible translations do not practice the historical judgment necessary to distinguish between circumstances and events of an ancient time and contemporary ethnic-religious-social realities, with the result that anti-Judaism in the modern sense of the term is needlessly fostered through biblical texts.[55]

Because of its gravity, the claim cannot be lightly dismissed. The Bauer-Danker lexicon, however, goes no way toward substantiating it. That the damage caused is said to be incalculable detours us around the specifics of the translation's *Wirkungsgeschichte* ("history of effect"). That is, they offer no concrete example of how the *translation* has unintentionally fostered anti-Judaism. Having read the NT many times before becoming acquainted with the mass of secondary literature, I never supposed that it authorized animosity toward the Jewish people. Nor, in speaking with many acquaintances who know Scripture well, have I witnessed any such transfer. This is anecdotal, of course, but the personal experience raises a question of methodology. To say that the translation "Jews" encourages hostility toward modern Jews, however unintentionally, begs for a standard of measurement.

I am inclined to think that the translation is a surface issue and that eliminating any mention of Jews in the NT would not have any appreciable effects in diminishing hatred of Jews today. Anti-Semitism has not been eradicated in the English-speaking world. But were we to compare the treatment of Jews before the Bible translations of the sixteenth and early seventeenth centuries that gloss Ἰουδαῖοι with "Jews" with their misfortunes in England in the Middle Ages before a vernacular translation was available, relations have improved considerably. The cause of this state of affairs is surely to be found in a conglomeration of social and political factors unrelated to practices in Bible translation. Correlation in this case, as so often, is not causation, nor should it be presumed in the opposite direction. The choice of translation is not to be credited or blamed without good cause.[56]

The reverse side of the ethical argument is that the translation "Judean" runs the risk of severing the ancient from the modern people. Jesus and his disciples are no longer Jews but Judeans and/or Galileans. We are left with a "Jew-free" NT.[57] Of course, this is not the intention of its advocates in the academic realm, who are typically concerned with historical accuracy or fidelity to ancient groups' own sense of self-identity. But an internet search will show its potential for misunderstanding and misuse. In short, against the best intentions of translators, anti-Semites are likely to find their fodder whatever the translation.[58]

The other impetus for "Judean" is more properly historical, though sometimes tethered to concerns about the effect of the text at the popular level. There are several inflections of this common theme. Shaye J. D. Cohen, to take a prominent example, locates a shift in the meaning of Ἰουδαῖος from an ethno-geographic signifier to a more markedly religious or cultural term sometime in the second century BCE, the Maccabean revolt and Hasmonean conversion of the neighboring Idumeans and Itureans being watershed moments in that process. The possibility of Gentile conversion meant a reconceptualization of Jewish identity as a religion.[59] After this point, "Jew" becomes the best translation. Cohen's separation of ethnicity and religion has been criticized as anachronistic or overly compartmentalized.[60] But the notion of a historical and cultural transition in the life of the Jewish people which calls for a shift in English translation informs several other arguments for "Judeans" in a first-century context. "Jews," it has been said, reflects an identity that has been so shaped by the destruction of the temple, failure of the revolts against Rome, the emergence of rabbinic culture and piety, and subsequent historical developments that it is no longer appropriate for first-century Ἰουδαῖοι.[61] Their identity was tied to homeland and temple in a way that their descendants was not. "Judeans" therefore better captures their sense of collective identity.

One of the most cogent critiques of this type of caesura comes, incidentally, from another advocate of the translation "Judean," Steve Mason. Mason's influential essay on the subject is in the first place a justification of the translation "Judean" adopted for some volumes of the Brill Josephus translation and commentary series. Given the article's length, it is almost inevitable that one will find particulars with which to cavil, but I take its central point to be beyond reasonable doubt: Jews of antiquity thought of themselves and were thought of by others to constitute an ἔθνος—a people, a nation. Their counterparts were Egyptians, Syrians, Greeks, Phoenicians, and so forth.[62] Even as Christian heresiologists went some way in attempting to reify Judaism as an outmoded and ossified religious system, many ancient writers, from Origen to the emperor Julian, still knew the Jews as a people, comparable to the other peoples of the world with their customs, patron deities, and ways of life.[63] The Maccabean revolt, the disastrous wars against Rome, and the loss of the Jerusalem cult, momentous as they were, do not mark any radical change in that respect. The Jewish people, like any other with so long a history, experienced the tides of fortune, the fell clutch of chance, the rise and fall of empires.

In some ways, continuity and discontinuity are matters of perspective, but if we were able to survey Jews of, say, the seventh century CE, I imagine that they would have felt no yawning gap, no decisive break between themselves and their ancestors.[64] True, patterns of worship had evolved. The Jewish people had to accommodate themselves to new political arrangements, but this had already been happening long before, and much continued as it had, particularly for those who had already been living in the diaspora for some time. For those cultural indicia which underwent change or faded out over time, there were others (circumcision of male children, dietary practices, synagogue services, and celebration of holidays, for example) that persisted and persist to this day. And, above all, the Jewish people have looked and continue to look upon the ancient Ἰουδαῖοι as their forebears, despite the changes that inevitably accompany several millennia of human history. At the risk of overstatement, the call to reserve "Jew" for the post-Second Temple period would be as if someone decided that we needed new names as we matured into adults, since our childhood selves were so unlike what we had become. As individuals, we have an unbroken sense of self from very early on in our development, and the same is true for many communities. If "Judean" is to be preferred, I suggest this ought to be done on Mason's grounds, that is, as a way to engage the categories of the ancients, to enter into their world of thought and discourse, not as a way to accentuate the historical distance between ancient and modern Jews. Mason, as he has clarified, in no way intends to drive a wedge between them.[65]

I am not ready to follow suit, however, not because of any fault in Mason's historical analysis but because of the resonances of "Judean" in English. Scanning any number of dictionaries, we find that "Judean" means a native or inhabitant of the land of Judea.[66] So if a non-Jew living outside of Judea were to resettle and raise children in Jerusalem, they would be Judeans. But if, say, a first-century Thracian couple had made the long trek to Judea and had children there, neither they nor their offspring would be Ἰουδαῖοι unless they underwent circumcision and adopted the Jewish way of life. As far as I know, nowhere in ancient literature is a non-Jewish resident in Judea named a Ἰουδαῖος.[67] In that sense, it is not coterminous with our "Judean."[68] In English, to be a Judean is not to be a member of a certain people but to live in a certain place; to be a Ἰουδαῖος in the ancient world was to be a member of a people with a homeland in a certain place. Mason, of course, is well aware that Ἰουδαῖος is not strictly geographical and of the fact that many Ἰουδαῖοι lived far afield from the province of Judea and had done so for generations. The reader of his commentaries will quickly realize this when he or she comes across Judeans in Antioch, or Alexandria, or Rome. In context, there is little risk of confusion, but it requires some stretching of English usage.

Now it must be conceded that "Egyptians" (Αἰγύπτιοι), "Syrians" (Σύροι), and other ethnonyms often fall prey to the same misunderstanding, as we tend to employ them loosely for any inhabitant of those lands, whereas ancient authors differentiated between Αἰγύπτιοι, for example, and the other ethnic communities living in Egypt. A similar imprecision happens often enough in contemporary discourse. While we might speak of Turkish Kurds without much thought, the expression would probably irritate a good number of Turks and Kurds themselves, who in their respective languages speak rather of Kurds in Turkey. If we tolerate the ambiguity in other cases, perhaps the same may be allowed for "Judean."

Nonetheless, it seems to me that "Jew" captures the complexities of ancient Jewish identity just as well without having to massage English usage. Although many may think predominantly in terms of religious categories, today "Jew" remains both a religious marker and more than that. It is membership in a people, a culture, and a belief system all intermingled and configured in different ways by Jewish communities and individuals.[69] For as much as Jewish identity and religion have been intertwined historically, and for as much as non-Jews might think first of Jewish religious distinctives, there are today many Jewish secularists, whose identity as Jews is not in question. And though their claims are often challenged, there are people (few in number, to be sure) who profess a Jewish identity but also believe that Jesus is the Messiah and Son of God. One can convert to Judaism. They did so also in antiquity, conceptualized then as the transference to a new people, not unlike an adoption. In practice, this all gets incredibly complicated because Jews (and non-Jews) differ in the stress placed on each aspect of identity.[70] Yet for its overlap with the modern category of religion, Jewish identity is not reducible to that category. In that respect, the first century is not far from the twenty-first.

In objection, it might be argued that "Jew" obscures the relationship between people and ancestral homeland that is inherent in the Greek, Aramaic, and Hebrew. Philip F. Esler holds that since territory and people were so commonly associated in the ancient Mediterranean world, "to translate Ἰουδαῖοι with a word such as 'Jews' in this context therefore represents a particularly blatant type of exceptionalist argument that is probably reason enough to reject it."[71] It is likely fair to say that to the native English speaker, "Judean" will more readily evoke the territory of Judea than does "Jew," but it is easy to press the point too strongly. It is not as if "Jew" has lost all aural resonance with "Judea." We have lost a "d" in the process of transmission from Latin through Old French to English, one that survives in other European languages. Surely such a small elision cannot be of so great a consequence.

"Jew" *is* the organic progression of the ancient term into English, attested several centuries before "Judean." No one had to argue for it. No conscious differentiation was made in the course of the history of the English language to set it off from other ethnonyms. And if the link between the people and the land of their ancestors has been occluded, it seems to me that this is more a result of the antiquity of the Jewish diaspora than of translation. That is, when Jews had been living away from Judea for many centuries, the immediate association with the land was probably dampened, though we must always ask in whose eyes. Many Jews still lived in Judea after the wars with Rome, even if they were banned from Jerusalem for over two centuries, and those in the diaspora continued to commemorate their people's past, which of course meant memories of Jerusalem and Judea as the ancestral homeland. For the person who has a rudimentary grasp of Jewish history, the relationship between "Jew" and "Judea" will not be lost. I am not entirely averse to "Judean," then, if adopted for the sake of historical consciousness, but on the whole, I see no reason to jettison the more traditional "Jew." We shall see in due course if the Fourth Gospel requires a different approach.

NOTES

1. Kaufmann Kohler, "New Testament," *JE* 9:251.
2. A position exemplified by Rudolf Bultmann, for whom the Johannine Jews are the representatives of unbelief and the foils to Christian faith. See especially Rudolf

Bultmann, *The Gospel of John: A Commentary*, trans. G. R. Beasley-Murray (Philadelphia: Westminster, 1971 [orig. 1941]), 86–87.

3. The respective quotations are from R. Alan Culpepper, "Anti-Judaism in the Fourth Gospel as a Theological Problem for Christian Interpreters," in *Anti-Judaism and the Fourth Gospel*, ed. Reimund Bieringer, Didier Pollefeyt, and Frederique Vandecasteele-Vanneuville (Louisville: Westminster John Knox, 2001), 81; Alan F. Segal, *Two Powers in Heaven: Early Rabbinic Reports about Christianity and Gnosticism*, SJLA 25 (Leiden: Brill, 1977), 217; Adele Reinhartz, "'Jews' and Jews in the Fourth Gospel," in *Anti-Judaism and the Fourth Gospel*, 214.

4. C. K. Barrett, *The Gospel of John and Judaism*, trans. D. Moody Smith (Philadelphia: Fortress, 1975), 72.

5. So James D. G. Dunn, "The Question of Anti-Semitism in the New Testament Writings of the Period," in *Jews and Christians: The Parting of the Ways AD 70 to 135*, ed. James D. G. Dunn, WUNT 66 (Tübingen: Mohr Siebeck, 1992), 197.

6. So also, Martinus C. de Boer, "The Depiction of 'the Jews' in John's Gospel: Matters of Behavior and Identity," in *Anti-Judaism and the Fourth Gospel*, 143–44; Jan van der Watt and Jacobus Kok, "Violence in a Gospel of Love," in *Coping with Violence in the New Testament*, ed. Pieter de Villiers and Jan Willem van Henten, Studies in Theology and Religion 16 (Leiden: Brill, 2012), 163–83; Jan van der Watt, "'Is Jesus the King of Israel?': Reflections on the Jewish Nature of the Gospel of John," in *John and Judaism: A Contested Relationship in Context*, ed. R. Alan Culpepper and Paul N. Anderson, RBS 87 (Atlanta: SBL Press, 2017), 39–56, at 52–53.

7. A position well summed up by Ernst Käsemann (*The Testament of Jesus: A Study of the Gospel of John in Light of Chapter 17*, trans. Gerhard Krodel [Philadelphia: Fortress, 1968], 59–60) who states forthrightly that Jesus in the Fourth Gospel does not love the world. Love for the brothers does not even encompass love for one's neighbor but is restricted to the community of believers.

8. Along these lines are the studies of Enno Edzard Popkes, *Die Theologie der Liebe Gottes in den johanneischen Schriften: Zur Semantik der Liebe und zum Motivkreis des Dualismus*, WUNT 2/197 (Tübingen: Mohr Siebeck, 2005); Francis J. Moloney, *Love in the Gospel of John: An Exegetical, Theological, and Literary Study* (Grand Rapids: Baker Academic, 2013).

9. Rodney Stark and William Sims Bainbridge, *The Future of Religion: Secularization, Revival, and Cult Formation* (Berkeley: University of California Press, 1985), 49–62.

10. Another way to express this is to observe that deviance is not only behavioral but also cognitive. That is, ideas, beliefs, and attitudes can depart from the norms of a reference group just as behaviors can. See, for example, Robin D. Perrin, "Cognitive Deviance: Unconventional Beliefs," in *The Handbook of Deviance*, ed. Erich Goode (Malden, MA: Wiley Blackwell, 2015), 401–21; Erich Goode, *Deviant Behavior*, 12th ed. (New York: Routledge, 2019), 266–97. Deviant behaviors and beliefs, in turn, may elicit a wide range of societal reactions and counter-reactions that manifest themselves in diverse patterns of social interaction.

11. This much seems abundantly clear from the Gospel, but see also Miroslav Volf, "Johannine Dualism and Contemporary Pluralism," in *The Gospel of John and*

Christian Theology, ed. Richard Bauckham and Carl Mosser (Grand Rapids: Eerdmans, 2008), 19–50.

12. So also John Ashton, *The Gospel of John and Christian Origins* (Minneapolis: Fortress, 2014), 3, n. 2.

13. This phenomenon is known as the intergroup sensitivity effect. Members of a group tend to react to criticism from those within the group less defensively than if it comes from outsiders. See, for example, Matthew J. Hornsey, Tina Oppes, and Alicia Svensson, "'It's OK if We Say It, but You Can't': Responses to Intergroup and Intragroup Criticism," *European Journal of Social Psychology* 32 (2002): 293–307; Matthew J. Hornsey and Armin Imani, "Criticizing Groups from the Inside and the Outside: An Identity Perspective on the Intergroup Sensitivity Effect," *Personality and Social Psychology Bulletin* 30 (2004): 365–83. Matthew J. Hornsey, "Kernel of Truth or Motivated Stereotype? Interpreting and Responding to Negative Generalizations About Your Group," in *Stereotype Dynamics: Language-Based Approaches to the Formation, Maintenance, and Transformation of Stereotypes*, ed. Yoshihisa Kashima, Klaus Fiedler, and Peter Freytag (New York: Lawrence Erlbaum Associates, 2008), 317–38; Robbie M. Sutton, Tracey J. Elder, and Karen M. Douglas, "Reactions to Internal and External Criticism of Outgroups: Social Convention in the Intergroup Sensitivity Effect," *Personality and Social Psychology Bulletin* 32 (2006): 563–75.

14. As John Ashton (*Understanding the Fourth Gospel*, 2nd ed. [Oxford: Oxford University Press, 2007], 64) has memorably put it in response to Hartwig Thyen's statement that the Gospel is stamped with a deeply ambivalent love-hate relationship toward Judaism: "Even if we ignore the easy substitution of the ambiguous word *Judentum* ('Judaism'/'Jewry') for John's specific οἱ Ἰουδαῖοι, there remains the clear implication that the evangelist was somehow torn between love and hatred (*Haß/Liebe*) in his feelings towards those he thus names; whereas in fact there is no love and little sympathy, only hostility tinged with fear." The retort is to Hartwig Thyen, "'Das Heil kommt von den Juden,'" in *Kirche: Festschrift für Günther Bornkamm zum 75. Geburtstag*, ed. Dieter Lührmann and Georg Strecker (Tübingen: Mohr Siebeck, 1980).

15. This is not to say that the intended readers of the Gospel necessarily knew these passages, only that there is a range of possible emotional and intellectual responses to Jesus's words in John 8. It should also be observed that in this passage Jesus speaks of a particular group of Jews, not of the Jewish people generally.

16. Indeed, there is a strong current within the Christian tradition that differentiates between a person's actions, which may be reprehensible and need to be called out as such, and the person him- or herself who has inherent dignity as someone made in the image of God. The command to love one's enemies in the Synoptic tradition and in Paul embodies a similar ethical stance.

17. So, Wayne A. Meeks, "The Man from Heaven in Johannine Sectarianism," *JBL* 91 (1972): 44–72.

18. Among those who regard the Fourth Gospel as an irredeemably anti-Jewish text are Rosemary Radford Ruether (*Faith and Fratricide: The Theological Roots of Anti-Semitism* [New York: Seabury, 1974], 111–16) and the Jewish social scientist Micha Brumlik ("Johannes: Das judenfeindliche Evangelium," in *Teufelskinder oder*

Heilsbringer: Die Juden im Johannes-Evangelium, ed. Dietrich Neuhaus, 2nd ed., Arnoldshainer Texte 64 [Frankfurt am Main: Haag & Herchen, 1993], 6–21).

19. The quote is from Steve Mason, "Jews, Judaeans, Judaizing, Judaism: Problems of Categorization in Ancient History," *JSJ* 38 (2007): 457–512, at 458.

20. John Farrell, *The Varieties of Authorial Intention: Literary Theory Beyond the Intentional Fallacy* (Cham: Palgrave Macmillan, 2017).

21. It should be noted that Wimsatt and Beardsley's famous essay on the intentional fallacy ("The Intentional Fallacy," *Sewanee Review* 54 [1946]: 468–88) was concerned with the standard of literary judgment of poetry. It was not a programmatic statement about a speaker or author's intention in ordinary acts of communication. Not only so, but Wimsatt and Beardsley do not deny that an author's intention can be inferred from a poem. What they object to are appeals to authorial intentions which cannot be detected from the poem itself. See Farrell, *Varieties of Authorial Intention*, 41–43.

As a pragmatic matter, we communicate with others to express meaning because we want to be understood and believe others have the capacity to understand what we mean. And as hearers, we naturally assume a communicative intention. We assume that the sounds and symbols coming from the communicator are meant to tell us something. They are the vehicles for the speaker or writer to convey meaning.

22. Farrell, *Varieties of Authorial Intention*, 31. See also within biblical studies, Ben F. Meyer, *Critical Realism and the New Testament* (Allison Park, PA: Pickwick, 1989), 17–56; Jonathan Bernier, *Aposynagōgos and the Historical Jesus in John: Rethinking the Historicity of the Johannine Expulsion Passages*, BibInt 122 (Leiden: Brill, 2013), 25; Wally Cirafesi, *John Within Judaism: Religion, Ethnicity, and the Shaping of Jesus-Oriented Jewishness in the Fourth Gospel*, AJEC 112 (Leiden: Brill, 2021), 3–5. As a matter of general observation, the field of biblical studies would be hollowed out if we were barred from questions like: "What did the author or authors mean? What were the historical and social forces that shaped the author's thought? Why did the author or authors choose to communicate in this way? What was the author trying to achieve?"

23. Similarly, Mark Allan Powell ("Narrative Criticism: The Emergence of a Prominent Reading Strategy," in *Mark as Story: Retrospect and Prospect*, RBS 65 [Atlanta: SBL Press, 2011], 19–44, at 27) states: "A significant distinction may be drawn, however, between imposing an extraneous notion of authorial intent upon a narrative and deriving an intrinsic notion of authorial intent from a narrative."

24. It might be argued that what matters is the effect of the act of communication on others, and that the author's intention is therefore not worthy of serious study. Such a position, however, represents a value judgment that lies outside the realm of historical analysis. It is effectively a moral claim that may be supported or contested on philosophical, social, and political grounds.

25. Similarly, Christine Hayes, "Paul 'Within Judaism,'" *Ancient Jew Review*, https://www.ancientjewreview.com/read/responding-to-paul-within-judaism, Sept. 14, 2022.

26. James D. G. Dunn, "The Embarrassment of History: Reflections on the Problem of 'Anti-Judaism' in the Fourth Gospel," in *Anti-Judaism and the Fourth*

Gospel, 41–60; idem, *The Partings of the Ways between Christianity and Judaism and their Significance for the Character of Christianity*, 2nd ed. (London: SCM, 2006), 206–14; Motyer, *Your Father the Devil? A New Approach to John and "the Jews*,*"* Paternoster Biblical and Theological Studies (Carlisle: Paternoster, 1997); idem, "The Fourth Gospel and the Salvation of Israel: An Appeal for a New Start," in *Anti-Judaism and the Fourth Gospel*, 83–100; idem, "Bridging the Gap: How Might the Fourth Gospel Help Us Cope with the Legacy of Christianity's Exclusive Claim over against Judaism?" in *The Gospel of John and Christian Theology*, 143–67; Craig S. Keener, *The Gospel of John: A Commentary*, 2 vols. (Peabody, MA: Hendrickson, 2003); Cirafesi, *John Within Judaism*. See also Christopher M. Blumhofer, *The Gospel of John and the Future of Israel*, SNTSMS 177 (Cambridge: Cambridge University Press, 2019); Christopher A. Porter, *Johannine Social Identity Formation after the Fall of the Jerusalem Temple: Negotiating Identity in Crisis*, BibInt 194 (Leiden: Brill, 2022); Andrew J. Byers, *John and the Others: Jewish Relations, Christian Origins, and the Sectarian Hermeneutic* (Waco, TX: Baylor University Press, 2021); Stewart Penwell, *Jesus the Samaritan: Ethnic Labeling in the Gospel of John*, BibInt 170 (Leiden: Brill, 2019); Jan van der Watt, "'Is Jesus the King of Israel?'"

27. Cirafesi, *John Within Judaism*, 279. By focusing upon the Gospel in its relation to Jews and Judaism, I do not mean to isolate it from other religious and social currents in the Greco-Roman world nor to deny the mutual influence of Greek and Jewish cultures in the Hellenistic era. Indeed, the religious outlook of the Fourth Gospel has much in common with developments that Jonathan Z. Smith has discerned in the diasporic expression of native religions in the Hellenistic era. In particular, the Fourth Gospel appears to detach proper worship of God from land and cultic site (4:23-24) and has a decided emphasis on the salvation of the individual from a world under the power of sin. See Jonathan Z. Smith, "Birth Upside Down or Right Side Up?" *HR* 9 (1970): 281–303; idem, "Native Cults in the Hellenistic Period," *HR* 11 (1971): 236–49. Helmut Koester (*History, Culture, and Religion of the Hellenistic Age*, vol. 1 of *Introduction to the New Testament*, 2nd ed. [Berlin: de Gruyter, 1995], 148–96) chronicles this persistence and change in Hellenistic-era religion with an eye specifically to the historical context of the NT. Nevertheless, as these concerns do not directly impinge upon the nature of the Gospel's polemic or the fourth evangelist's ethnic self-identification, they fall outside the scope of the present study. To the extent that the Gospel participates in these wider religious phenomena, it does so always with reference to Israel's Scriptures and Jewish tradition.

28. Adele Reinhartz, *Cast Out of the Covenant: Jews and Anti-Judaism in the Gospel of John* (Lanham, MD: Lexington Books/Fortress Academic, 2018). See also Jonathan Numada, *John and Anti-Judaism: Reading the Gospel in Light of Greco-Roman Culture*, McMaster Biblical Studies Series 7 (Eugene, OR: Pickwick, 2021). Numada's analysis is more reserved than Reinhartz's, but he too sees in the Gospel of John a socio-rhetorical program of disaffiliation from Jewish identity. John reduces the normative fit of Jewish social identity to reduce its salience for the Johannine audience, replacing an ethnic identity with a "Christologically centered social identity" (23-30, at 30). "The Jews," in this reading, serve as representatives of unbelief.

29. As Luther advises in the notorious *On the Jews and Their Lies* (1543).

30. Although Rudolf Bultmann only proposed three main written sources for the Gospel of John, his commentary is a prime example of the tendency to divide and rearrange the text as it has been received. D. Moody Smith devoted a book to sorting out Bultmann's method and textual decisions: *The Composition and Order of the Fourth Gospel: Bultmann's Literary Theory*, Yale Publications in Religion 10 (New Haven: Yale University Press, 1965). Another fine example is F. R. Hoare, *The Original Order and Chapters of St. John's Gospel* (London: Burns, Oates & Washbourne, 1944), whose theories of displacement are ingenious but implausible. A more recent work within this tradition is M.-E. Boismard and A. Lamouille, *Un évangile préjohannique*, EBib 17, 3 vols. (Paris: Gabalda, 1993).

31. The development is traced by Richard A. Burridge, *What Are the Gospels? A Comparison with Graeco-Roman Biography*, 2nd ed. (Grand Rapids: Eerdmans, 2004), 3–24.

32. The emergence of narrative-critical approaches to the Fourth Gospel is most often associated with R. Alan Culpepper's *Anatomy of the Fourth Gospel: A Study in Literary Design*, FF (Philadelphia: Fortress, 1983). That is not to say that earlier scholars showed no interest in the Gospel as a work of literature. See Mark Stibbe, ed., *The Gospel of John as Literature: An Anthology of Twentieth-Century Perspectives*, NTTS 17 (Leiden: Brill, 1993).

33. Eugen Ruckstuhl and Peter Dschulnigg, *Stilkritik und Verfasserfrage im Johannesevangelium: Die johanneischen Sprachmerkmale auf dem Hintergrund des Neuen Testaments und des zeitgenössischen hellenistischen Schrifttums*, NTOA 17 (Göttingen: Vandenhoeck & Ruprecht, 1991). The book expands upon Ruckstuhl's earlier study *Die literarische Einheit des Johannesevangeliums: Der gegenwärtige Stand der einschlägigen Forschungen*, Studia Friburgensia 2/3 (Freiburg: Paulusverlag, 1951).

34. As D. A. Carson has argued in his review of Ruckstuhl and Dschulnigg's book (*JBL* 113 [1994]: 151–52), the stylistic arguments do not in themselves invalidate source- and redaction-critical theories. However, whoever intends to substantiate their theories of literary development via differences in style between compositional layers faces a momentous challenge. It is interesting to note, in this respect, that Tom Felton and Tom Thatcher ("Stylometry and the Signs Gospel," in *Jesus in Johannine Tradition*, ed. Robert T. Fortna and Tom Thatcher [Louisville: Westminster John Knox, 2001], 209–18) largely pass over Ruckstuhl and Dschulnigg's work when trying to prove that the hypothesized Signs Source has a distinct style of its own.

35. Schweizer, *Ego eimi: Die religionsgeschichtliche Herkunft und theologische Bedeutung der johanneischen Bildreden, zugleich ein Beitrag zur Quellenfrage des vierten Evangeliums*, FRLANT 2/38 (Göttingen: Vandenhoeck & Ruprecht, 1939); Jeremias, "Johanneische Literarkritik," *TBl* 20 (1941): 33–46; Menoud, *L'Évangile de Jean d'après les recherches récentes*, 2nd ed., CahT 3 (Neuchatel: Delachaux & Niestlé, 1947).

36. Known as such at least since the articles of Eduard Schwartz, "Aporien im vierten Evangelium," *Nachrichten von der königlichen Gesellschaft der Wissenschaften zu Göttingen* 63 (1907): 342–72; 64 (1908): 115–48, 149–88, 497–650.

37. Martin Hengel, *The Johannine Question*, trans. J. Bowden (London: SCM, 1989); Ashton, *Understanding*.

38. At the very least, the author of the Fourth Gospel knew of Synoptic-like traditions and sayings, as C. H. Dodd sought to show in *Historical Tradition in the Fourth Gospel* (Cambridge: Cambridge University Press, 1963). The sorting out of memory, tradition, and invention and the implications of that task for the historical reliability of the Fourth Gospel continue to occupy scholars in the field. This is evident in the work of the John, Jesus, and History Group of the Society of Biblical Literature, which resulted in three books: Paul N. Anderson, Felix Just, S. J., and Tom Thatcher, eds., *Critical Appraisals of Critical Views*, vol. 1 of *John, Jesus, and History*, SymS 44 (Atlanta: Society of Biblical Literature, 2007), *Aspects of Historicity in the Fourth Gospel*, vol. 2 of *John, Jesus, and History*, ECL 2 (Atlanta: Society of Biblical Literature, 2009), and *Glimpses of Jesus through the Johannine Lens*, vol. 3 of *John, Jesus, and History*, ECL 18 (Atlanta: SBL Press, 2016).

39. This is not a position I take, but it more forcefully illustrates the problem.

40. Bultmann hypothesized a written "Revelation Discourse Source" (*Offenbarungsredenquelle*) which lay behind Jesus's extended speeches in the Fourth Gospel. This was one aspect of Bultmann's source-critical theory that never gained much traction.

41. This will be considered in ch. 4.

42. This is especially true of the water-drawing and candle-lighting rituals associated with the Feast of Tabernacles, which serve as points of contact in Jesus's speeches in John 7–8.

43. As aptly illustrated, for example, by Catrin H. Williams, "John, Judaism, and 'Searching the Scriptures,'" in *John and Judaism*, 77–100. For a more extensive case study in Johannine exegesis, see Peder Borgen, *Bread from Heaven: An Exegetical Study of the Concept of Manna in the Gospel of John and the Writings of Philo*, NovTSup 10 (Leiden: Brill, 1965).

44. There is also the question of a Semitic coloring in the language of the Gospel. In past generations, some even argued that the Gospel was originally composed in Aramaic. See C. F. Burney, *The Aramaic Origin of the Fourth Gospel* (Oxford: Clarendon, 1922). Burney's thesis has not won wide support, but a certain Semitic influence on Johannine style seems unmistakable.

45. The Jewish character of the Gospel of John is one of J. L. Martyn's fundamental insights in *History and Theology in the Fourth Gospel*. The book first appeared in 1968 but has gone through several editions. See Martyn, *History and Theology in the Fourth Gospel*, 3rd ed., NTL (Louisville: Westminster John Knox, 2003). It is why, besides his identification of the Johannine synagogue expulsion with the rabbinic "Blessing of the Heretics," he regarded the history of the Johannine community as a chapter in the history of Jewish Christianity. Even someone like Reinhartz, who believes that the Gospel is anti-Jewish in intent and effect, acknowledges that "the Gospel of John reflects deep and broad knowledge of Jerusalem, Jewish practice, and methods of biblical interpretation." Adele Reinhartz, "The Gospel according to John," in *The Jewish Annotated New Testament*, ed. Amy-Jill Levine and Marc Zvi Brettler (Oxford: Oxford University Press, 2011), 152–96, at 153–54. In *Cast Out of*

the Covenant, as well, Reinhartz imagines the Gospel's implied author as a Greek-speaking Jew from Asia Minor who had "absorbed not only the knowledge that is common to Jews of his time and place, but also a Jewish way of seeing the world" (*Cast Out*, xxix), but who no longer identified as a Jew.

46. To be sure, some scholars will only speak of an implied author. While the construct of an implied author has its hermeneutical advantages, given the non-fictional character of the Gospels, I will not hesitate to speak of a real flesh-and-blood author who penned the Gospel of John. On the potential for and necessity of co-operation between narrative and historical criticism, see the vigorous arguments of Petri Merenlahti and Raimo Hakola, "Reconceiving Narrative Criticism," in *Characterization in the Gospels: Reconceiving Narrative Criticism*, ed. David Rhoads and Kari Syreeni, JSNTSup 184 (Sheffield: Sheffield Academic Press, 1999), 13–48. They state (p. 34): "In light of the Gospels themselves and the way most readers read them, critical attempts to analyze the Gospels as narrative communication should not restrict readers' interests to the exclusive storyworlds of the Gospels."

At a minimum, the actual author of the Fourth Gospel (1) lived in the first-century Mediterranean, (2) knew the Greek language, (3) believed that Jesus was the Messiah, and (4) had a working knowledge of Jewish beliefs, practices, and traditions.

47. Adolf Schlatter, *Die Sprache und Heimat des vierten Evangelisten*, BFCT 4 (Gütersloh: Bertelsmann, 1902), 7.

48. The hypothesis that the Fourth Gospel was composed in a setting of conflict between church and synagogue has a much longer history. Already Moritz von Aberle, "Über die Zweck des Johannesevangeliums," *TQ* 42 (1861): 37–94; Carl Weizsäcker, *Untersuchungen über die evangelische Geschichte: Ihre Quellen und den Gang ihrer Entwicklung*, 2nd ed. (Tübingen: Mohr Siebeck, 1901); Wilhelm Wrede, *Charakter und Tendenz des Johannesevangeliums* (Tübingen: Mohr Siebeck, 1903).

49. I have taken the quoted phrase from J. Louis Martyn, "The Johannine Community among Jewish and Other Early Christian Communities," in *What We Have Heard from the Beginning: The Past, Present, and Future of Johannine Studies*, ed. Tom Thatcher (Waco, TX: Baylor University Press, 2007), 184. I do not intend here to criticize Martyn, for in context he is reflecting upon the tendency among some earlier exegetes to downplay the historical and social context of the Gospel, but it is worth noting at the outset the problem of historical specificity.

50. So Gérald Caron, *Qui sont les Juifs de l'Évangile de Jean?* Recherches 35 (Saint-Laurent, QC: Bellarmin, 1997).

51. Many of the considerations outlined in what follows parallel the treatment of the debate by Jason A. Staples, *The Idea of Israel in Second Temple Judaism: A New Theory of People, Exile, and Israelite Identity* (Cambridge: Cambridge University Press, 2022), 11–20.

52. Important contributions to the question of translation include Shaye J. D. Cohen, *The Beginnings of Jewishness: Boundaries, Varieties, Uncertainties*, Hellenistic Culture and Society 31 (Berkeley: University of California Press, 1999); Philip F. Esler, *Conflict and Identity in Romans: The Social Setting of Paul's Letter* (Minneapolis: Fortress, 2003), 40–76; Mason, "Jews, Judaeans, Judaizing," 457–512; Daniel

R. Schwartz, "'Judaean' or 'Jew'? How Should We Translate *Ioudaios* in Josephus?" in *Jewish Identity in the Greco-Roman World/Jüdische Identität in der griechischrömischen Welt*, ed. Jörg Frey, Daniel R. Schwartz, and Stephanie Gripentrog, AGJU 71 (Leiden: Brill, 2007), 3–27; idem, *Judeans and Jews: Four Faces of Dichotomy in Ancient Jewish History* (Toronto: University of Toronto Press, 2014), 3–10; David M. Miller, "Ethnicity, Religion and the Meaning of *Ioudaios* in Ancient 'Judaism,'" *CBR* 12 (2014): 216–65. The matter is far from settled, as Adele Reinhartz's contribution to *Marginalia* ("The Vanishing Jews of Antiquity," http://marginalia.lareviewofbooks.org/vanishing-jews-antiquity-adele-reinhartz/, June 24, 2014) and the ensuing debate that it sparked would indicate.

53. Another option proposed for the Gospel of John is to place "Jews" in quotation marks, signaling to the reader that what the Fourth Gospel means by it is not typical.

54. Although sometimes used interchangeably, there has been a move among some theologians to differentiate between anti-Judaism as a theological stance and anti-Semitism as hatred of the Jewish people, the latter at times more narrowly defined as the product of modern racial ideologies. See Edward H. Flannery, "Anti-Judaism and Anti-Semitism: A Necessary Distinction," *JES* 10 (1973): 581–88; Robert Morgan, "Susannah Heschel's Aryan Grundmann," *JSNT* 32 (2010): 439–46. Not all find the distinction germane, however. So, for example, Susannah Heschel in response to Morgan ("Historiography of Antisemitism versus Anti-Judaism: A Response to Robert Morgan," *JSNT* 33 (2011): 258–60.

55. BDAG, 478; similarly, Malcolm Lowe, "Who Were the Ἰουδαῖοι?" *NovT* 18 (1976): 130; Esler (*Conflict and Identity*, 68) questions the morality of the translation "Jews" but on the grounds that it does not honor the memory of ancient Ἰουδαῖοι in a way that accords with their own sense of self.

56. Similarly, Jonathan Klawans, "An Invented Revolution," *Marginalia*, http://marginalia.lareviewofbooks.org/invented-revolution-jonathan-klawans/, Aug. 26, 2014.

57. So Amy-Jill Levine, *The Misunderstood Jew: The Church and the Scandal of the Jewish Jesus* (San Francisco: HarperOne, 2006), 160.

58. So also Klawans, "Invented Revolution."

59. Cohen (*Beginnings of Jewishness*, 340) argues that "religion overcame ethnicity," though an ethnic component to the term did not fade out entirely.

60. See, among others, Esler, *Conflict and Identity*, 73–74; Mason, "Jews, Judaeans, Judaizing," 494–95, 505–6; Seth Schwartz, "How Many Judaisms Were There? A Critique of Neusner and Smith on Definition and Mason and Boyarin on Categorization," *Journal of Ancient Judaism* (2011): 208–38.

61. Among others, Bruce J. Malina and Richard L. Rohrbaugh, *Social-Science Commentary on the Gospel of John* (Minneapolis: Fortress, 1998), 44–46; Esler, *Conflict and Identity*, 63–67; John H. Elliott, "Jesus the Israelite Was Neither a 'Jew' nor a 'Christian': On Correcting Misleading Nomenclature," *JSHJ* 5 (2007): 119–54.

62. So too Philip F. Esler, "Judean Ethnic Identity in Josephus' *Against Apion*," in *A Wandering Galilean: Essays in Honour of Seán Freyne*, ed. Zuleika Rodgers,

Margaret Daly-Denton, and Anne Fitzpatrick McKinley, JSJSup 132 (Leiden: Brill, 2009), 73–91.

63. Mason, "Jews, Judaeans, Judaizing," 489–510.

64. Similarly, Klawans, "Invented Revolution." By analogy, English society today might be said to be shaped more by the events of the twentieth century than those, say, of the sixteenth, but, as far as I can tell, no one is arguing for a change in nomenclature.

65. Steve Mason, "Ancient Jews or Judeans? Different Questions, Different Answers," *Marginalia*, http://marginalia.lareviewofbooks.org/ancient-jews-judeans-different-questions-different-answers-steve-mason/, Aug. 26, 2014.

66. So, for instance, *OED*, s.v. "Judaean/Judean," 8:291.

67. See also Schwartz, "'Judaean' or 'Jew'"? 14–15.

68. Likewise, idem, *Judeans and Jews*, 6.

69. So, ibid., 91–92; Reinhartz, "Vanishing Jews."

70. This is borne out by two surveys conducted by the Pew Research Center, one of American Jews (2013) and the other of Israeli Jews (2016). Among other questions, respondents were asked whether, for them Jewish identity was mainly a matter of ancestry/culture, religion, or all three and what elements they deemed essential to being Jewish. In both surveys, the majority characterized Jewish identity as a matter of ancestry/culture, but there was significant variation among different groups of Jews. American and Israeli Jews also diverged on several of the elements regarded as essential to Jewish identity. See Pew Research Center, "A Portrait of Jewish Americans," http://www.pewforum.org/files/2013/10/jewish-american-full-report-for-web.pdf and "Israel's Religiously Divided Society," http://pewforum.org/files/2016/03/Israel-Survey-Full-Report.pdf.

71. Esler, *Conflict and Identity*, 63.

Chapter 1

The Johannine Christians and Their Jewish Neighbors

A Tale of Two Religions?

Writing over three-quarters of a century ago, the great English commentator Sir Edwyn Hoskyns remarked upon the near anonymity of the author and intended readers of the Fourth Gospel, eclipsed as they are by the evangelist's single-minded concentration on the Word become flesh:

> But where did the original readers of the Fourth Gospel once stand? What was in their minds? In what direction or directions were they moving? These are urgent, pressing questions. Yet the precise character and standing, not of the author only, but even of his readers, are obscure . . . It is therefore extremely difficult to gain from the gospel any direct information concerning its original readers, and for this reason it is hard to come by the key to its historical understanding.[1]

This was not an admission of total ignorance, for Hoskyns presses on to give some account of the life setting of the Gospel despite the difficulties of the task. But what is remarkable about the baronet's resigned comments is how far removed from them we are today. In the opinion of many, experts in Johannine literature and NT generalists alike, the historical key for which Hoskyns was searching has been discovered: the book and its peculiar ideas belong to a community of ethnically Jewish believers in Jesus who, because of their devotion to Jesus, had come into conflict with the Jewish religious establishment in the closing decades of the first century CE.[2]

I have already had occasion to mention J. Louis Martyn's seminal *History and Theology in the Fourth Gospel*. Martyn was not the first to explain the Johannine attitude toward the Jews as the residual effect of conflict with the synagogue, but in the words of D. Moody Smith, his reconstruction was the first to achieve "sustained flight."[3] The methodological starting point of the book, and what time and usage have shown to be Martyn's most enduring contribution, is that the Fourth Gospel is at once a story about Jesus (what Martyn calls the *einmalig* level) and a story about the birth and maturation of the Johannine community, above all its growing pains as it found itself harassed and its existence threatened by the synagogue.[4] The showcase in *History and Theology* for the two-level reading is the dramatic healing of the man born blind in John 9. Jesus is said to stand in for a preacher in the Johannine community, the man born blind for a Christian convert, and the Pharisees for the Jewish council in John's own city who had aligned themselves against the nascent Christian movement.[5]

As an important clue to this second level of meaning, though by no means its sole support, Martyn famously points to John 9:22 (cf. 12:42 and 16:2): "For the Jews had already agreed that anyone who confessed Jesus to be the Messiah would be put out of the synagogue (ἀποσυνάγωγος γένηται)."[6] Such punitive measures against Jewish believers, states Martyn, are scarcely imaginable in Jesus's own lifetime and are to be correlated rather with the "blessing of the heretics" (the Birkat Haminim) thought to have been added to the Twelfth Benediction of the Jewish Amidah prayer under the direction of Rabban Gamaliel II at the Judean city of Yavneh sometime between 80 and 115 CE.[7] For Martyn, these events form part of the history of Jewish Christianity.[8] That is to say, the members of the Johannine community were Jews who had come to believe that Jesus was the long-awaited Messiah and who were ultimately barred from the synagogue as their estimation of Jesus swelled. The inference often drawn is that the Johannine Christians, having suffered so traumatically at the hands of their compatriots, now relinquished their own identity as Jews. Or if the separation was not yet final, it was nevertheless in process. As Martyn states: "To express it theologically, they cease even to be 'Jews' and become instead—like Nathanael—'truly Israelites' who now constitute the *new* 'his own' because the stranger has come from above and has chosen them out of the world/synagogue."[9]

Although some of the more adventurous aspects of Martyn's community reconstruction have fallen by the wayside, in its essential contours it has been more than warmly received, endorsed in some form by such luminaries as Raymond E. Brown, John Ashton, and R. Alan Culpepper. The theory's most vulnerable component (Wayne A. Meeks has called it a "red herring") has proven to be the identification of being made ἀποσυνάγωγος with the Birkat Haminim, though, as Ashton observes, this in itself does not damage the overall integrity of the proposal.[10] Others, writing in what Jonathan Bernier has recently described as the neo-Martynian tradition, take the Gospel's notices of Jewish opposition and persecution of the Christian community as projections intended to create and reinforce the community's identity over against the Jews.[11]

For all the adjustments and adaptations that have been made to Martyn's two-level reading, the scenario of a subsociety of ethnically Jewish believers in Jesus that had come to sever ties with its Jewish roots has on the whole remained intact. Brown writes of the community's post-expulsion identity: "The Johannine Christians were expelled from the synagogues . . . and told that they could no longer worship with other Jews; and so they no longer considered themselves Jews despite the fact that many were of Jewish ancestry."[12] Similarly, for Ashton what was initially a family row had escalated beyond that: "To speak of the Johannine group as Ἰουδαῖοι is to fail to take seriously the deliberate alienation-effect of the use of this term in the Gospel."[13] "The decisive break between Judaism and Christianity," concludes Culpepper, "had already occurred, at least in the Johannine setting."[14] And for those who consider the violence suffered to be more imagined than real, it is still part of a process of religious separation between Jews and the Johannine believers who became increasingly alienated from their brethren. Thus despite her measured skepticism about the historicity of Jewish persecution of Johannine believers, Adele Reinhartz is in agreement that the Fourth Gospel witnesses to a definitive rift between Judaism and Christianity on the local level.[15] "In following Jesus," she continues, "Jews relinquish the ethnic and national categories that hitherto marked their lives."[16] Along similar lines, Raimo Hakola argues that the Johannine quest for self-definition led the evangelist "to create an autonomous symbolic universe" detached from fundamental aspects of traditional Jewish practice and belief.[17] Although Hakola stresses the ambiguity of the Gospel's relationship with the Jews and Judaism, the trajectory is one from the inside out. Through this process of self-definition, the Johannine community "no longer understood themselves in terms of Jewish identity."[18]

THE FOURTH GOSPEL AND INTRA-JEWISH POLEMIC

There are, nonetheless, a number of interpreters who still see it fit to classify the polemic in the Gospel as a family quarrel or as neuralgic admonishments designed to goad contemporary Israel to repentance. James Dunn, for example, situates the Fourth Gospel and its criticism of the Ἰουδαῖοι within the factionalism of late first-century Judaism confronted with the loss of the temple and sacrificial cult.[19] Bereft of a central symbol of their corporate identity and grappling with the theological ramifications of the disaster, the Jewish community took a renewed interest in the question of revelation, of who had the authority "to speak in God's name with God's voice."[20] Against this background, says Dunn, it is hard not to hear the Gospel of John as an attempt to fill that void. The answer to the political and spiritual turmoil, the privileged locus of revelation which addresses the hopes and fears of God's people, is the man Jesus of Nazareth. The debate is still one between Jewish factions, or rather between the Johannine Christians and mainstream Jewish society with which it remained in dialogue. The Fourth Gospel "does not presuppose two monoliths, Judaism and Christianity, clearly distinct and clearly separate in identity, denouncing each other in anathemas and open hostility."[21] So for Dunn, John's acerbic statements about the Jews more nearly resemble intra-Jewish polemic, more like the Dead Sea Scrolls or Psalms of Solomon than the anti-Jewish prejudices of Tacitus and the Latin satirists or the tirades of the patristic-era Adversus Judaeos literature.

The view that the Gospel of John speaks to the concerns of the Jewish people in the period between the two revolts against Rome is taken to its furthest end by Stephen Motyer. Following the lead of Dunn, Motyer identifies seven "points of sensitivity" in the text: the temple and festivals, the law of Moses, revelation, Judea and the Jews, the formation of faith, signs, and the argumentative style of many of the Gospel's dialogues.[22] Heard by Jews, especially those of Judea, still wrestling with the loss of the temple but on the path toward a reconstituted religious life, the Gospel functioned as a direct appeal "to persuade them that Jesus is the Christ who can meet the particular needs of Israel."[23] The Gospel's purpose, as Karl Bornhäuser, W. C. van Unnik, and J. A. T. Robinson had maintained before the entrenchment of the two-level reading, was evangelistic, so that it must be read as an appeal coming from within Israel to co-religionists: "Jew speaking to Jew, in just the same way as the authors of 4 Ezra and 2 Baruch tried to minister to the needs of their fellow-Jews by publishing their own solutions in written form."[24] In the Gospel's pages is announced a renewal program for a troubled Israel, a project whose goal was to restore what had fallen, not to strike down its battered remnants as they tried to raise themselves up once more from the rubble.

While it has sometimes been maintained that the earliest stages of the Gospel's development have their *Sitz im Leben* in the context of a Jewish mission (one thinks above all of Robert T. Fortna's setting for the hypothesized Signs Source), Motyer is likely to face an uphill battle convincing interpreters that the Gospel in something like its present form will have functioned effectively as a missionary tract directed toward non-believing Jews.[25] We might nonetheless settle for something in between the Fourth Gospel as a "letter of repudiation" against Judaism and an evangelistic manifesto meant to convince hardened Israel.[26] The mediating position is well represented in Craig S. Keener's commentary. Keener identifies the Gospel's intended audience as believing Jews who reside in Asia Minor, the traditional resting place of the apostle John. They had indeed faced some resistance from the synagogue authorities, but the rupture with the Jewish community was by no means complete. Nor had the Johannine Christians consciously placed themselves outside of Judaism:

> John was not, of course, claiming that the church had "replaced" Jewish Israel; he was claiming that it was Jewish and that it continued the faithful remnant of Israel that had always existed. The Jewish Christians still saw themselves as part of Judaism.[27]

Within this orbit of scholars, we may also place Wally Cirafesi, who has shown perhaps more thoroughly than anyone else how the Fourth Gospel engages the key markers of ancient Jewish identity. Cirafesi's *John Within Judaism* seeks to understand the Fourth Gospel not merely against the background of ancient Judaism but as situated within the diverse Jewish social, cultural, and religious landscape of antiquity. He argues that the Gospel of John negotiates with aspects of Jewish identity such as land, cult, genealogy, and law in modes recognizable from other ancient Jewish texts, placing the Fourth Gospel on the diasporic end of Jewish identity in contrast to a priestly oriented Judaism. The Gospel's invective is not against Judaism *in se* but against a certain expression of it, which is represented by the *Ioudaioi* in the narrative.[28]

This line of interpretation, however, eventually runs headlong into John's presentation of the Jews. While I concur with Cirafesi that the question of the Fourth Gospel's relationship to Jewishness cannot be reduced to its use or non-use of the term *Ioudaioi*, an exegetical account of its usage must feature prominently within that broader conversation.[29] There are ways in which the rhetorical strategies of the Gospel of John resemble the writings of the Yaḥad or Philo or the rabbis, but no other Jewish text in antiquity speaks so pervasively and so critically of "the Jews." The editors of *Anti-Judaism and the Fourth Gospel* describe it as a "virtually irresolvable question."[30] If the Fourth Gospel witnesses to an inner-Jewish conflict, why would one side call the other "the Jews"? Why would a self-consciously Jewish author speak so critically about "the Jews" when other terms (Pharisees, chief priests, etc.) were at his disposal? Does this Johannine peculiarity not vitiate attempts to read John within the Jewish tradition? Indeed, the very pertinent observations of Dunn, Motyer, Keener, Cirafesi, and others could also be readily accommodated within a Martynian schema. On this model, the evangelist/ community speaks Jewishly, as it were, because its origins are Jewish, but the Gospel's rhetoric about the Jews evinces an estrangement from the larger Jewish community. Its facility with the categories of Jewish discourse and identity formation reflects the community's past but does not tell the full story of its present and future.[31] So, how do we differentiate between a Jewish author who continued to live and write from within a Jewish identity and one who was nourished in the Jewish tradition but had moved beyond it in some fashion?

"John's statements about οἱ Ἰουδαῖοι," acknowledges Keener, "are too strong to dismiss as internal polemic without further explanation."[32] Dunn submits that the Johannine Christians ceded the name "Jews" to their opponents in the synagogue, preferring in its stead the name "Israel."[33] The rejoinder is that if this were the case, it is hardly meaningful to hang on to the tag line "intra-Jewish," since these believers no longer numbered themselves among the Jews or reckoned them as their own.[34] And if so, it seems to me that the "breakdown of ecumenical relations," which Dunn sees as on the horizon, ought to be regarded as a fait accompli in the sense that the Johannine community now regarded the Jews as outsiders.[35]

Motyer, for his part, pursues a more philologically oriented approach, drawing upon suggestions put forward by Wilhelm Lütgert and Bornhäuser in the early twentieth century.[36] Whereas the "hub sense" of Ἰουδαῖος is all those who so identify and who adhere to the religion of Judea (whether or not they live there), an important derived reference is "the particularly strict, Torah- and Temple-centered religion found especially (but not exclusively) in Judea and Jerusalem," or in Bornhäuser's more succinct but less diplomatic formulation, "the Torah fanatics."[37] In context, the Ἰουδαῖοι of the Fourth Gospel *are* often religious authorities centered in Jerusalem and zealous for the traditions of their forefathers, as I will argue in the next chapter. On the other hand, one would be hard-pressed to show that any ancient Jewish sources, from the early post-exilic era to the age of the Amoraim and beyond, use the appellation Ἰουδαῖος to isolate a specific party within Judaism. And if this was not established usage, the question naturally follows why John would craft a persuasive appeal to Jews while criticizing their leaders in those very terms.

If the answer to this most perplexing of Johannine riddles is not to be found at the philological level, perhaps it resides on the literary plane in the Johannine love of irony.[38] The evangelist and the community on whose behalf he speaks had not given up the name "Jews," proposes Keener, but put the epithet to service as a subtle way of undermining the authority of the community's detractors, a sort of subaltern strategy of resistance to a more powerful class which was arrogating to itself the authentic embodiment of Jewish identity.[39] We shall see shortly that on most other fronts in the war over Israel's heritage, the evangelist is on the offensive. Jesus's enemies claim to cherish the Scriptures, but their inability to hear his word exposes their assertion as bluster. They rest themselves on a proud lineage, but their murderous intentions demonstrate that they are not truly Abraham's children, and so on. Then, too, it must be asked whether the transformation of

Ἰουδαῖοι into a kind of passive-aggressive swipe at non-believing Jews will not have resulted in its eventual renunciation by the Johannine Christians themselves.[40]

Similarly, Andrew Byers argues that with the phrase οἱ Ἰουδαῖοι, John provocatively targets those in the narrative who would rigidly restrict salvation to the physical people of Israel. The evangelist's use of the term Ἰουδαῖοι, states Byers, "undermines not an ethnic group, but an envisaged social identity that is, in his view, wrongly restrictive."[41] With its firm basis in Johannine literary technique, this solution has much to commend it, but one wonders if it is overly subtle even for the "spiritual Gospel," as Clement of Alexandria famously described the Fourth Gospel.[42] Byers, for example, avers that John is likely targeting a specific set of ideas held only by a limited group of Jews amidst a narrative populated by other Jews with different or undefined religious commitments.[43] But then why does the evangelist not opt for a term that more narrowly circumscribes that subset of Jews?[44] If some Jews insisted on genealogical purity for inclusion in the covenant people of God while others did not, the evangelist could have achieved the goal of delegitimizing exclusionary social practices by a more direct route. It might be questioned, moreover, whether the restriction of covenant membership to Jews really stands at the forefront of the contentious exchanges in the Fourth Gospel. Though matters of genealogy arise in the course of the narrative, Jesus's opponents never express the view that God's covenantal protection could extend only to ethnic Jews.[45] What they consistently object to, rather, are the claims that Jesus makes about himself. Finally, if John is thoroughly invested in deracializing soteriology and ecclesiology, then it may be that he has not relativized ethnicity, as Byers contends, but abolished it.[46] The *Ioudaioi* are not criticized for misprioritizing the place of ethnicity but for assigning it any value at all. Perhaps the evangelist calls readers into a new divinely generated transethnic social identity precisely to disaffiliate them from the Jews, as Reinhartz argues.[47]

While a consistent reading of the Gospel of John as the product of a self-consciously Jewish author cannot be dismissed out of hand, these lingering questions leave us at an impasse. To reprise the question posed above: How do we differentiate between a Jewish author who writes within the Jewish tradition and an erstwhile Jew who had forged a new identity? What I hope to show in this study is that it is not only possible to read the Gospel of John as the work of a self-consciously Jewish author, but that it is more plausible than the alternative. There are deficits in the religious-schism model which have not yet received due scrutiny, and there are alternative models for the Johannine language about the Jews which are more compelling.

CRACKS IN THE FOUNDATION OF THE TWO-LEVEL READING

We begin, then, with some general remarks about the weaknesses of the two-level reading which Martyn pioneered.[48] I have noted a tendency to disassociate the ἀποσυνάγωγος passages from the Birkat Haminim, or to deny their historicity altogether. Another set of critiques is more radical (in the etymological sense of that word) and thus represents a more serious challenge to the two-level reading strategy. Some have abandoned the whole enterprise of retrieving communal histories from what purport to be stories about Jesus as methodologically unsound, since it proceeds as if the Gospels were occasional letters rather than a form of Greco-Roman biography.[49] Thus even if directed toward a local church or circle of disciples, there is no warrant in the Gospel genre for reading it as a cipher for the experiences of second- and third-generation Christians. The story of Jesus will have been relevant to its first readers and hearers for its own sake, as those who professed faith in Jesus will have wanted to know about the one they revered as Lord and Savior of the world. The Gospels, it has been further argued, were written for many or all Christians, meant to circulate widely among believers in the Mediterranean basin.[50] Still others have eschewed attempts to extrapolate the life, loves, and hates of the Johannine community as inconsistent or unduly selective in which passages are allowed a place in the process of reconstruction.[51]

Although I cannot examine each critique in detail, their cumulative force has begun to erode the methodological foundations for reading the Gospel as simultaneous *vita Christi* and encoded community annals.[52] The chief methodological crux, in any event, is the extent to which the Gospel of John correlates with its social setting. The Fourth Gospel and its symbolic structures must reflect something of the world in which it originated and in which it was first received, as all texts do. But between the acknowledgment of that fact and Martyn's historical allegory, there is much room to maneuver.[53] What sustains the two-level reading is the sense that it seems to make of the Gospel, the placement of its Jewish and allegedly anti-Jewish elements into a single, evolving social matrix. To the extent that it does not perform this task, the methodological objections against the theory loom larger.

In what follows, I deploy some now well-established paradigms of Jewish ethnic reasoning in antiquity in the service of answering a neglected but important question. Does the religious-schism model yield a consistent reading of the Gospel's attitude toward the Jews? I shall argue that it does not, precisely in its assumption that the fourth evangelist had come to see faith in Jesus and membership in the Jewish *ethnos* as incompatible. On sociohistorical grounds, it is questionable that a group of first-century Jewish believers in Jesus would have renounced their identity as Jews, leaving it to their enemies as a name of opprobrium. And on literary grounds, the image of a break between two religions sits uneasily with John's self-understanding as the legitimate heir to the faith of Israel.

THE RELIGIOUS SCHISM REVISITED

John Ashton opens *The Gospel of John and Christian Origins* with an anecdote about the philosopher Edith Stein, a Jewish convert to Roman Catholicism and Carmelite nun.[54] Stein and her sister Rosa were deported to Auschwitz in early August 1942 and executed in the gas chambers not long after their arrival. Beatified in May 1987 and canonized just over a decade later in October 1998 as St. Teresa Benedicta of the Cross, Stein is a recognized saint of the Catholic Church. Ashton recounts a tense conversation between Edith and her mother, a devout Jew, during the synagogue service on Yom Kippur sometime after her conversion in the early 1920s. Upon the recitation of the Shema, the central confession of the Jewish liturgy, Stein's mother leaned over and whispered to her daughter, "Do you hear? Your God is One, and only One." For Ashton, the exchange serves as a vivid encapsulation of the dividing line between Judaism and Christianity, a thread that he traces all the way back to the Fourth Gospel.[55] The doctrines of Incarnation and Trinity to which historically the fourth evangelist contributed so much mark Christianity as distinct from the other Abrahamic faiths and make it irreconcilable with Judaism.

As an entrée to the problem of the emergence of the Christian religion from Judaism, the example of Edith Stein is, in one sense deeply ironic. Even after her conversion, she never ceased to consider herself a Jew.[56] They were still her own people. She had a foreboding of sharing in their collective fate.[57] Stein, of course, is many centuries removed from the writing of the Fourth Gospel, but her lasting conviction that she belonged to the Jewish people rattles our air-tight categories. That the Gospel witnesses to a religious dispute, to competing claims about revelation, salvation, and access to God is undoubtedly true. Is it also a dispute between two religious communities? Would the evangelist have thought in those terms?

The fact that religious conversion is common to our experience and native to our mode of social description lends a kind of self-validation to a narrative in which Jews shed their former identity to reemerge with a distinctively Christian one. So interpreted, the Gospel of John witnesses to the embryonic stages of the disambiguation of Christianity from Judaism into the discreet socio-religious entities with which we are familiar. Or if we prefer the more antagonistic imagery, it is the story of an ugly divorce between the two.[58] The members of the Johannine community had converted from one religion to another and were therefore Jews no longer. Although we might corroborate this story by pointing to examples of Jews, past or present, who have willingly placed themselves outside of the Jewish fellowship, there is a confounding phenomenon that flows directly counter to this, namely, ethnic Jews who believe in Jesus but hold fast to their Jewish identity and heritage, men and women like Edith Stein.

These individuals and congregations, frequently maligned on both Jewish and Christian sides, are worth study in their own right.[59] But what is to be observed here is the holding together of identities that many judge to be incompatible. Being a Christian and being a Jew in this conceptualization are not mutually exclusive. A person is a Jew by birth and ancestry, a member of the Jewish people. A similar rationale seems to underlie the traditional halakic opinion that children born to an apostate (or apostates) still contract valid Jewish marriages.[60] That is, as far as marital relations are concerned, they are treated as Jews even if their parents have defected from Judaism.[61]

The conceptualization of Jewish identity as something dependent upon lineage is revealing both because it illustrates the complexities of Jewish self-understanding and because it is likely the understanding that prevailed in antiquity. As we have already seen, the Jews of the ancient world were accorded status as an ἔθνος. Jewish authors assumed as much, both those writing in Greek and those writing in Hebrew or Aramaic with corresponding terms.[62] What distinguished the inhabited world's diverse ἔθνη from other types of associations and institutions, and what made them species of the same social genus, is the myth of common ancestry. We might liken an ἔθνος to an imagined family, believed to have at its hoary beginnings an ancestor from whom the current members of the group are descended. This social formation was typically attended by a number of other characteristic marks: a group name, the myth of a common homeland, a shared history and customs, and national deities, to name some of the most salient.[63]

For the Jews, all of these were memorialized in their sacred writings, the patrimony of the people since the exilic period.[64] They believed that they had common ancestors Abraham, Isaac, Jacob, and Judah, a common homeland in Judea with its capital city and holy place, a shared national story about the people's origins, movements, misfortunes, and restoration, the common customs of circumcision, Sabbath observance, and dietary laws, among others, and a God who was Lord of all peoples but who had elected them as his special possession. According to their founding documents, Israel was a privileged nation, set apart from the others, but a nation all the same.[65] The Jews were more than a cult, or a form of piety, or a philosophy despite all the overlap with these.

In fact, against the tendency of some to emphasize multiple, shifting meanings of the term Ἰουδαῖος, it might be argued that in a general sense it was much less ambiguous than today. No Jewish author or work that has survived antiquity repudiates the myth of common ancestry even if a few try to graft foreign cultural heroes into the family tree.[66] No known Jewish author denies the shared corporate historical experiences even if some are more interested in their spiritual meaning.[67] None of them disputes that their ancestors' homeland was in the province that the Romans knew as Iudaea. For all the local coloring of customs and practice, the diversity in native languages, and the multiplicity of what we would call religious beliefs, the myth of common ancestry and thus of a physical bond with all other Jews seems to have been close to invariable.[68] To borrow the apostle Paul's metaphor, they were a single tree, made up of many branches, but in their mind all sharing the same roots (Rom 11:16–24).

Within this conceptual framework, the binary opposition of Jew and Christian looks incongruent, even a touch absurd. "Being a Judaean," as Mason concludes,

> and being a follower of Jesus were incommensurable categories, rather like being a Russian or a Rotarian, a Brazilian or a Bridge player. Scholars know this well, but our continued use of "religion," as if this were the *genus* of which "Judaism" and "Christianity" were two *species* tends to de-historicize and obfuscate the matter.[69]

In principle, someone born a Jew who had come to believe that Jesus was the promised Messiah had no decision to make whether to remain a Jew. And had he or she renounced his or her Jewish identity, most logically it would have been to don an alternative mode of ethnic self-identification. The plausibility of a transition in Johannine self-understanding from Jews to something other than Jews, then, rises and falls in proportion to its satisfaction of two conditions: (1) that some at this period thought that one could not believe in Jesus and remain a Jew, and (2) that this community of ethnically Jewish believers accepted and internalized that premise.[70] Neither of these should be assumed in light of the preceding considerations.

The Pincer Movement: Developments among Gentile Christians

If a reasonable case is to be made for the fulfillment of either condition, it is for the first. Although in theory Jewish identity and belief in Jesus initially belonged to different epistemological planes, two developments pushing in from opposite ends make matters more complicated. It has been argued that Gentile Christian authors come to remake Jewish identity in their own generic image, twisting it into Christianity's heretical counterpart.[71] Mason traces the beginnings of this development to Ignatius of Antioch and Tertullian in the second century. To some extent, a discursive transformation of this sort cannot be doubted. Christian authors begin to treat Judaism as a form of piety, or a system of philosophy abstracted from the common life of the Jewish people whose principles could not be reconciled with the Christian faith. It is by such a transformation that the fourth-century church father Epiphanius of Salamis, the indefatigable watchdog against heresy, could arrange Judaism alongside Barbarism, Hellenism, and Scythianism as overarching categories of theological error dissolved with the coming of Christ (*Pan.* 1–4).

Yet we should not overlook the fact that many of these same Christian authors never redefine Jewish identity in its entirety. Eusebius of Caesarea might reduce Judaism to an abstract theological system for the sake of facile contrast with the true divine philosophy, Christianity (*Dem. ev.* 1.2.1–2), but it is not because he has forgotten that the Jews are a living, if humbled, ἔθνος.[72] And for all the reified systemization with which Epiphanius overlays his heresiological project, he still recognizes that the Jews are the physical descendants of Abraham, and so does not cleanly dissect the Jewish faith from the Jewish people.[73] Earlier authors such as Tertullian and Origen tend to think of the Jews not as adherents of a religion per se but as a homeless and rejected people whose covenant with God has been annulled, the vacancy having been quickly filled by the mass incoming of the Gentiles into God's new covenant.[74] For someone like Tertullian, it was not so much that Judaism was a "system of postulates" as it was the reduction of Jewish identity to Torah observance, the now outmoded way of life of a God-forsaken nation.[75] Part of the reason that Christian authors begin to regard Jewish and Christian identity as mutually exclusive is because adherence to the law of Moses, for many of them the *sine qua non* of being a Jew—indeed, the virtual definition of Judaism—becomes increasingly seen as inimical to faith in Christ. In that respect, the Christian inclination to define themselves over against the Jewish people was not an artificial project of self-definition. It grew out of their exegetical engagement with the Gospels and Pauline epistles, fostered by a kind of dispensationalist theology that made the Mosaic law and the sacrificial system into a temporary provision.

Hardening as time progressed, this attitude is on full display by the fourth and fifth centuries.[76] Epiphanius decries all attempts at compromise between obedience to the Torah and Christian faith as inherently heretical and gross distortions of the orthodox truth (*Pan.* 29.8–9). A Jew who comes to believe in Jesus and enters the communion of the church through baptism surrenders the former name along with the practice of Jewish rites.[77] Jerome assumes the same, ridiculing the Nazoraeans for mixing belief in Jesus with observance of the Torah. Trying to be both Christians and Jews, they are for that very reason neither (*Epist.* 112.4.13).[78]

But this development among Gentile Christians is rather remote from the circumstances of the Fourth Gospel, nor was it the universal opinion of the churches in the first or second century. Our evidence is riddled with holes, but we are able to see all the same that not all Christian authors of this period, to say nothing of the mass of anonymous faithful, shared the sensibilities of Epiphanius and Jerome. Ignatius of Antioch, it is true, tries to erect a wall between his constructs of Christianity (Χριστιανισμός) and Judaism (Ἰουδαϊσμός) and thus ostensibly between being a Jew and being a Christian: "It is absurd to profess Christ Jesus, and to Judaize. For Christianity did not embrace Judaism, but Judaism Christianity, so that every tongue which believes might be gathered together to God" (*Magn.* 10).[79] The very fact that he feels it necessary to combat such Judaization suggests that not all were as worried about their intermingling as he.[80]

By comparison with Ignatius, the mid-second century convert and apologist Justin Martyr comes across as more lenient. He too believes that the time for the law of Moses has passed, its ordinances put into permanent abeyance with the coming of Christ. He nonetheless permits Jewish believers to adhere to the Torah, provided that they do not compel Gentile believers to do the same (*Dial.* 47). If these brothers from the circumcision are a bit stubborn in holding on to antiquated traditions, they are not for that reason heretics to be excluded from the communion of the saints. From Justin's statements we may surmise that the growing church was divided over the status of Torah-observant Christ believers. Justin believes that they will be saved and encourages association with them as kinsmen and brethren, but he knows of others who refuse to extend them this hospitality.[81]

But above this, the guiding element in most models of Johannine community history is a setting of conflict with fellow Jews. It was the guardians of Jewish orthodoxy, so to speak, who exerted pressure on the Johannine Christians in their midst. Or at least this is what these believers thought in their moments of existential angst. Relations between ethnically Jewish believers and Gentiles are perhaps on the horizon in the Fourth Gospel, as well as persecution from "the world," but resistance from non-Jewish brethren is surely not one of the Gospel's "points of sensitivity." If we are to make any headway in assessing the first condition, we must therefore turn to the Jewish side of the pincer movement.

The Pincer Movement: Possible Developments among Non-Christian Jews

There is, as Mason says, a certain incongruence in the categories "Jew" and "Christian" as it pertains to ancient modes of social organization. At the same time, belonging to an ἔθνος was often so closely associated with the observance of ancestral customs and laws that perceived aberration from them or adoption of foreign practices was tantamount to betrayal of one's own people.[82] We might illustrate the interconnection between belief, praxis, and ethnic identity by returning to Mason's lighthearted (or perhaps slightly satirical) comment about Brazilians and Bridge players. The two quite obviously belong to very different spheres of social identity, neither inherently coterminous nor inherently incompatible. But let us suppose that Bridge is the national pastime of Brazil, played by most everyone from childhood on, and thus part and parcel of Brazilian national identity. Nonconformist behavior is likely to elicit some form of disapproval from one's peers. The situation is exacerbated if the preferred card game is associated with another nation, if, say, all Columbians play Canasta but not Bridge. The Brazilian who enjoys the former over the latter begins to look unpatriotic, perhaps even a threat to Brazilian society, especially if relations between the two nations have soured. It is because of such a tight association of behavior and ethnic belonging that Roman authors sometimes express dismay at the proliferation of foreign cults and customs, including those of the Jews, among the Roman populace.[83] Those who attached themselves to these strange, even odious, practices were forsaking the way of life of their ancestors, despising their fathers' gods, and imperiling the welfare of the state. Tacitus's remarks in *Hist.* 5.4.1 about Jewish proselytes are telling: "Those who are converted to their way of life accept the same practice, and the earliest habit they adopt is to despise the gods, to renounce their country, and to regard their parents, children, and brothers as of little consequence."[84] It is this same sort of crisis that arguably sparked the Maccabean revolt. To the more conservative segments of Jewish society, embracing the Greek way of life or ceasing to observe Torah struck at the very heart of what it meant to be a Jew. Failure to share in the ancestral customs amounted to a proverbial stab in the back.[85]

Central to the Jewish religious tradition, of course, is the worship of Yahweh alone and the refusal to participate in the cults of foreign gods, even if not all Jews were equally scrupulous. So, to some Jewish onlookers, a group of ethnic Jews who venerated Jesus as the pre-existent Son of God must have aroused suspicion. If, in Johannine self-understanding, they were the faithful remnant of God's people, to other Jews they were in danger of apostasy or had already left the fold. The charge, in fact, is recorded in the Fourth Gospel. In the eyes of Jesus's enemies, the man is a deceiver (7:12) and a blasphemer (10:33) who, by divine decree, must be put to death because he had the audacity to declare himself the Son of God (19:7). No one who follows him can claim to be a disciple of Moses, as the Jewish authorities are made to imply in 9:28. The author of the Gospel in no way accepts the charges, as we shall see.

When we transpose the accusations against Jesus in the Gospel to accusations against the Johannine community at the time of the evangelist, as the two-level reading instructs us to do, we are able to see how, even in antiquity being Jewish and believing in Jesus could be construed as mutually exclusive. The Johannine Christians, it was thought, had transgressed the bounds of proper Jewish belief and were leading the people wildly astray.[86] Expressed syllogistically, the logic of the local Jewish authorities responsible for putting the Johannine Christians out of their company could have run as follows: 1) Jews believe in one God and worship none other beside him. 2) These people who say they are Jews make Jesus out to be God's equal. 3) Therefore they are not Jews but have betrayed their God and their people.

The possible short circuit in the syllogism comes in the deduction. It is not certain that the Jewish leadership actually will have denied that Johannine Christians were Jews. Jewish sources that deal with apostates are not always explicit about the person's post-defection status. Known defectors, such as Dositheos son of Drimylos and Antiochus of Antioch, are certainly scorned as traitors. The former, a Jew by birth according to 3 Macc 1:3, later "changed his religion and apostatized from the ancestral traditions." The latter, Josephus tells us, left off observance of the Torah to ape the worship and customs of the Greeks, so zealous to demonstrate his hatred for the old way of life that he actively persecuted the Jewish community of Antioch in the aftermath of the war against Rome (*J.W.* 7.47–60). If his Jewish ancestry cannot be denied, he has for all intents and purposes made himself a Gentile.[87] But are such apostates thought of as former Jews or simply as bad Jews whose disloyalty to nation and kin has earned them the disdain of their Jewish compatriots?[88]

In rabbinic literature, both apostates—those who no longer keep the commandments—and heretics—those whose interpretation of Torah diverges from that of the rabbis—continue to belong technically to Israel, though in almost all other respects, it is prescribed that they be treated like or worse than non-Jews.[89] We might say that as a matter of birth, their Jewish status is granted, while in social interaction, this counts for next to nothing.[90]

The difference between non-Jewish status and ostracism despite retention of that status is not very pronounced, and the social consequences are effectively the same, but for the present task, the shades of nuance are potentially significant. Granted the synagogue-expulsion hypothesis, will the Jewish leadership of John's city have reproved the Johannine believers as non-Jews or rather as Jewish sinners and renegades? In the latter case, being a faithful Jew, but not a Jew per se, and following Jesus will have been seen as incompatible. The Johannine avowal of Jewish identity will have been assaulted indirectly, rather than openly denied.[91] The action, moreover, would only have represented the judgment of one Jewish community, not of a universal synagogue, as if a unified institution existed in the first century.[92] The fulfillment of the first condition thus remains an open question. The Gospel itself does not supply the means to make so fine a distinction.

Former Jews? The Lack of Ancient Precedent

It is the second condition that is less probable and whose dearth of support jeopardizes the internal stability of Martyn's reconstruction. The deficit is both external and internal to the Gospel. It is external insofar as we have no precedent for Jewish believers in Jesus in antiquity relinquishing the name Ἰουδαῖοι. Reliable information about these groups in the first few centuries of the Common Era is hard to come by. We know directly of the so-called sects of the Ebionites and Nazoraeans only from the church fathers who regard their faith as flawed or denounce them as outright heretics. The lack of sympathy and suspect inferences as the literary tradition grows make sifting fact from polemical fiction no small task. The common denominator in this tradition from Irenaeus to Jerome is the existence of sects who live like Jews but profess some manner of belief in Jesus, whether itself heretical or in harmony with the orthodox faith. According to Irenaeus, the Ebionites deny the virgin birth (*Haer.* 3.21.1; 4.33.4; 5.1.3). Hippolytus accuses them of making Christ into a mere man, like us in all respects (*Haer.* 7.22). Origen mentions two types of Ebionites who are split about the virgin birth but regulate their lives like the Jewish multitude (*Cels.* 5.61). Jerome equates the Ebionites with a sect he knows as Nazoraeans and judges their Christology to be sufficiently Christian but their practice damnably Jewish (*Epist.* 112.13). Epiphanius ascribes a bizarre mélange of beliefs about Christ to the Ebionites (*Pan* 30.3) but professes ignorance about the Nazoraeans' Christology (*Pan.* 29.7.6).

Of the relevant sources, Epiphanius alone claims that one of these sects, the Nazoraeans, has given up the name "Jews."

> But these same sectarians whom I am discussing here disregarded the name of Jesus, and neither called themselves Jessaeans, kept the name of the Jews, nor termed themselves Christians—but "Nazoraeans" supposedly from the name of the place "Nazareth." But they are Jews in every way and nothing else. (*Pan.* 29.7.1)[93]

It has been argued that Epiphanius accurately reflects Nazoraean self-understanding since the bishop's personal opinion is that the Nazoraeans are defective Jews.[94] He does in fact appear to preserve some trustworthy information about this group in *Pan.* 29.7. The Nazoraeans use both the Old and New Testaments, observe the law of Moses, affirm the resurrection of the dead, God's creation of the world, and Jesus's Sonship, and they are versed in the

Hebrew tongue. At the very least, this section has the semblance of historical plausibility.[95] Nonetheless, it is unlikely that the bishop of Salamis was personally acquainted with the Nazoraeans, not enough in any case to know whether their Christology was acceptably orthodox.[96]

If Epiphanius had a good source for current Nazoraean beliefs, he is much more in the dark about their origins. In tracing the alleged sect's history, the *doctor confusus* does nothing to allay the reputation that has long dogged him.[97] Part of the agenda in the *Panarion* is to create a genealogical tree of heresy and heretics. The Nazoraeans, according to Epiphanius, were the successors to the Cerinthians and precursors to the Ebionites. But the bishop runs into several problems. He does not know their precise relationship to the former: "Next after these come the Nazoraeans, at the same time as they or even before them—either together with them or after them, in any case their contemporaries. I cannot say more precisely who succeeded whom" (*Pan.* 29.1.1).[98] Even so, he is confident that the two groups held similar ideas, although the only point of contact is that Cerinthus is said to have adhered to part of the Jewish law. Epiphanius must also confront the fact that all of Jesus's earliest disciples were called Nazoraeans and therefore struggles to explain how the genuine followers of the apostles and these so-called followers bore the same name.[99]

Slowed by several digressions, Epiphanius reports the sect's beginnings as follows: they were Jews attached to the law, but, having heard Jesus's name and the miracles wrought by the apostles, they came to faith in Christ, though without a true understanding of him. The Christians at the time, says Epiphanius, were called Jessaeans (an interesting case of confusion and conflation in its own right) after Jesse, the father of David, or after Jesus.[100] These parvenus to the faith, however, did not keep that name, but adopted that of Nazoraean after the place of Jesus's upbringing. The history is patently artificial and probably devoid of any historical value. The allegation that the Nazoraeans did not keep the name "Jews" comes as a summary of the sect's origins before he relates their present character and location in *Pan.* 29.7.2–29.7.7. That it tells us about their self-identification is doubtful. It seems, rather, that Epiphanius has inferred this from the fact that they are named "Nazoraeans" and that they believe in Jesus, thus setting them apart from the Jews. He refutes his own faulty deduction.

I have cautioned against taking Epiphanius at his word about Nazoraean self-identity in part because of his own biases, though that does not permit us a facile rejection of everything he says. But most crucial is the fact that he was not an insider to any of the movements he describes and therefore not in an advantageous position to speak on the matter. There is one other figure, much closer in time to John, of whom this cannot rightfully be said and whose self-understanding as a result is of utmost importance: the self-styled apostle to the Gentiles.[101] The view has sometimes been maintained, and has its able defenders still today, that Paul consciously left his identity as a Jew behind when he put on Christ. His conversion, that momentous turn from persecutor to apostle, meant the end of his former religious and ethnic existence.[102] How otherwise could he become a Jew to the Jews (1 Cor 9:19-23)?[103] So perhaps he had already come to think of himself and other Christians as something like a third race, "neither Jew nor Gentile" in Christ, as he writes in Gal 3:28.[104]

That Paul, along with the authors of Ephesians and 1 Peter, sowed the seeds for the notion of Christians as a third race is clear enough.[105] That this meant the obliteration of Paul's own ethnic identity is not. Alongside passages like 1 Cor 9:19-23 and Gal 3:28, which might seem to imply that Paul had discarded his identity as a Jew (his chameleon-like missionary antics a symptom of the negation of any ethnic affiliation by the transcendent meta-identity of being in Christ), stand others in which he asserts membership in or solidarity with the Jewish people.[106]

In Gal 2:15, Paul recounts having confronted Peter in Antioch over the latter's withdrawal from communal meals with Gentile converts in the following words: "We are Jews by nature and not sinners from among the nations." It is an appeal elicited by the exigencies of the moment, but there is little warrant from the text for supposing that Paul is dissembling, becoming like a Jew to win back his brethren from the error of their ways, or that being Jewish "by nature" implies a present status as non-Jews.[107] The essence of the rebuke to Peter is that not even those of Jewish stock, physical descendants of Abraham and heirs to the covenant, are justified by the works of the law. Thus demanding Torah observance of Gentiles as if this were a prerequisite to their adoption as children of God and communion with Jewish believers constitutes a flagrant violation of the Gospel message that we are justified by faith in Christ.[108]

Paul, to be sure, writes earlier in Galatians of his former conduct in Ἰουδαϊσμός (often translated "Judaism") (1:13). This behavior entailed persecution of the church and zeal for the ancestral traditions. It is clear that Paul reckons his advancement in Ἰουδαϊσμός as something of the past. The pursuit of Ἰουδαϊσμός, however, is not necessarily the equivalent of being a Jew. That is, in Gal 1:13, Paul makes a statement not about his ethnic identity but about his once ardent concern to live according to the laws and traditions of the Jewish people, a concern which he has reevaluated in light of Christ. But the best barometer for whether Paul intended to initiate a program that dispensed with natural ethnic identities is Rom 9–11. When Paul refers to himself as an Israelite in 11:1, from the seed of Abraham, of the tribe of Benjamin, he is speaking about his membership in the Jewish ἔθνος.[109] They are his kinfolk according to the flesh (9:33; 11:14), whom he hopes to save through his calling as the apostle to the Gentiles. Belonging to the people of Israel relative to Christ may count for loss (Phil 3:5-8), but it is not thereby engulfed or stripped of all salvation-historical significance.[110] That Paul has physical Israel in mind through to the doxology that crowns ch. 11 receives confirmation from 11:28-31, for here the Israelites are said to be at present God's enemies, handed over to disobedience, so that God may have mercy on them. Thus in Romans, a letter that is unarguably one of the most mature expressions of Paul's thought, he presents himself as an ethnic Israelite in Christ.

What of the ethnonym "Jew" itself? Paul's statements about Israel "according to the flesh" in Rom 9–11 are anticipated in Rom 3:1-8, but there he expounds on the advantages of being a Jew. Paradoxically, and what has at times been felt a misstep in the apostle's reasoning, these advantages are said to be much in every way (3:2, πολὺ κατὰ πάντα τρόπον).[111] But the list of Jewish privileges is immediately curtailed after the first in v. 2, cut off by a digression on God's justice in judging sinners. The topic of Israel's prerogatives is not reprised until Rom 9:4-5, which again plunges Paul into the labyrinths of theodicy. Paul's charge in Rom 3:9-20 that Jew and Gentile alike are under the power of sin also finds its counterpart in 11:30-32. God has handed all people over to disobedience, even his covenant people Israel. And just as in Rom 3:21-31 God's response to human sinfulness is to extend his grace, received through faith in Jesus Christ, so in 11:30-32 the solution to the plight of human disobedience is God's mercy, divine favor experienced as the pardoning of transgression and rescue from God's righteous anger. Because of the correspondences, any divorce between Paul's self-identification as an ethnic Israelite and that as a Jew is unwarranted.[112] The two passages share so many themes and Paul's thought swirls about in such similar ways that Rom 9–11 may be seen as an extension of what Paul began but did not fully pursue in Rom 3.

It is probable, moreover, that Paul includes himself among the Jewish people in Rom 3:9, even if this is not as straightforward as Gal 2:15. Because what immediately precedes in Rom 3:5-8 concerns the glory that comes to God through his righteous judgment and the pretext that this fact might give to sinners to transgress deliberately, some have interpreted the question in v. 9 as Paul's restatement of human responsibility: "Are we making excuses? Not at all!"[113] In Greek, the question is comprised of a single verb, προεχόμεθα. In the middle voice it can indeed bear the meaning of putting something forward as a pretext, though the absence of a direct object in Rom 3:9 makes this less tenable.[114] On the other hand, the common rendering, "Are we any better off?" requires the verb to have a meaning that properly belongs to the active voice.[115]

Despite the unexpected middle voice, the second interpretation commends itself as the superior.[116] In v. 8 Paul has already headed off the pernicious reasoning that doing evil will redound to God's glory, and the reply that Jews and Greeks are all under sin in v. 9 is out of place if the problem at hand is still the tension between the culpability of sinners and the display of God's righteousness in judging sin. The fact that sin holds dominion over all people does not explain how wrongdoing merits judgment when it inadvertently enhances God's truthfulness. Rather, in v. 9, Paul returns to the question with which the section begins, anticipating a riposte to his claim that the Jews enjoy great advantages. Paul therefore asks, "Are we (Jews) any better off (than the gentiles)?" for that might seem to be the implication of v. 2. The response is either, "Not at all," or "Not entirely," depending on how one understands οὐ πάντως. "Not entirely," in my opinion, respects the word order and falls precisely upon the line that Paul tries to straddle. The privileges that the Jewish people have received as gifts from God are not trivial. Paul does not at all want to deny their worth. Yet these advantages, great as they are, do not confer righteousness. In one vital respect, Jews and Gentiles are on the same footing: they are under the power of sin and stand in need of the mercy of God which he poured out in Christ.

To the extent that Paul created a third race, it appears that it was, as E. P. Sanders puts it, "against his own conscious intention."[117] He thought of himself as a Ἰουδαῖος even after his experience of the risen Jesus.[118] If that is so, and if Epiphanius's report is historically unreliable as I have suggested, then the search for ancient analogues to the alleged Johannine renunciation of the name Ἰουδαῖοι comes up empty. It would be precarious, if not fallacious, to build a positive argument on the basis of this silence. What this means, however, is that the fulfillment of the second condition rests entirely on whatever evidence we can extract from the Fourth Gospel.

Former Jews? The Johannine "Sectarian" Mentality

In view of the foregoing considerations, the evangelist's self-perception takes on paramount importance. Where does he position himself in relation to Israel's heritage? We do not need to search long to see that it is in continuity with the seminal figures of Israel's history and its Scriptures. The author portrays faith in Jesus not as an innovation but as the fulfillment of God's promises to Israel. Because all of the patriarchs and prophets testify to Jesus, unbelief entails not only rejection of him but rejection of them by proxy. The Johannine reflex is swift and uniform: "You search the Scriptures because you think that in them you have eternal life; and it is they that testify on my behalf" (5:39-40). "If you believed Moses, you would believe me, for he wrote about me. But if you do not believe what he wrote, how will you believe what I say?" (5:46-47).[119] "If you were Abraham's children, you would be doing what Abraham did (8:39).... Your ancestor Abraham rejoiced that he would see my day; he saw it and was glad" (8:56). "If God were your Father, you would love me, for I came from God and now I am here" (8:42).

I spoke above about a pincer movement against Jewish believers in Jesus that challenged the legitimacy of their faith and practice. The Johannine Jesus executes a pincer movement of his own, simultaneously denying Israel's heritage to his opponents and appropriating that legacy to those who follow him. Whether or not properly a sect in sociological terms, the Johannine community exhibits what according to Stark and Bainbridge is one of this social formation's distinguishing marks: a self-understanding as "something old," as an "authentic, purged, refurbished version" of the parent faith.[120] Against this, it might be objected that John subordinates Moses, Abraham, and the Scriptures so entirely to Jesus that he divests them of all importance, dispensing with the old wineskins in the process. In the sense that the Johannine Jesus overshadows all others, this is partially correct, but to put it in such terms is to confuse a theological judgment about Christianity's proper relationship with Judaism with Johannine self-understanding. The evangelist's stance is that those who believe in Jesus have been faithful to God and obedient to all of his servants and messengers.[121] And we can almost hear voices in the Gospel retorting, "You are sorely mistaken. We are the rightful heirs to God's covenant with Israel."

So why in this shouting match would the Johannine community have suddenly lost its voice when it came to the ethnonym "Jews"? Here it is crucial to remember that the evangelist, by nearly all accounts, had been born and raised a Jew. It is a foundational premise of the synagogue-expulsion hypothesis and of the religious-schism model more generally. While we know of Gentile Christian authors who simultaneously claim Israel's legacy and jettison the name "Jew," it is much harder to explain why an ethnically Jewish evangelist/community who otherwise aggressively affirms continuity with Israel's past would make that same move.[122] The tension is made all the more acute when we observe that the evangelist nowhere tries to conceal that Jesus himself is a Jew and that the names "Israel" and "Israelite" are consistently positive in the Fourth Gospel.[123] It is a basic tenet of Johannine Christology that the Jews are Jesus's own people, even on the off chance that "his own" (οἱ ἴδιοι) of the prologue refers to humanity in general.[124] Jesus, handed over to Pilate by his own people and his own chief priests (18:35), dies as the king of the Jews. And it is as a Jew that Jesus declares to the Samaritan woman at Jacob's well that "salvation is from the Jews" (4:22). Striking here is not only the asseveration itself, on its own a potent reminder of the complexity of the Johannine attitude toward the Jews, but the "we" (ἡμεῖς) of 4:22a.[125] When Jesus states, "We worship what we know," he speaks as a member of the Jewish people. The entire dialogue of 4:1-26 hinges upon this. The Samaritan woman expresses her bewilderment at Jesus's request for a drink in exactly those terms: "How is it that you, a Jew, ask a drink of me, a woman of Samaria" (4:9)? If the evangelist does not try to disguise that the Son of God sent by the Father is in the flesh a Jew or excise it out of embarrassment over the community's past, why would the ethnically Jewish members of the Johannine community have renounced it for themselves?[126]

As for the name "Israel," we must take into consideration not only that it bears positive connotations but also that the evangelist does not transform it into code language for the church or contrast it with the ethnonym Ἰουδαῖος.[127] A case in point is the description of Nicodemus in John 3. According to v. 1, he is a "leader of the Jews," but in the course of the winding conversation, Jesus addresses him as the "teacher of Israel" (3:10). Because at this point in the narrative Nicodemus is only a curious sympathizer, "Israel" must mean the natural people, the nation of Israel. Again, he who is hailed by the crowds as "the king of Israel" at the triumphal entry (12:13) is executed as "king of the Jews," the two expressions carrying roughly the same meaning.[128] So when Jesus penetrates into Nathanael's inner being and announces, "Behold, truly an Israelite in whom there is nothing false (1:47)," it is not the creation of a new identity, a spiritualized Israel that floats free from ethnic bonds, or a *tertium quid* that constitutes its own people or race, but the affirmation of an already existing one.

Because of the semantic overlap between Ἰσραηλίτης and Ἰουδαῖος in the Fourth Gospel, the distinction between being "truly Israelites" and being "Jews," as Martyn frames it, seems artificial.[129] So, too, Christopher Blumhofer's hypothesis that John envisions a future for Israel in contradistinction to the *Ioudaioi* is difficult to maintain. According to Blumhofer, the evangelist exploits a semantic gap between the terms "Jew" and "Israel" already present in Second Temple Jewish literature. Following Shemaryahu Talmon, he posits a distinction between the *Ioudaioi* as a creedal-national community (the inner-group) and Israel as a broader historical and theological entity (the in-group). The terms, he says, "are not inherently coextensive, but the extent to which they overlap (or do not) corresponds to a broader assessment of the relationship between a particular historical and theological community and an idealized theological and historical people, Israel."[130] As an example of this distinction, Blumhofer points to the Yaḥad. Because of their struggle with a Judean inner-group, the covenanters avoided the term "Jew" and expressed ambivalence toward the house of Judah. They positioned themselves as the inner-group as they sought to bring the in-group Israel into its eschatological future.[131] The *Ioudaioi*, that is to say, were not the only claimants to the center of Israel. Blumhofer discerns a comparable theological and rhetorical ploy in the Fourth Gospel where the author imagines a future for Israel without the *Ioudaioi* as the inner-group.

Blumhofer is correct that "Israel" and "Jew" were not mere synonyms in most Second Temple Jewish literature, but Talmon's dichotomy between an inner-group and in-group does not provide the best framing for the difference. Rather, as I have argued elsewhere, and as Jason Staples has convincingly shown, Jewish authors of the period continue to see "the Jews" as a subset of Israel.[132] They are descendants of the southern tribes and thus only part of the twelve-tribe collective. The texts of the Yaḥad show an awareness of that difference, but they do not drive a wedge between the house of Judah and Israel. According to Staples, while the Yaḥad prefers "Israel" terminology, it does not identify itself as the "true Israel" but rather as a faithful remnant and vanguard of the eschatologically restored nation.[133] "Judah," for its part, has not become a negative or outsider term in the scrolls. As with Israel, the Yaḥad recognizes both righteous and wicked within the house of Judah, and carefully employs subset language to demarcate various groups.[134] Blumhofer's claim that the scrolls attest to an inner-group that positions itself against the house of Judah does not bear itself out. Likewise, the Gospel of John nowhere sets "Israel" and "Jew" in opposition to each other. "Israel" only appears five times in the narrative, and as we have seen, when it does appear, it refers to the physical nation and/or its members, sometimes in parallel with the term "Jews." Nicodemus is both a "leader of the Jews" and a "teacher of Israel." Nathanael is truly an Israelite, and Jesus is a Ἰουδαῖος.[135]

CONCLUSION

Proponents of the synagogue-expulsion theory generally agree that the Johannine Christians repudiated identification as Jews as a result of excommunication. Culpepper likens this transition to a divorce. In the process of separation, these believers forged a new religious identity but took all the valuables of the house as their own.[136] I would emend the imagery. What the Fourth Gospel asserts is that the house itself has belonged all along to those who hear Jesus's voice. The evangelist had no intention of conceding it to another. Or to put it in more technical terms, the tradents of the Johannine tradition score high on Stark and Bainbridge's index of antagonism, but they do so by presenting themselves more as a faithful remnant than as a new religion that invalidates the old.

The model of a local parting of the ways between Jews and the disciples of Jesus requires that John and the community for which he writes were pugilists through and through but had, on this point, lost their fighting spirit. They would in effect be saying: "We are faithful to Moses. We are faithful to the prophets. We are faithful to the Scriptures. We are the children of Abraham. We are truly Israelites. The Word made flesh was a Jew. But we are not

Jews." For a community of ethnically Jewish believers in Jesus, supposedly struggling to create social boundaries, a disjuncture in self-identity of this kind would be markedly idiosyncratic. Devoid of reliable external evidence and pushed up against the evangelist's "sectarian" mentality, the premise that the Gospel of John reflects a schism in which the evangelist or members of the Johannine community fashioned a new identity to the exclusion of their former identity as Jews loses some of its stability. At least, it opens up the need for reassessment.

NOTES

1. Edwyn Clement Hoskyns, *The Fourth Gospel*, ed. Francis Noel Davey (London: Faber & Faber, 1940), 49–50. The book was published posthumously from Hoskyns's incomplete notes.

2. So John Ashton, *Understanding,* 1st ed. (Oxford: Oxford University Press, 1991), 109: "It is largely because of his [Martyn's] work that one can say that this area of Johannine research (that is, the one concerned with audience and situation) has been roughly mapped out. What remains is a matter of adjusting a few details and filling some gaps." The second edition of *Understanding* drops the entire first part of the original ("Questions and Answers") and so also omits this particular statement. D. Moody Smith ("The Contribution of J. Louis Martyn to the Understanding of the Gospel of John," in *History and Theology*, 14, n. 30) refers to Martyn's thesis as a paradigm, "part of what students imbibe in standard works . . . as knowledge generally received and held to be valid."

3. Smith, "Contribution of J. Louis Martyn," 6.

4. Martyn leaves the German *einmalig* untranslated but points out in a note (*History and Theology*, 40, n. 22) that it means something like the "back there" level of the story.

5. Ibid., 40–45.

6. Ibid., 46–49. The synagogue expulsion mentioned in the Gospel of John was associated with the Birkat Haminim as early as Moritz von Aberle, "Über die Zweck"; later, but before the publication of *History and Theology*, Kenneth L. Carroll, "The Fourth Gospel and the Exclusion of Christians from the Synagogues," *BJRL* 40 (1957): 19–32; Wolfgang Schrage, "ἀποσυνάγωγος," *TWNT* 7:848-52.

7. Martyn, *History and Theology*, 51–66. "Blessing" is a euphemism for a curse, as in Job 2:9 ("Bless God and die"), directed in this case against *minim* (heretics), presumably including, but not limited to, Jewish Christ followers.

8. The term "Jewish Christians" is ideologically freighted, and its precise referent is sometimes unclear, as scholars have defined and redefined it. I believe it could be retained as a neutral description of ethnic Jews in antiquity who professed some form of faith in Jesus. This leaves out the question of Torah observance and allows space for a spectrum of Christological views. That is, one could employ the term in a sense analogous to Oskar Skarsaune's phrase "Jewish believers in Jesus."

See Skarsaune, "Jewish Believers in Jesus in Antiquity—Problems of Definition, Method, and Sources," in *Jewish Believers in Jesus: The Early Centuries*, ed. Oskar Skarsaune and Reidar Hvalvik (Peabody, MA: Hendrickson, 2007), 3–21.

However, to avoid confusion and the ideological entanglements in the history of research, I have only retained the term when necessary to accurately represent previous scholarly use of the category. For discussion and critique of the nomenclature, see, among others, Matt Jackson-McCabe, *Jewish Christianity: The Making of the Christianity-Judaism Divide* (New Haven: Yale University Press, 2020); Annette Yoshiko Reed, *Jewish-Christianity and the History of Judaism*, TSAJ 171 (Tübingen: Mohr Siebeck, 2018); and Daniel Boyarin, "Rethinking Jewish Christianity: An Argument for Dismantling a Dubious Category (to which is Appended a Correction of My *Border Lines*)," *JQR* 99 (2009): 7–36.

9. J. Louis Martyn, "Glimpses into the History of the Johannine Community: From its Origin through the Period of Its Life in Which the Fourth Gospel Was Composed," in idem, *History and Theology*, 157.

10. Wayne A. Meeks, "Breaking Away: Three New Testament Pictures of Christianity's Separation from the Jewish Communities," in *"To See Ourselves as Others See Us": Christians, Jews, "Others" in Late Antiquity*, ed. Jacob Neusner and Ernest S. Frerichs, Scholars Press Studies in the Humanities 9 (Chico, CA: Scholars Press, 1985), 102. Seminal studies of the "blessing" that contributed to the decline in confidence in its pertinence to the Gospel of John include Peter Schäfer, "Die sogenannte Synode von Jabne: Zur Trennung von Juden und Christen im ersten/zweiten Jh. N. Chr.," *Judaica* 31 (1975): 54–64, 116–24; Reuven Kimelman, "*Birkat Ha-Minim* and the Lack of Evidence for an Anti-Christian Jewish Prayer in Late Antiquity," in *Aspects of Judaism in the Greco-Roman Period*, ed. E. P. Sanders, Albert I. Baumgarten, and Alan Mendelson, vol. 2 of *Jewish and Christian Self-Definition*, ed. E. P. Sanders (Philadelphia: Fortress, 1981), 226–44; also the more recent study of the history of the benediction by Ruth Langer, *Cursing the Christians? A History of the Birkat Haminim* (Oxford: Oxford University Press, 2012), 16–40.

Ashton (*Understanding*, 2nd ed., 33) states that Martyn's thesis is at most buttressed by the identification of being made ἀποσυνάγωγος with the synagogue curse. That Ashton is essentially correct is seen in the fact that in Martyn's unpublished dissertation ("The Salvation-History Perspective in the Fourth Gospel," [PhD diss., Yale, 1957]), which contains the germ of many of the ideas in *History and Theology*, he had not yet proposed the identification.

11. Bernier, *Aposynagōgos*, 49–52. Among advocates of this position, Bernier (ibid., 13) lists Adele Reinhartz, Raimo Hakola, Warren Carter, and Tom Thatcher.

12. Brown, *The Community of the Beloved Disciple* (New York: Paulist, 1979), 41.

13. Ashton, *Understanding*, 108.

14. R. Alan Culpepper, "The Gospel of John and the Jews," *RevExp* 84 (1987): 282; similarly idem, "The Gospel of John as a Threat to Jewish-Christian Relations," in *Overcoming Fear between Jews and Christians*, ed. James H. Charlesworth, Frank X. Blisard, and Jerry L. Gorham, Shared Ground among Jews and Christians 3 (New York: Crossroad, 1993), 36–37.

15. Reinhartz, "'Jews' and Jews," 213–27.

16. Ibid., 224; Reinhartz makes this argument especially forcefully throughout *Cast Out of the Covenant*. See also eadem, "Forging a New Identity: Johannine Rhetoric and the Audience of the Fourth Gospel," in *Paul, John, and Apocalyptic Eschatology: Studies in Honour of Martinus C. de Boer*, ed. Jan Krans et al., NovTSup 149 (Leiden: Brill, 2013), 123–34. Reinhartz holds that Samaritans, Gentiles, and ethnic Jews were among the Gospel's intended audience, so that the process of identity formation entails the separation of Johannine Christians not only from Jews but from any other ethno-religious entity.

17. Raimo Hakola, *Identity Matters: John, the Jews and Jewishness*, NovTSup 118 (Leiden: Brill, 2005), 235–36.

18. Ibid., 231.

19. Dunn, "Embarrassment of History," 43–46.

20. Ibid., 49.

21. Ibid., 53. David Rensberger ("Anti-Judaism and the Gospel of John," in *Anti-Judaism and the Gospels*, ed. William R. Farmer [Harrisburg, PA: Trinity International, 1999], 120–57) takes a similar stance, though he moves the conflict a bit further down the road. The Fourth Gospel stands at the dividing line of Judaism and Christianity, occupying a transitional period between inner-Jewish sectarian protest and a full-blown religious schism.

22. Motyer, *Your Father the Devil?* 35–73.

23. Ibid., 73.

24. Ibid., 212. Motyer revives the position of Bornhäuser, *Das Johannesevangelium: Eine Missionsschrift für Israel*, BFCT 2/15 (Gütersloh: Bertelsmann, 1928); W. C. Van Unnik, "The Purpose of St. John's Gospel," *SE I* (Berlin: Akademie, 1959), 382–411; J. A. T. Robinson, "The Destination and Purpose of St. John's Gospel," *NTS* 6 (1960): 117–31.

25. Robert T. Fortna, *The Gospel of Signs: A Reconstruction of the Narrative Source Underlying the Fourth Gospel*, SNTSMS 11 (Cambridge: Cambridge University Press, 1970); idem, *The Fourth Gospel and Its Predecessor: From Narrative Source to Present Gospel* (Philadelphia: Fortress, 1988). Motyer himself (*Your Father the Devil?* 7) recognizes that the position he wishes to defend will strike many as prima facie improbable.

26. "Letter of repudiation" (*Absagebrief*) is how von Aberle ("Über die Zweck," 94) had phrased it.

27. Keener, *Gospel of John*, 1:200.

28. Cirafesi, *John Within Judaism*, 1–26.

29. Ibid., 95. Similarly, Christopher Blumhofer (*John and the Future of Israel*, 11) states that "readers need to make sense of both John's constructive engagement with Israel's tradition and its polemic toward the *Ioudaioi*."

30. Reimund Bieringer, Didier Pollefeyt, and Frederique Vandecasteele-Vanneuville, "Wrestling with Johannine Anti-Judaism: A Hermeneutical Framework for the Analysis of the Current Debate," in *Anti-Judaism and the Fourth Gospel*, 3–37, at 22–23.

31. As John Van Maaren remarks (review of *John Within Judaism*, by Wally Cirafesi, *RBL* [2023]: 362–65, at 365): "Cirafesi convincingly argues that John's

Ioudaioi have the characteristics of a priestly-oriented form of Judaism, but it is more difficult to demonstrate that the text advocates an alternative form of Judaism (as Cirafesi argues) rather than something else. Since the *Ioudaioi* are not explicitly distinguished from another group of exemplary *Ioudaioi*, their narrative characterization could be a caricature of the entire *ethnos* and not meant to designate one particular type."

32. Keener, *Gospel of John*, 1:216.

33. Dunn, *Partings*, 191–92, 209. This is based in part on Dunn's understanding of "Israel" as a title that expressed identity in relation to God, while "Jew" emphasized distinction in relation to others. Any neat division of "Israel" and "Jew" into insider and outsider names respectively, however, is questionable. See my "'Israel' and 'Jew' as Markers of Jewish Identity in Antiquity: The Problems of Insider/Outsider Classification," *JSJ* 45 (2014): 80–99; Staples, *Idea of Israel*, 25–53.

34. Mark Goodwin ("Response to David Rensberger: Questions about a Jewish Johannine Community," in *Anti-Judaism and the Gospels*, 168–71) raises a similar objection against Rensberger, asking whether, as far as it relates to the Gospel of John, the transitional period between an inner-Jewish struggle and that between two religions had not already ended.

35. Dunn, "Embarrassment of History," 53.

36. Wilhelm Lütgert, "Die Juden im Johannesevangelium," in *Neutestamentliche Studien: Georg Heinrici zu seinem 70. Geburtstag*, UNT 6 (Leipzig: Hinrichs, 1914), 147–54; Bornhäuser, *Missionsschrift*, 141. Ashton (*Understanding*, 69–78) also builds upon these suggestions as well as on Daniel Boyarin's "The Ioudaioi in John and the Prehistory of 'Judaism,'" in *Pauline Conversations in Context: Essays in Honor of Calvin J. Roetzel*, ed. Janice Capel Anderson, Philip Sellew, and Claudia Setzer, JSNTSup 221 (London: Sheffield Academic, 2002), 216–39.

37. Motyer, *Your Father the Devil?* 56; similarly Cornelis Bennema ("The Identity and Composition of Οἱ Ἰουδαῖοι in the Gospel of John," *TynBul* 60 [2009]: 239–63) who identifies the Johannine Jews as "a particular religious group of Torah- and temple-loyalists found especially, but not exclusively, in Judaea" (242).

38. The evangelist's fondness for the literary device of irony is well detailed in Paul D. Duke, *Irony in the Fourth Gospel* (Atlanta: John Knox, 1985).

39. Keener, *Gospel of John*, 1:218–28; similarly, but independently, de Boer, "Depiction of 'the Jews,'" 141–57.

40. De Boer ("Depiction of 'the Jews,'" 156–57) states explicitly that the Johannine Christians eventually renounced the name "Jews" for themselves, the irony contributing to the creation of a new social reality. Keener does not press this idea as far as de Boer, but some of his arguments carry him in that direction. He compares the situation of the Johannine community to a hypothetical group of Christians who consider themselves heirs to the faith but are rejected by the wider Christian community: "The minority might respond by calling themselves 'true Christians' to distinguish themselves from the 'false' ones . . . or more to the point here, they might relinquish the title altogether to their opponents . . . The second solution appears to be the one chosen by the author of the Fourth Gospel" (*Gospel of John*, 1:219).

41. Byers, *John and the Others*, 45–94, at 61.

42. Clement so describes the Fourth Gospel in the now lost *Hypotyposes*. The information comes to us through Eusebius of Caesarea, *Hist. eccl.* 6.14.5–7.

43. Byers, *John and the Others*, 86.

44. A similar question may be asked of Cirafesi. If the Gospel criticizes a *type* of Judaism, namely, a priestly-oriented Judaism that was not representative of all Jews in antiquity, then why not level that criticism with other terms (chief priests, teachers of the law, scribes, Pharisees, etc.)?

45. Byers (*John and the Others*, 87), for example, writes that many of the negative occurrences of the term "the Jews" are associated with resistance to the universalizing scope of covenant belonging. Yet even in John 8, where matters of genealogy come most to the fore, the debate is not over whether non-Jews may be included in the people of God or on what basis. While Jesus does implicitly undermine the role of genealogy in determining covenant membership, the contentious exchange revolves around Jesus's identity and the paternity of his opponents. Any "anxiety over a Torah mission to gentiles" (Cirafesi, *John Within Judaism*, 102; cf. 110) seems remote from the concerns of the passage.

46. Byers, *John and the Others*, 58–64.

47. Similarly, Numada, *John and Anti-Judaism*, 115–16. According to Numada, John reduces the attraction of Judaism and Jewish social identity for the Gospel's audience, creating a new theocentric identity based on the Gospel's Christology.

48. The course of the debate and the challenges to Martyn's two-level reading are thoroughly recounted in Wally V. Cirafesi, "The Johannine Community Hypothesis (1968-Present): Past and Present Approaches and a New Way Forward," *CBR* 12 (2014): 173–93; idem, "The 'Johannine Community' in (More) Current Research: A Critical Appraisal of Recent Methods and Models," *Neot* 48 (2014): 341–64.

49. Among others, Stephen C. Barton, "Can We Identify the Gospel Audiences?" in *The Gospels for All Christians: Rethinking the Gospel Audiences*, ed. Richard Bauckham (Grand Rapids: Eerdmans, 1998), 173–94. With respect to the Fourth Gospel in particular, Motyer, *Your Father the Devil?* 24–31; Trond Skard Dokka, "Irony and Sectarianism in the Gospel of John," in *New Readings in John: Literary and Theological Perspectives*, ed. Johannes Nissen and Sigfred Petersen, JSNTSup 182 (Sheffield: Sheffield Academic, 1999), 85–91; Tobias Hägerland, "John's Gospel: A Two-Level Drama?" *JSNT* 25 (2003): 309–22; Edward W. Klink III, *The Sheep of the Fold: The Audience and Origin of the Gospel of John*, SNTSMS 141 (Cambridge: Cambridge University Press, 2007), 107–51. Doubts have also been raised about the existence of a Markan community by Dwight N. Peterson (*The Origins of Mark: The Markan Community in Current Debate*, BibInt 48 [Leiden: Brill, 2000]).

50. This is the central thesis of Richard Bauckham, "For Whom Were Gospels Written?" in *Gospels for All Christians*, 9–48. Klink's *Sheep of the Fold* is an extension of Bauckham's work on the Gospel of John.

51. So, for example, Thomas L. Brodie, *The Quest for the Origin of John's Gospel: A Source-Oriented Approach* (New York: Oxford University Press, 1993), 15–21; Motyer, *Your Father the Devil?* 25–28; Adele Reinhartz, "The Johannine Community and Its Jewish Neighbors: A Reappraisal," in *Literary and Social Readings of the Fourth Gospel*, ed. Fernando F. Segovia, vol. 2 of *What is John?* SymS 7

(Atlanta: Scholars Press, 1998), 111–38; eadem, *Befriending the Beloved Disciple: A Jewish Reading of the Gospel of John* (New York: Continuum, 2001), 37–53.

52. Similarly, Cirafesi, "'Johannine Community' in (More) Current Research," 361.

53. The methodological difficulties in correlating ideas or systems of symbols, and the texts which carry them, with particular social structures and patterns of interaction are adumbrated in Bengt Holmberg, *Sociology and the New Testament: An Appraisal* (Minneapolis: Fortress, 1990), 118–44, 125–28 on the Gospel of John. According to Holmberg (ibid., 142), the quest for correlations between texts and social situations is not "invalid or hopeless" but it must start from "good factual knowledge about social data" and "the realization of how complex and subtle such relationships typically are."

54. Ashton, *Gospel of John and Christian Origins*, 1.

55. Ibid., 1–3.

56. I say in one sense because if we think in terms of Judaism and Christianity as religious systems, then someone like Edith Stein did not adhere to both, but this just shows that being a Jew and practicing Judaism are not entirely symmetrical. So also Jacob Neusner, "Defining Judaism," in *The Blackwell Companion to Judaism*, ed. Jacob Neusner and Alan Avery-Peck (Oxford: Blackwell, 2000), 4–5. That Stein still thought of the Jews as her own people is documented by Waltraud Herbstrith, *Edith Stein: A Biography* (San Francisco: Harper & Row, 1985), 62–67; Sarah Borden, *Edith Stein*, Outstanding Christian Thinkers (London: Continuum, 2003), 139–40: "It is, ironically, after her conversion to Catholicism that Stein identifies herself most strongly with the Jewish people, taking pride in her heritage and regularly insisting on her own Jewishness."

57. Herbstrith, *Edith Stein*, 62–67. In a letter dated October 31, 1938, Stein compares herself to Esther, "taken from among her people precisely so that she might represent them before the king," as Borden (*Stein*, 139) reports.

58. This is the imagery of John T. Townsend, "The Gospel of John and the Jews: The Story of a Religious Divorce," in *Antisemitism and the Foundations of Christianity*, ed. Alan T. Davies (New York: Paulist, 1979), 72–97; appropriated also by Culpepper, "Anti-Judaism in the Fourth Gospel," 69.

59. Scholarship on ancient "Jewish Christian" groups is voluminous. Much less has been written about modern movements—whether their history of development, theology, or religious practice—though that appears to be changing. See from a wide variety of perspectives, Dan Cohn-Sherbok, *Messianic Judaism* (London: Cassell, 2000); Michael R. Darby, *The Emergence of the Hebrew Christian Movement in Nineteenth-Century Britain*, SHR 128 (Leiden: Brill, 2010); David Rudolph and Joel Willitts, eds., *Introduction to Messianic Judaism: Its Ecclesial Context and Biblical Foundations* (Grand Rapids: Zondervan, 2013).

60. Thus, for instance, *Shulchan Aruch*, Even HaEzer 44:9. Joseph Karo also states in Even HaEzer 44:9 that the betrothal of an apostate to a Jewish woman is valid, and thus the wife of the convert must still receive a bill of divorce in order for the marriage to be dissolved. The halakhic standing of the apostate him- or herself is fraught with tension, but according to Jacob Katz (*Exclusiveness and Tolerance:*

Studies in Jewish-Gentile Relations in Medieval and Modern Times, Scripta Judaica 3 [London: Oxford University Press, 1961], 71), the Talmudic dictum that "although Israel has sinned, he is Israel" (b. Sanh. 44a) has become, since the time of Rashi, "a standard ruling in connexion with the definition of the status of the apostate."

61. See further Yona Reiss, "Halakhic Views toward Different Jews," in *The Relationship of Orthodox Jews with Believing Jews of Other Religious Ideologies and Non-Believing Jews*, ed. Adam Mintz, Orthodox Forum (New York: Ktav, 2010), 243–58.

62. Terms such as עם, גוי, and אמה.

63. John Hutchinson and Anthony D. Smith ("Introduction," in *Ethnicity*, ed. John Hutchinson and Anthony D. Smith, Oxford Readers [Oxford: Oxford University Press, 1996], 6–7) settle on six marks that ἔθνη habitually exhibit: a common proper name for the group, a myth of common ancestry, a shared history or memories of a common past, a common culture, a historical homeland, and a sense of communal solidarity. See also Cirafesi, *John Within Judaism*, 37–51; David Goodblatt, "Ancient Jewish Identity," *Ancient Jew Review*, https://www.ancientjewreview.com/read/2018/10/24/ancient-jewish-identity, Oct. 24, 2018.

64. I speak here of memorialization, but it has also been argued that the direction of influence went the other way. According to David Goodblatt (*Elements of Ancient Jewish Nationalism* [Cambridge: Cambridge University Press, 2006], 28–48), it was Scripture that "provided the foundation and the building blocks for constructing the beliefs in shared descent and common culture" (29). In either case, Scripture was a vital component of Jewish self-understanding by the first century CE.

65. This is classically articulated when Israel is at Mount Sinai preparing for God's appearance in glory. The Israelites are to be God's treasured possession, a holy nation (גוי קדוש, Exod 19:6). This understanding of Israel is everywhere in evidence in ancient Jewish literature, including the rabbinic corpus, where Israel is the nation *par excellence*, as Sacha Stern observes (*Jewish Identity in Early Rabbinic Writings*, AGJU 23 [Leiden: Brill, 1994], 8).

66. On the pervasiveness of the myth of common ancestry in the texts of this period, see Goodblatt, "Ancient Jewish Identity." Reflecting on the practice of referring to Judaisms in the plural, Goodblatt remarks: "In my view what we have are people of (believed) shared ancestry emphasizing or modifying different elements of a common culture." Some Jewish authors were creative in their synthesizing of Jewish and non-Jewish lineages. The Hellenistic Jewish author Artapanus, for example, identifies Moses with the mythical Greek singer Musaeus, and Cleodemus Malchus makes the descendants of Abraham through Keturah the founders of Assyria and Africa.

67. For which Philo of Alexandria is famous. David T. Runia (*Philo and the Church Fathers: A Collection of Papers*, Supplements to Vigiliae Christianae 32 [Leiden: Brill, 1995], 213) writes: "It cannot, in the first place, be said that Philo totally dehistoricizes God's revelation to Moses and his relation to the Patriarchs. There is no doubt in his mind that Abraham, Isaac, Jacob, and later Moses were real, if clearly exceptional men." See also Martha Himmelfarb, *A Kingdom of Priests: Ancestry and Merit in Ancient Judaism* (Philadelphia: University of Pennsylvania

Press, 2006), 143–59. According to Himmelfarb, Philo sometimes restrains himself from allegorizing the cult and priesthood because he did not want to undermine these institutions.

68. That is not to say that all ancient Jews saw the value of kinship and ancestry equally. See again Himmelfarb, *Kingdom of Priests*, 3–4. Nevertheless, the assumption of common ancestry may be seen as one aspect of what E. P. Sanders has called "Common Judaism." That is, there were beliefs and behaviors like monotheism, the practice of circumcision, Sabbath observance, and so forth that were shared by most Jews of the time. See E. P. Sanders, *Judaism: Practice and Belief, 63 BCE-66 CE* (Philadelphia: Trinity International, 1992); Wayne O. McCready and Adele Reinhartz, eds., *Common Judaism: Explorations in Second-Temple Judaism* (Minneapolis: Fortress, 2008). The belief in common ancestry is, of course, closely associated with the conviction that God chose Israel as his special possession among the nations, a belief that Dunn (*Partings*, 29–32) identifies as one of the "four pillars of Second Temple Judaism."

69. Mason, "Jews, Judaeans, Judaizing," 512.

70. I say "from Jews to something other than Jews" to avoid the objection that the label "Christian" is anachronistic in this context. If we would like to stay close to Johannine self-descriptors, the contrast might be couched as "Jews" versus "the children of God."

71. So, most vociferously, Daniel Boyarin, "Justin Martyr Invents Judaism," *CH* 70 (2001): 427–61; idem, "The Christian Invention of Judaism: The Theodosian Empire and the Rabbinic Refusal of Religion," *Representations* 85 (2004): 21–57; idem, *Border Lines: The Partition of Judaeo-Christianity* (Philadelphia: University of Pennsylvania Press, 2004).

72. So in bks. 1 and 2 of *Ecclesiastical History,* Eusebius speaks occasionally of the Jews' history and misfortunes as a nation (1.6.6; 2.6.1; 2.26.1) as it relates to the history of the church. He does so, of course, rather condescendingly; the disasters that befell the Jewish people were predicted by Christ and are just desserts for their rejection of him and his apostles.

73. In *Pan.* 8.4.1, he states that Jews are "Abraham's lineal descendants and the heirs of his true religion." In 8.3.5, he connects the name "Jews" with the tribe of Judah to which David belonged, the people of Israel from David's time taking on the additional title of "Jews."

74. For example, Origen, *Cels.* 2:8; Tertullian, *Adv. Jud.* 1. See also Mason, "Jews, Judaeans, Judaizing," 472–5, 504–5.

75. According to Mason (ibid., 474), Christian authors from Tertullian on treat Judaism as a "system of postulates." One can see what he means, but it should not be forgotten that Tertullian's construct of *Iudaismus* includes practices such as circumcision, the dietary laws, and other regulations from the law of Moses. That is, it is not a purely intellectual endeavor.

76. The intensification in the rhetoric of Christian authors intent on disassociating the Christian faith from the Jewish people and their traditions is amply documented by Andrew S. Jacobs in *Remains of the Jews: The Holy Land and Christian Empire in Late Antiquity* (Stanford: Stanford University Press, 2004), 21–55. According to

Jacobs, Christian authors of the fourth century defame the Jews in the service of a totalizing imperial discourse that aimed to relegate perceived deviants and dissenters to an inferior status within a grand narrative of Christian triumph.

77. This is implied in his discussion of the Jewish convert Joseph of Tiberias, from whom he has received information about gospels written in Hebrew (*Pan.* 30.5-12). In general, it is obvious from Epiphanius's treatment of the Ebionites and Nazoraeans that he thinks of being a Jew and Christian as mutually exclusive.

78. The occasion of the statement is a disagreement between Augustine and Jerome on Paul's rebuke of Peter in Gal 2. Jerome had argued that the whole encounter was a pious ruse, since Peter was no longer observing Jewish customs. Augustine caviled at the notion of righteous deception, maintaining that the apostles kept to the Jewish law, though such was not permitted to believers after them. Jerome subsequently argues (112.4.14) that all those who adhere to the ancestral customs of the Jews, whether from among the Jews or the Gentiles, and profess to follow Christ will be cast into the pit of perdition. See Jacobs, *Remains*, 56–102.

79. Cf. *Phild.* 6, with further discussion in Mason, "Jews, Judaeans, Judaizing," 470.

80. So also Judith Lieu, "'The Parting of the Ways': Theological Construct or Historical Reality?" *JSNT* 56 (1994): 114; eadem, *Image and Reality: The Jews in the World of the Christians in the Second Century* (Edinburgh: T&T Clark, 1996), 40. Over two and a half centuries later, in the 380s CE, John Chrysostom, preaching in Antioch, still feels it necessary to admonish Christians who participate in the Jewish feasts, thus revealing the continuing appeal of Jewish customs among at least a segment of the Christian population. See Pieter W. van der Horst, "Jews and Christians in Antioch at the End of the Fourth Century," in *Christian-Jewish Relations through the Centuries*, ed. Stanley E. Porter and Brook W. R. Pearson (London: T&T Clark, 2004), 228–38.

81. So also Lieu, *Image and Reality*, 138–89. Lieu suggests that by taking a moderate position on Torah observance by Jewish converts, Justin may also be seeking to bring Gentile Christians who had adopted some Jewish practices back into the mainstream church.

82. As Mason observes, "Jews, Judaeans, Judaizing," 462, 505–10. So also Goodblatt, "Ancient Jewish Identity." This is certainly not restricted to the ancient world. Maykel Verkuyten (*The Social Psychology of Ethnic Identity*, European Monographs in Social Psychology [Hove: Psychology Press, 2005], 77) states almost axiomatically that "departures of cultural practices are typically defined as a loss or abandonment of one's own culture and a betrayal of one's own people or group." See also the observations of Cirafesi (*John Within Judaism*, 80–94) about the interplay of genealogy and culture in constructions of ancient Jewish identity.

83. Many of the pertinent sources are laid out by Benjamin Isaac, *The Invention of Racism in Classical Antiquity* (Princeton: Princeton University Press, 2004), 225–47, 440–91 for prejudices against the Jews. I do not thereby mean to imply that all foreign religious rites, cults, and practices were deplored, only that this tolerance was not boundless.

84. Similarly, Juvenal *Sat.* 14.100-104. On the other side, there is Philo (*Virtues,* 102–3), who lauds incomers to the Jewish community.

85. This is implied, for instance, in 1 Macc 1:41-64; 2 Macc 4:11-17.

86. So Martyn, *History and Theology,* 69–83. According to Martyn, the Jewish authorities in John's city had charged Johannine missionaries with being "beguilers" who were leading the people to the worship of another alongside God. The prohibition of this behavior and the dire consequences for engaging in it are set forth in Deut 13.

87. These figures and other alleged apostates are treated in greater detail in John M. G. Barclay, "Who Was Considered an Apostate in the Jewish Diaspora?" in *Tolerance and Intolerance in Early Judaism and Christianity,* ed. Graham N. Stanton and Guy G. Stroumsa (Cambridge: Cambridge University Press, 1998), 80–98; also Stephen G. Wilson, *Leaving the Fold: Apostates and Defectors in Antiquity* (Minneapolis: Fortress, 2004), 23–65.

88. In favor of the first, at least in Josephus's mind, is that the Samaritans are said to be apostates from the Jewish nation (*Ant.* 11.340) but are very plainly something other than Jews. However, he also regards them as foreign settlers from Mesopotamia.

89. Sacha Stern, *Jewish Identity,* 105–12; Lawrence H. Schiffman, *Who Was a Jew? Rabbinic and Halakhic Perspectives on the Jewish Christian Schism* (Hoboken, NJ: Ktav, 1985), 41–49.

90. Stern, *Jewish Identity,* 105: "On the one hand, the apostate remains permanently and irreversibly 'Israel' . . . On the other hand . . . rabbinic sources ignore by and large the Jewish identity of the apostate, and emphasize as much as possible his affinity with the non-Jews." Similarly, for *minim* (ibid., 112).

91. Keener (*Gospel of John,* 1:218-19) speaks of a "functional claim" on the part of the Jewish authorities that the Johannine Christians were no longer Jewish. The status of these believers as Jews was not denied, but they were made to feel unwelcome in the synagogue. For present purposes, it is best to keep any actual claims of the synagogue leaders and the implications of their actions conceptually distinct, though it must be allowed that the Johannine Christians could have perceived social ostracism as a denial of their standing as Jews.

92. According to Cirafesi ("Rethinking John and 'the Synagogue' in Light of Expulsion from Public Assemblies in Antiquity," *JBL* 142 [2023]: 677–97), the synagogue expulsion referred to in the Gospel of John has more to do with the contentious politics of public assemblies than with a separation from Judaism *tout court.* That is, the synagogue does not stand in for Judaism. It could still be asked, though, how members of a putative Johannine community might have responded to a perceived denial of the authenticity of their embodiment of Jewishness, even if at the local level.

93. Frank Williams, trans., *The Panarion of Epiphanius of Salamis: Book I (Sects 1-46),* 2nd ed., Nag Hammadi and Manichaean Studies 63 (Leiden: Brill, 2009), 128.

94. So Martinus C. de Boer, "L'Évangile de Jean et le christianisme juif (nazoréen)," in *Le déchirement: Juifs et chrétiens au premier siècle,* ed. Daniel Marguerat, MdB 32 (Geneva: Labor et Fides, 1996), 179–202; idem, "The Nazoreans: Living at the Boundary of Judaism and Christianity," in *Tolerance and Intolerance,* 239–63.

95. So also Edwin K. Broadhead, *Jewish Ways of Following Jesus: Redrawing the Religious Map of Antiquity,* WUNT 266 (Tübingen: Mohr Siebeck, 2010), 177–78; Ray A. Pritz, *Nazarene Jewish Christianity: From the End of the New Testament Period until Its Disappearance in the Fourth Century* (Jerusalem: Magnes, 1988), 36.

96. So also A. F. J. Klijn and G. J. Reinink, *Patristic Evidence for Jewish-Christian Sects,* NovTSup 36 (Leiden: Brill, 1973), 52; Petri Luomanen, *Recovering Jewish-Christian Sects and Gospels,* Supplements to Vigiliae Christianae 110 (Leiden: Brill, 2012), 62; Pritz, *Nazarene Jewish Christianity,* 35.

97. This goes back at least as far as John Toland in the early eighteenth century, as F. Stanley Jones points out in "The Genre of the Book of Elchasai: A Primitive Church Order, Not an Apocalypse," in *Historische Wahrheit und theologische Wissenschaft: Gerd Lüdemann zum 50. Geburtstag,* ed. Alf Özen (Frankfurt am Main: Lang, 1996), 87; of Epiphanius's handling of the Nazoraeans, Broadhead (*Jewish Ways of Following,* 174–75) concludes that the portrayal is "particularly confused and unsubstantiated."

98. Williams, Panarion *of Epiphanius,* 123.

99. The epithet Nazarenes is applied to the followers of Jesus in Acts 24:5. Epiphanius confuses the name of a sect with the general designation in Aramaic for followers of Jesus, nomenclature still current in Arabic and Hebrew. See Wolfram Kinzig, "The Nazoraeans," in *Jewish Believers in Jesus,* 468–71.

100. Epiphanius seems to have taken his Jessaeans from Philo's Essenes, mentioned in *Contempl. Life* 1 and *Good Person* 75–87, conflating them with the Theraputae by misreading or misremembering Philo's opening remarks in *The Contemplative Life.* Since Eusebius of Caesarea had identified the Theraputae as Christian ascetics in *Hist. eccl.* 1.17, Epiphanius reasons that the Ἐσσαῖοι, or Ἰεσσαῖοι as he remembers them, were none other than early Christians and concocts an etymology that links the name with Jesse or Jesus. It is also worth noting that one of his etymologies for the name Jesus is "healer," perhaps derived in a roundabout way from the name "Theraputae." Further discussion on the source of Epiphanius's confusion in Aline Pourkier, *L'hérésiologie chez Épiphane de Salamine,* Christianisme antique 4 (Paris: Beauchesne, 1992), 439–47.

101. Ps.-Clem. Recognitions 1.27-71 presents one other possible first-hand source for Jewish-Christian self-understanding, as it or parts of it are usually regarded as a distinct literary unit that originated in Jewish-Christian circles. In Recognitions 1.50 and in the Latin version of 1.53, Peter does speak of "us" and "the Jews" as apparently separate groups, which might be taken as evidence of Jewish-Christian renunciation of the name "Jews." But the multiple layers of redaction of the Pseudo-Clementine literature mean that this argument could only be sustained if it could be shown with confidence that these particular statements belong to the source behind 1.27-71 and not to the author of the hypothesized *Grundschrift* or of the Recognitions itself. F. Stanley Jones, for example, assigns the middle of 1.44.1 to the middle of 1.53.4 to the author of the *Grundschrift* since its reintroduction of Clement and dialogical style are characteristic of the rest of the romance but strikingly different from the surrounding material. See idem, *An Ancient Jewish Christian Source on the History of Christianity: Pseudo-Clementine Recognitions*

1.27-71, Texts and Translations 37, Christian Apocrypha 2 (Atlanta: Scholars Press, 1995), 134–36. It should be noted, moreover, that in the Syriac text of Recognitions 1.32.1, Abraham is called a man of "our race, the Hebrews, who are also called the Jews."

102. Wilhelm Wrede, best known for his work on the Messianic secret motif in the Gospel of Mark, determines that for Paul faith in Jesus is "no more a form of the Jewish faith, but a new faith" (*Paul*, trans. Edward Lummis [London: Philip Green, 1907], 168). Similarly, Jürgen Becker (*Paul, Apostle to the Gentiles*, trans. O. C. Dean [Louisville: Westminster John Knox, 1993]) describes Paul after his encounter with the risen Jesus as a "former Jew." The position has been again defended by Love L. Sechrest, *A Former Jew: Paul and the Dialectics of Race*, LNTS 410 (London: T&T Clark, 2009).

103. James D. G. Dunn, "Who Did Paul Think He Was? A Study of Jewish-Christian Identity," *NTS* 45 (1999): 182: "Paul speaks as one who does not acknowledge 'Jew' as his own given identity, or as an identity inalienable from his person." Similarly, D. A. Carson, "Mystery and Fulfillment: Toward a More Comprehensive Paradigm of Paul's Understanding of the Old and the New," in *The Paradoxes of Paul*, ed. D. A. Carson, Peter T. O'Brien, and Mark A. Seifrid, vol. 2 of *Justification and Variegated Nomism*, WUNT 2/181 (Tübingen: Mohr Siebeck, 2004), 402.

104. Indeed, 1 Cor 9:19-23 in particular could be readily interpreted to mean that Paul occupies a third position, neither Jew nor Gentile. C. K. Barrett (*A Commentary on the First Epistle to the Corinthians*, 2nd ed., BNTC [London: Black, 1971], 211) comments that Paul "could become a Jew only if, having been a Jew, he had ceased to be one and became something else." If that is the correct inference, the problem becomes how to reconcile this passage with those that will be considered below, in which Paul identifies himself as a member of the physical people of Israel. It should be noted, however, that Paul says that he became "like a Jew." Although it is thereby implied that at other times he was somehow not "like a Jew," this may not be transparent to the question of Paul's ethnic self-identification. Since 1 Cor 9:19-23 deals with Paul's behavior, I suggest that the passage may simply mean that among the Jews, Paul lived like a Jew (cf. Gal 2:14), not that he would have answered the question, "Are you a Jew," with a "Yes" in some settings and a "No" in others.

105. "Third race" language and related metaphors for social belonging in early Christian literature are treated thoroughly in Denise Kimber Buell, *Why This New Race: Ethnic Reasoning in Early Christianity* (New York: Columbia University Press, 2005); see also Judith Lieu, *Christian Identity in the Jewish and Graeco-Roman World* (Oxford: Oxford University Press, 2004), 239–68. An early instantiation of this concept can be found in Aristides's *Apology*, which in the Greek version speaks of three classes of worshipers: Jews, Christians, and polytheists (2.2); similarly Clement of Alexandria, *Strom.* 6.5.

106. Several distinctions are important to keep in mind in what follows. First, I am not concerned with how others viewed Paul but with his own self-understanding. For many of Paul's Jewish peers, the man was a sinner or apostate. See John M. G. Barclay, "Paul among Diaspora Jews: Anomaly or Apostate?" *JSNT* 60 (1995): 89–120; idem, *Jews in the Mediterranean Diaspora from Alexander to Trajan (323 BCE–117*

CE) (Berkeley: University of California Press, 1996), 381–98. But this gives us no indication of what Paul thought about himself. Barclay, for instance, states that Paul never lost his sense of belonging to the Jewish people despite the skepticism and resistance with which he was often met (*Jews in the Mediterranean Diaspora*, 395); similarly, Alan F. Segal, *Paul the Convert: The Apostolate and Apostasy of Saul the Pharisee* (New Haven: Yale University Press, 1990), 125–26.

Second, the guiding question is not so much whether Paul abandoned his Jewish identity but whether he saw himself as a Jew. The first phrasing is more ambiguous, since there are many dimensions in which Paul's Jewishness could be considered, as Lionel J. Windsor notes in *Paul and the Vocation of Israel: How Paul's Jewish Identity Informs his Apostolic Ministry, with Special Reference to Romans*, BZNW 205 (Berlin: de Gruyter, 2014), 3–4.

107. Sechrest (*Former Jew*, 150–51) holds that the qualification "by birth/nature" means that Paul no longer considered them to be Jews. She supports this by observing that Gal 2:15 speaks of the ἔθνη whereas Paul elsewhere refers to his converts as former Gentiles (1 Thess 4:3-5; 1 Cor 12:1-2). In Rom 11:13, on the other hand, the apostle addresses his audience as "you Gentiles," mitigating the force of the argument. In any case, it seems hard to maintain Sechrest's inference since in Gal 2:14 Paul recounts having rebuked Peter for inconsistency. Peter is compelling non-Jews to adopt Jewish customs while he, a Jew (Ἰουδαῖος ὑπάρχων), does not even live Ἰουδαϊκῶς.

108. My understanding of this passage, and of Paul's train of thought in Galatians more generally, agrees in the main with that of Stephen Westerholm, *Perspectives Old and New on Paul: The "Lutheran" Paul and His Critics* (Grand Rapids: Eerdmans, 2004), 366–84.

109. With Jörg Frey, "Paul's Jewish Identity," in *Jewish Identity in the Greco-Roman World*, 290.

110. So also, David J. Rudolph, *A Jew to the Jews: Jewish Contours of Pauline Flexibility in 1 Corinthians 9:19-23*, WUNT 2/304 (Tübingen: Mohr Siebeck, 2011), 32.

111. C. H. Dodd (*The Epistle of Paul to the Romans*, MNTC 6 [London: Hodder & Stoughton, 1960], 68) states that the logical reply should be "None," but that Paul's ingrained Pharisaism or patriotism has hindered him from following through on his own premises. I say that Paul's statements in Rom 3:1-2 are paradoxical because, in the preceding section (2:17 29), he seems to undercut Jewish privilege. If Paul is inconsistent, I see no grounds for supposing that he is being disingenuous, reasserting Jewish privilege to placate some in the Roman church.

112. This is further supported by Paul's bifurcation of humanity into Jews and Gentiles (Rom 9:24) and Israel and the Gentiles (9:30-31; 11:11). Thus, when Paul locates himself on the Israelite side of the divide in 11:1, logic would dictate that he also places himself on the Jewish side of the parallel formula.

113. So Sechrest, *Former Jew*, 152; with a slightly different inflection, James D. G. Dunn, *Romans*, WBC 38 (Dallas, TX: Word, 1988), 1:144-47.

114. In agreement with C. E. B. Cranfield, *A Critical and Exegetical Commentary on the Epistle to the Romans*, ICC (London: T&T Clark, 1975), 1:188.

115. Though the middle is intelligible as a direct reflexive: "Are we holding ourselves in front?"

116. With Cranfield, *Romans*, 187–90; Douglas Moo, *The Epistle to the Romans*, NICNT (Grand Rapids: Eerdmans, 1996), 199–200; Brendan Byrne, *Romans*, SP 6 (Collegeville, MN: Liturgical Press, 1996), 115–16, 119. That the "we" in 3:9 refers to the Jews was also the understanding of Origen and John Calvin in their respective commentaries on Romans.

117. Sanders, *Paul, the Law, and the Jewish People* (Philadelphia: Fortress, 1983), 178.

118. This, incidentally, is also the assessment of the author of Acts, who has Paul plainly affirm before the Sanhedrin that he is a Jew (Acts 22:3). Calvin J. Roetzel comments in *Paul: A Jew on the Margins* (Louisville, Westminster John Knox, 2003), 4 that the apparent discrepancies "reflect more the ambiguity of living on the margin than they reveal actual contradictions."

119. The Johannine claim to continuity with Moses is also rightly accented by Cirafesi, *John Within Judaism*, 138–39.

120. Stark and Bainbridge, *Future of Religion*, 25. While I speak of a Johannine "sectarian" mentality, Byers (*John and the Others*) is right to question the "sectarian hermeneutic" which marked Johannine studies post-Martyn. Here, I simply mean to highlight the Gospel's assertion that those who truly learn from Israel's past and hear from Israel's God will come to Jesus.

121. From the outside, the Johannine devotion to Jesus may look like an innovation, so that it would not be entirely wrong to describe the putative community as "cult-like" in the sense of Stark and Bainbridge's model, as Fuglseth does in *Johannine Sectarianism*. So also, Numada, *John and Anti-Judaism*, 123–24. But these are not the terms in which the evangelist frames matters, and so an "etic" analysis of the community, as far as that would be possible for an ancient group whose existence is not known from sources outside the Gospel and Johannine epistles, might come to a conclusion at variance with the community's self-perception.

122. As Raimo Hakola (*Identity Matters*, 240) remarks: "It has never been strange to Christian anti-Jewish tradition based on supersessionism to hold to the Jewish Scriptures, or to maintain that Jesus was really a Jew, or, for that matter, to turn the Jewish people's sacred writings against them in accusations of hypocrisy, obstinacy, or blindness." Here, of course, Hakola has in mind Gentile Christian writers from the second century on. Interestingly, when Justin Martyr explicitly calls Christians the "true spiritual Israel," he also describes them as the γένος of Judah, Jacob, Isaac, and Abraham (*Dial*. 11).

123. The latter point is noted also by D. Moody Smith (*The Theology of the Gospel of John* [Cambridge: Cambridge University Press, 1995], 172–73). That the Gospel acknowledges Jesus's identity as a *Ioudaios* also presents problems for Byers' argument that the evangelist employs the term in order to ironically undermine the assertion of those Jews who held genealogical purity as a prerequisite for covenant membership.

124. The importance that the flesh which the Word assumes is Jewish is brought to the fore by Thomas Söding, "'Was kann aus Nazareth schon Gutes kommen?' (Joh

1.46): Die Bedeutung des Judeseins Jesu im Johannesevangelium," *NTS* 46 (2000): 21–41.

125. Of the declaration that "salvation is from the Jews," Ashton ("The Identity and Function of The Ἰουδαῖοι in the Fourth Gospel," *NovT* 27 [1985]: 49) remarks: "In fact there can be few phrases in the Gospel more capable of laying bare an exegete's basic presuppositions than this one: it sends the commentators flying in all directions."

126. Likewise Ashton, *Understanding*, 65, though for him this only heightens the tension with the less-than-favorable presentation of the Ἰουδαῖοι.

127. With John Painter, "The Church and Israel in the Gospel of John: A Response," *NTS* 25 (1978): 103–12, against Severino Pancaro, "'People of God' in St. John's Gospel," *NTS* 16 (1970): 114–29.

128. So also, Painter, "Church and Israel," 109–11.

129. Similarly, ibid., 111: "The distinction between Jew and Israelite does not seem to be significant for Johannine theology." Byers's claim (*John and the Others*, 74) that the name "Israel" is emblematic of positive responses to Jesus, while "Jews" becomes increasingly associated through the course of the narrative with negative responses, is subject to the same criticism, though Byers himself tempers too strong of a contrast (ibid., p. 75, n. 74).

130. Blumhofer, *John and the Future of Israel*, 11–28, at 25. Talmon's model also informs Daniel Boyarin's argument in "The Ioudaioi in John."

131. Blumhofer, *John and the Future of Israel*, 26–27.

132. Thiel, "'Israel' and 'Jew'"; Staples, *Idea of Israel*, 51–53.

133. Staples, *Idea of Israel*, 262–64.

134. Ibid., 259–63 and 277–78. It also bears noting that some scrolls speak of the rebellion and sin of "Israel"/"children of Israel." See, for example, CD I, 3–4; III, 13–14; IV, 13–18; 1QS I, 22–24; 4QpPs[a] ii 14; iii 12; 1QpHab 2:3-10.

135. If one were to make the case that "Israel" and "Jew" represent alternative identities in the Fourth Gospel, the difference would more likely fall along traditional biblical lines: the northern tribes of Israel vs. the southern tribes collectively known as the Jews. George Wesley Buchanan ("The Samaritan Origin of the Gospel of John," in *Religions in Antiquity*, ed. Jacob Neusner [Leiden: Brill, 1968], 149–74), for instance, places the origins of the Gospel of John among the Samaritans who regarded themselves as the descendants of the northern tribes.

136. Culpepper, "Anti Judaism in the Fourth Gospel," 69.

Chapter 2

Referents and Roles

The Johannine Jews as Microcosm

In an influential article on the Jews in the Fourth Gospel, John Ashton disentangles three questions that he says previous scholars had bundled together to ill effect: Who are the Johannine Jews (the term's *reference*)? What role or function do they fulfill within the narrative (the term's *sense*), and why does the evangelist regard them with such hostility? The first two, he says, belong to exegesis, the third to history. But as his own procedure reflects, exegesis and history are mutually dependent, so that any explanation of the evangelist's attitude toward the Jews can only proceed from a firm grasp of their characterization within the Gospel itself.[1]

As I stated in the Introduction, the Gospel's stylistic unity is suggestive of a strong individual hand at one of the terminal stages of its development. Therefore, I think it is best to begin with a synchronic approach to the Gospel's presentation of "the Jews," seeing if sense can be made of their characterization within the text as we have received it.[2] The sundry source-critical attempts to reconstruct the history of the Gospel as a living text, growing with and in the community that nurtured it, cannot be surveyed here.[3] I would not deny in principle the legitimacy of the approach, but it is a daunting task to integrate all the pertinent data into any given redactional scheme. To assign the so-called hostile uses of "the Jews" to a late stage in the Gospel's composition during or after the synagogue-expulsion crisis is not prima facie unreasonable, but then we would have to explain why an intelligent author would retain a statement like "salvation is from the Jews" if he had come to believe that opposition to Jesus was inherent to being a Jew.[4] Or what are we to make of the Jews of John 11 who are sympathetic, and some of whom even become believers? We would seem to be in need of another chapter in the community's history when the feud with the Jews had abated and communication was again possible.[5] Such loose ends do not necessarily invalidate source-critical approaches to the Gospel's presentation of the Jews, but they do cast some doubt on their utility, more so when we consider that an author let the varied portrayals of and statements about the Jews stand in the form of the Gospel that has come down to us.

THE COLLAPSE OF THE DIALECTIC: THE JOHANNINE JEWS AS REPRESENTATIVES OF UNBELIEF

Assessments of the role played by the Jews in the Fourth Gospel at times resemble a game of tug of war. On the one hand, it is often acknowledged that those named οἱ Ἰουδαῖοι respond to Jesus in a variety of ways and that some usages of the term "the Jews" in the Fourth Gospel are seemingly neutral, referring to Jewish festivals and customs.[6] On the other, the Johannine characterization of the Jews has been described as crushingly negative, generalizing, stereotypical, and grossly undifferentiated. Whereas the Synoptic Gospels preserve memories of Sadducees and scribes, teachers of the law and Pharisees, tax collectors, sinners, rich, and poor, John, so the reasoning goes, has jumbled them all together and put a homogenous label on what was in reality a motley crew.[7] They are now submerged into "the Jews."

The second strain of interpretation reaches at least as far back as the mid-nineteenth century, but it is Rudolf Bultmann who perhaps gave it its most incisive expression:

> The term οἱ Ἰουδαῖοι, characteristic of the Evangelist, gives an overall portrayal of the Jews, viewed from the standpoint of Christian faith, as the representatives of unbelief (and thereby, as will appear, of the unbelieving "world" in general) ... Οἱ Ἰουδαῖοι does not relate to the empirical state of the Jewish people, but to its very nature.[8]

The impression of total opposition that Bultmann captures so effectively has left its mark even on many scholars who recognize differences among the Ἰουδαῖοι of the narrative. R. Alan Culpepper's remarks are reflective of the tension. Having critiqued a symbolic interpretation for turning a blind eye to the division among the Jews in the Gospel, he nevertheless concurs with Bultmann:

> The Fourth Gospel stereotypes the rejection of Jesus as the response of the Jews. Even if οἱ Ἰουδαῖοι once denoted "the Judeans" or the Jewish authorities, the Gospel of John generalized and stereotyped those who rejected Jesus by its use of this term.[9]

This designation, he writes, "carries the burden of unbelief and the world's rejection of Jesus."[10] So, too, Robert Kysar: "Although the term *Ioudaioi* is used to refer to many different groups in the Gospel and from varying perspectives, the negative characterization inherent in the term serves the dualistic scheme of the Gospel in which it opposes the Christian believers."[11] Adele Reinhartz is no less forceful. Not only does the occurrence of "the Jews" in a variety of contexts tend to "blur the fine distinctions and nuances implied by these contexts," but the evangelist, she claims, consigns all Jews of the narrative to the negative pole of his dualistic mindset.[12] The Fourth Gospel promotes a rhetoric of binary opposition, which is expressed through its contrasting metaphors. Positive traits are associated with Jesus, while negative traits such as spiritual blindness and being from below are associated with the Jews who "exemplify and concretize the negative pole of these binaries."[13]

Although this way of categorizing all of the responses of those named οἱ Ἰουδαῖοι is not, strictly speaking, a return to Bultmann's classic articulation because of its attention to the socio-historical circumstances of the Gospel's composition, exegetically it comes close. The Jews' collective role is still to represent unbelief. Yet it must be asked whether this threatens to flatten out a deliberate Johannine tension.[14] That is, does the line of Johannine dualism run to one side of the Jews of the Gospel, or does it run through them? Certainly, on the surface of the text, there is not a unified Jewish response to Jesus. There are sympathizers like Nicodemus, who, if he is not a believer by John 19, nevertheless shows support for Jesus despite the opposition of his colleagues (7:50-52; 19:39-42). According to chs. 11 and 12, many of the Jews who had come to visit Mary and Martha put their faith in Jesus, which arouses the Sanhedrin to take decisive action against Jesus. And there is the persistent note of schism among the crowds about Jesus's identity (7:43-44; 10:19-21; 11:45-46).[15] Jesus's own Jewish identity, moreover, is integral to the Gospel's Christology, as we've seen.[16] A symbolic interpretation resolves these internal tensions, suggesting that, in the end, such responses to Jesus are deemed wholly inadequate by the evangelist—examples of Jewish obduracy and incomprehension.

I will argue, to the contrary, that the variety of Jewish stances toward Jesus in the Gospel of John need not and should not be resolved to one end of John's dualistic spectrum. The diversity in their portrayal is not superficial. The lines of Johannine dualism, that is to say, run through the Jews of the Gospel.[17] Others, to be sure, have advanced that general thesis. In what follows and in the next chapter, then, I will not be arguing for an entirely novel reading of the referents and role(s) of the Jews in the Fourth Gospel. Instead, I will be lending support to an existing interpretation by more firmly situating the Gospel's usage of the term "the Jews" in its ancient literary context. To see how the Gospel's critical statements about the Jews may stand alongside more positive characterizations, we must bring its usage of "the Jews" into sharper focus by comparison with other Jewish authors of the period.[18] The thrust of the following argument is not to disprove that the Jews in the Fourth Gospel are frequently Jesus's opponents. That they are is too plain to contest. It is to show rather that the appellation οἱ Ἰουδαῖοι, which seems to ring so general, does not subsume what might otherwise be regarded as positive and neutral references to "the Jews."

"THE JEWS" AND "THESE JEWS AS DETERMINED BY NARRATIVE CONTEXT"

In the methodological prolegomenon to an unpublished dissertation on the application of linguistic theory to the Johannine Jews, Terry Schram, like Ashton after him, differentiates between sense and reference.[19] For Ashton, as we have seen, "sense" means the role that the Jews play in the Gospel. As Schram employs it, "sense" is roughly equivalent to a word's lexical meaning, a basic grasp of what a word means to the extent that intelligible communication about it is possible, even if we have difficulty precisely defining it. So, to take up Schram's own example, we might struggle to define "chair" or have a different mental image of a chair than the person sitting next to us, but we have no trouble using the word "to refer to a variety of (somehow) recognizably similar things that constitute a class in the world of experience."[20] We have, on the whole, a good idea of what chairs are, the occasional oddity notwithstanding. A word's referent, on the other hand, is a particular instance of the general concept that it picks out, the activation of its lexical content to specify members of a class of objects in the real world. If I remark to someone that the chair is comfortable, presumably I have a definite chair in mind. I am not making a statement about all chairs everywhere, nor does this particular chair's luxurious quality adhere to the sense of the term.

Ancient authors acquainted with the Jewish nation and its customs had a good enough idea of what "Jews" meant to talk about them and be understood: a people like the other peoples of the world, having a common ancestral land, bound by a set of shared customs and traditions and by worship of the same God.[21] The precise referents of "Jews" or "the Jews," in contrast, frequently change without disrupting the word's sense. This is well illustrated in the literary corpora of the Alexandrian philosopher Philo and of the Jewish aristocrat, general, and prisoner of war turned historian, Flavius Josephus. For here, a bare "the Jews" meets us time and again, in reference to the Jewish people at large, but just as commonly, if not more so, to very restricted subsets of Ἰουδαῖοι. As Dunn observes:

Philo speaks regularly of the "nation of the Jews" or of Moses as "the lawgiver of the Jews." But in *In Flaccum* and *de Legatione ad Gaium* he can often use οἱ Ἰουδαῖοι to denote Jews who are more specifically defined by their context, as Jews of a particular region or city. Josephus in *The Jewish War* speaks typically of "the Jews" in opposition to such as Antiochus, Pompey, Herod and Pilate . . . but he can also speak with equal meaningfulness of "the Jews" of specific cities such as Alexandria or Damascus, or switch from specific to general reference (as in *JW* 2.532) without confusion.[22]

While Dunn's distinction between general and specific references does not map directly onto Schram's "sense" and "reference," as applied, they cover much the same ground.[23] In some passages, "the Jews" is more or less equivalent to the word's lexical meaning, such that we could substitute "the Jewish people" for οἱ Ἰουδαῖοι without doing any damage to the passage. When Philo or Josephus writes of the laws, customs, and feasts of the Jews, they are not picking out individual members or subsets of the collective. But on many occasions, the referent of "the Jews" contracts, so that we could gloss "the Jews" with "these Jews": "the Jews who resided in their [the Caesareans'] city" (*J.W.* 2.457, LCL), "the remnant of the Jews at Antioch" (*J.W.* 7.41), and so on. Of course, this is rather cumbersome to continually repeat and redundant at that, since context makes it clear which Jews are now acting. Thus, often in the place of these fuller constructions are just "Jews" or "the Jews."

Because circumscription of a word's reference by context is a normal part of both oral and written communication, we often pass it over unnoticed. So, when Josephus refers to the Jewish populace of Caesarea Maritima in the lead-up to the revolt, the defenders of Jotapata, Tiberias, Tarichaea, and Gamala during Vespasian's Galilean campaign, the combatants of Jerusalem during the siege, or the Jews of Antioch and Macheraus in its aftermath, all in their respective contexts as "the Jews," we know quite intuitively that he has particular subsets of the people in mind, some Jews rather than all Jews or Jews in general.[24] Philo exhibits the same tendency when recounting the fracas between Jews, Egyptians, and Greeks in Alexandria. "The Jews" of *Flaccus* 55 are consistently the Jews of Alexandria, and those of *Embassy* 155–161 are the Jews of Rome during the reign of Augustus.

Sometimes those named οἱ Ἰουδαῖοι exercise a representative function.[25] But this is not inherent to the literary convention. In fact, in a number of passages, it is evident that what "the Jews" say and do is not reflective of the will or character of the ἔθνος at large, as the following examples will show.

Jewish War 1.90-195

During the reign of Alexander Jannaeus, a growing number of malcontents, angered over his brutal treatment of political opponents, invited the Seleucid king Demetrius Eucaerus to help dislodge the king from his throne. Demetrius, all too happy about the instability in Judea, readily complies and ventures into Samaria. "The Jews," Josephus now informs us, "joined with their allies around Shechem (συνέμισγον οἱ Ἰουδαῖοι τοῖς συμμάχοις περὶ Σίκιμα)" (1.92). Josephus, we can be sure, has in sight only a sliver of the Jewish people. Not only were the combatants with Demetrius numbered in the low thousands, but Alexander, on his side, had "the part of the Jews that favored him to the number of 10,000 (παρῆν δὲ αὐτῷ καὶ τὸ εὐνοοῦν Ἰουδαϊκὸν εἰς μυρίους)" (1.93). When the two parties confronted each other, both kings, hoping to forestall the battle and gain a victory without the loss of any men, petitioned the soldiers on the other side, Alexander wanting to coax the Jews with Demetrius to return to him in peace, and Demetrius the Greek mercenaries whom Alexander had hired. Neither sovereign met with success: "Neither would the Jews," that is, the Jews allied with Demetrius, "abate their resentment nor the Greeks," that is, the Greek mercenaries accompanying Alexander Jannaeus, "their fidelity" (1.94).

Jewish War 1.141-151

The civil strife that plagues the Jews during Alexander's reign rears its ugly head once more just a decade or so later, the feud between Alexander's sons Hyrcanus and Aristobulus bringing Pompey into Judea and marking the end of Jewish independence. When the famed Roman general reaches the capital, those of Hyrcanus's party are eager to open the gates, while the supporters of Aristobulus, determined to hold out, take refuge in the temple. Upon Pompey's entrance into the city, a battle ensues between the Roman army and those holed up in the sanctuary. At one point, Josephus refers to this latter party as "the Jews," remarking in 1.45 that the Romans filled up the valley surrounding the temple while the Jews, that is, those Jews who were for Aristobulus, made an effort to repel them (τῶν Ἰουδαίων πάντα τρόπον εἰργόντων ἄνωθεν).

Jewish War 6.113-114, 136-148

Josephus is doggedly insistent throughout *Jewish War* that it was internal discord and not Roman aggression that was to blame for Jerusalem's downfall and, moreover, that brigands and tyrants—the Zealots, Simon bar Giora, and above all, John of Gischala—had overtaken all those in the city who were for peace, killing some and coercing others to do their will. It comes as no surprise, then, when Josephus reports in *War* 6.113-116 that many chief priests and a good number of the aristocracy that were left in Jerusalem, emboldened by Josephus's impassioned plea for surrender to the Romans, braved the fury of the rebels and jumped ship. Yet when Josephus returns in 136-48 to the battle at the gates of the temple, and in the ensuing scenes, the rebels are often engaged in combat against the Romans as "the Jews." Not only so, but they are characterized as disorderly and disastrously confused, running to and fro at random and without unity, traits which Josephus elsewhere says are alien to a genuinely Jewish disposition (6.17).

Summary of Examples

If the examples presented here risk redundancy, that is by design, for they show to be mundane in Josephus what is often contested when it comes to the Fourth Gospel. First, we must not confuse what "the Jews" do in any given scene or report with what the word itself means, to move from characterization at selected points to definition. If, as it happens often in *Jewish War*, the part of the Jews that opposes the Romans is called "the Jews," this does not mean that "Jew" has become a cipher for someone hostile to Roman rule. Josephus knows that some Jews were for peace. In fact, as noted above, he is anxious to prove to his readers that the peaceable majority were put into an impossible situation by a small band of extremists.[26] Of course, we may very well have to pardon Josephus for exaggerating. Wanting to put his people in the best possible light, he hurls the blame at alleged knaves and instigators to deflect it from the nation as a whole.[27] But none of this has to do with definition. The sense of the word "Jews" remains constant even as the behavior of those so named varies from episode to episode.

Second, the referents of οἱ Ἰουδαῖοι change frequently. They expand and contract depending on the context. Sometimes the actions and attitudes of "the Jews" are reflective of the broader Jewish populace or carried out on their behalf, but often they are not. When οἱ Ἰουδαῖοι in a given passage are equivalent to "these Jews as made known by context," we cannot justifiably predicate their actions to all Jews of all times and places. Josephus's usage of "the Jews" for so many actors in the narrative, with their own agendas and character, can hardly be part of a strategy of stereotyping or generalizing. An overall image of the Jewish people, to be sure, emerges out of the string of individual scenes, but the behavior of those named "the Jews" in any given passage need not and indeed does not always conform to it.[28]

FROM JOSEPHUS TO JOHN

There is a distinct challenge moving from here to the Fourth Gospel, for those literary conventions which I have shown to be unexceptionable in Philo and Josephus have appeared otherwise to many interpreters of the Gospel. How do we proceed without merely arguing in a circle? Admittedly, there is no way to prove that John's language about the Jews has affinities with Josephus or Philo at those points just enumerated, but by working inductively and observing the resemblances between the Fourth Gospel and these texts, some progress may be made in that direction. To avoid begging the question as much as possible, it will be best to move gradually from less controversial passages to the infamous statement in John 8:44 ("You are of your father the devil"). I will begin therefore not with the Jews but with the Samaritans.

On the Periphery of the Disturbance

In John 4, after an impromptu encounter with a Jewish man claiming to be the Messiah and revealing the secrets of her less-than-honorable past, a Samaritan woman departs from Jacob's well to report the remarkable conversation to her fellow villagers. Their interest piqued, they go out to meet him. Verse 39 tells us that many of the Samaritans from this village believed in Jesus on account of the woman's testimony, and so, having reached Jesus, they ask him to come and stay with them. Those who extend the invitation are referred to as "the Samaritans" (οἱ Σαμαρῖται) without anything further added (v. 40).

Now there is some ambiguity in the passage, since v. 30 seems to imply that everyone in the village came out, while vv. 39-40 could be construed to mean that only those who were persuaded by what the woman had to say made the short trip. Either way, the Σαμαρῖται of v. 40 are restricted to the people of Sychar, and perhaps to the many that believed the woman's words. Having established the identity of this group by context, the evangelist drops any modifying adjectives or prepositional phrases; the Samaritans from this village are now "the Samaritans." Is this positive response to Jesus indicative of a widespread Samaritan acceptance of the stranger from heaven, intended to make the unbelief of the Jews stand out all the more starkly? It has been so read by a number of scholars, but the Gospel says nothing more about the Samaritans, either good or bad, the accusation that Jesus is a Samaritan (and demon-possessed) aside.[29]

If in John 4:40 οἱ Σαμαρῖται are narrowly the inhabitants, or some of the inhabitants, of Sychar, there is still perhaps some uncertainty whether the evangelist makes their reception of Jesus representative for all Samaritans, though on the basis of what I have said thus far, the inference is tenuous. No such thing can be said about the response of the Jews in ch. 11. John 11:33 holds the honor of being the shortest verse in the Bible, a mere two words, in English as in Greek: "Jesus wept." The setting is the raising of Jesus's friend Lazarus. Jesus, so unprecedentedly confident, so supremely self-assured of his identity and mission throughout the Gospel, is now overwhelmed at the sight of the tomb and of the accompanying mourners. The tears flow. The outpouring of emotion is met with a sympathetic response: "See how he loved him!" The sympathizers are simply "the Jews" (v. 36).

If we move back to v. 19, the context makes clear who these Jews are. Many Jews, we are told, had come to visit Mary and Martha to comfort them over the loss of their brother. Upon Jesus's agonizingly delayed arrival, Mary rushes out to meet him, which prompts "the Jews who were with her in the house, consoling her (οἱ οὖν Ἰουδαῖοι ὄντες μετ' αὐτῆς ἐν τῇ οἰκίᾳ καὶ παραμυθούμενοι αὐτήν)" to follow (11:31). When Mary reaches Jesus, she is overtaken by grief and begins to weep. Jesus, seeing her weeping and "the Jews who came with her (τοὺς συνελθόντας αὐτῇ Ἰουδαίους)" also weeping, can no longer hold back his emotions (11:32-33). The Ἰουδαῖοι of v. 36 are none other than this small contingent of Jewish mourners, in fact, only a part of them, since in short order there is a division among them, some openly cynical about a man who could open the eyes of the blind but would not arrive in time to heal a friend (v. 37). The relationship between Jesus and these Jews is far from the rancorous debates of 5:10-47 or 8:31-59. The Jews in ch. 11 sympathize with him. Some even believe in him (v. 45). Those in chs. 5, 8, and 10 seek to murder him. Although all are referred to as οἱ Ἰουδαῖοι, they do not comprise the same subset of the Jewish people.

From John 11, we must venture one step closer to the fault line. If "the Jews" of John 11:36 are meant to signify only some of the Jews who had accompanied Mary to Lazarus's tomb, it is natural to ask whether the actors are similarly restricted throughout the Gospel. One of the curious features of the synagogue-expulsion passages is that they assign the ban to the Jews in 9:22 and to the Pharisees in 12:42. John 9:16 and 10:19 reverse the interchange, the first reporting a division among the Pharisees, the second predicating this schism of the Jews. Within the story of the healing of the man born blind itself, the interrogators are the Pharisees from 9:13-17 and the Jews from v. 18 onward.

Whatever the pre-history of the passage, if it had any, the narrator has made a concerted effort to craft the episode into a dramatic whole.[30] From the disciples' query about the blind man in v. 1 to the man's climactic confession and worship of Jesus as the Son of Man in v. 38, each scene builds the tension, centered, like so much of the Gospel, upon the question of Jesus's identity. Verse 24 states, "Again (πάλιν) they summoned the man who had been blind." This πάλιν joins the first phase of the investigation in vv. 13-17 with the second in vv. 24-34, just as the blind man's sarcastic retort to the Jews, "I have already told you, and you did not listen" (9:27), looks back to v. 15, where the Pharisees serve as the ringleaders of the investigation. If we couple these exegetical clues with the same type of literary device just observed in John 11, then the change in terminology is of little consequence.[31] The referent of "the Jews" in 9:18-34 are the Pharisees of 9:13-17, as context demands. It is for this reason that the synagogue ban ascribed to the Jews in 9:22 is assigned to the Pharisees in 12:42.

The referent of "the Jews" in ch. 9 overlaps partially with those named οἱ Ἰουδαῖοι in the Passion Narrative, where the designation at times refers to a coalition of the Pharisees and chief priests and at other times to the chief priests alone. The evangelist reminds the reader in 18:14 that Caiaphas was "the one who had advised the Jews" to arrest Jesus, alluding to the meeting of the Pharisees and chief priests in 11:45-63, which sprung these final events into motion. The "servants of the chief priests and Pharisees (ἐκ τῶν ἀρχιερέων καὶ ἐκ τῶν Φαρισαίων ὑπηρέτας)" sent to arrest Jesus in 18:3 become "the servants of the Jews (οἱ ὑπηρέται τῶν Ἰουδαίων)" in 18:12. As the narrative progresses, the Pharisees disappear, and "the Jews" alternates with "the chief priests" during the trial scene before the conflicted Pilate (19:6, 15). "The Jews" of the Passion Narrative, therefore, are the Jerusalem-based leaders among whom the chief priests are most prominent. And yet even here the referent quickly expands and contracts without formal notice from the evangelist, as the "many Jews" of 19:20 who read the *titulus* on the cross presumably refer to passers-by distinct from the chief priests, who in v. 21 are themselves named "chief priests of the Jews." So, if we are to ask about the referent of "the Jews" in chs. 9, 11, and 18–19, we must give at least five separate answers: those who had come to comfort Mary and Martha, the Pharisees, the Pharisees and chief priests, the chief priests alone, and the Jewish people in general.

At the Epicenter: "Your Father is the Devil" (John 8:44)

Now we come to the epicenter: John 8:44, according to some, the most anti-Jewish statement in the NT.[32] Even were John 8:31-59 not fissured with exegetical problems, its aftershock alone in the sad history of anti-Semitism would compel the exegete to come with fear and trembling.[33] But whom does Jesus charge with being offspring of the evil one? To begin with, it is ambiguous whether "the Jews who had believed in him (τοὺς πεπιστευκότας αὐτῷ Ἰουδαίους)" in 8:31 are part of the many who believed in Jesus in 8:30. If so, this does indeed bode ill for the Jews of the rest of the narrative. The problem is exacerbated because the perfect participle πεπιστευκότας can bear the sense either of a perfect, a state persisting into the present, or a pluperfect, a past condition which no longer holds. Grammatically, neither is to be given priority.[34] Context, therefore, must dictate which sense is most appropriate.

Any answer to these questions must account for the meteoric rise in hostility against Jesus. The narrative never builds up to their unbelief. Jesus knows from the outset that they have sinister designs (8:37). The expedient of an immature faith that Jesus now exposes is incommensurate with the severity of the conflict. It is not that their faith is shallow. Jesus does not accuse them of naively clinging to his signs at the expense of his words. He accuses them of nothing less than intent to murder. If the sudden burst of unexplained animosity is not just a deficiency in the evangelist's story, then we must look for the spark which has set off this explosion. The intensity of the exchange right from the start pushes us toward identifying these "Jews who had believed" as former followers of Jesus, who at some point had fallen away.[35]

But if that is so, how has the reader been prepared for it? Terry Griffith argues that at the heart of the invective of John 8:31-59 is apostasy, and the apostates are the defectors of 6:60-71 who, incensed at Jesus's claim to be the bread of life, no longer follow him.[36] To them Jesus holds out the possibility of return, but their lot has already been cast against their former rabbi.[37] Griffith's suggestion brings the polemic in John 8:31-59 into contact with one of the Gospel's ancillary themes, though in truth it is one aspect of the central theme of belief and unbelief, namely, the absolute necessity of holding fast to Jesus and the gravity of defection or betrayal.

This is first dramatized in John 6, where the report of disciples turning away from Jesus is closely connected with the betrayal of Judas, the archetypal apostate. Outside of John 8, in fact, Judas is the only figure in the narrative to be associated with the devil (6:70; 13:27), and it is precisely at the point of betrayal that the devil is said to enter into him. Unbelievers may stand under God's judgment for their refusal to come to the light, but the Gospel's most scathing denunciations are reserved for traitors.

Aligned with this is the prominence of the motif of "remaining" in John 8:31-59, a theme which resurfaces in the true vine discourse of ch. 15 as well as in 1 and 2 John, where the secessionist crisis is front and center. In John 8, Jesus defines true discipleship as an abiding relationship. The slave to sin does not remain in the household, but Jesus the Son remains there forever and is therefore able to free those who believe in him and make them children of God. "The Jews who had believed in him" bear the brunt of Jesus's rebuke because they have failed to abide. Although it would be methodologically precarious to read John 8 as a literary artifice created in order to decry Jewish-Christian defectors from the Johannine community and warn others tempted to leave the fold, it is fair to say that the pericope sets a pattern of opposition that applies in broad strokes to later Christians.[38] No servant is greater than his or her master. If some disciples fell away and turned against Jesus, this is only to be expected to repeat itself in other settings where the same dynamic of faith and unbelief plays itself out.

All this is to say that the author does not indict the entire Jewish people, a charge which, as I have already suggested, would leave us with more problems than it solves. We cannot intelligibly read John 8:31-59 as if it nullifies the more positive portrayal of the Jews in, say, chs. 11 and 12.[39] Just as in 11:36 "the Jews" is shorthand for a narrow subset of the people, so throughout 8:31-59 "the Jews" are strictly the ones who according to v. 31 had (once) believed in him. Nor, for that matter, does the accusation of diabolical paternity in John 8:44 annul the declaration that salvation is from the Jews, as if a fossil from a bygone age had been inexplicably left lying *in situ*. Salvation does indeed come from the Jewish people, as the Messiah is one of their own and as to them God's will and word have been revealed. For the evangelist, it is not that all Jews, insofar as they are Jews, are the progeny of the devil, but that these Jews who intend to take Jesus's life are imitators of the primeval murderer.[40]

REFERENTS IN RETROSPECT

We could move back from the epicenter and walk through each passage in search of the referents of οἱ Ἰουδαῖοι, but it would be superfluous. "The Jews" in John are often various subsets of Jews. Those who persecute Jesus in ch. 5 are not the same group as the Jews in ch. 6, who are at first more perplexed than hostile, arguing among themselves. The Jews who attempt to stone Jesus in ch. 8 are not the Jews who come to believe in him in chs. 11 and 12. And these are all of a different nature than explanations of Jewish customs or a title such as "king of the Jews." Here the results of the present study join with those of Wendy E. S. North: "The evidence suggests that John uses the expression 'the Jews' in a *general* sense, that is to say, as a term which can accommodate within its scope people with different responses toward Jesus as well as different social groups."[41] Sometimes the phrase has all Jews without qualification in view, as in the explanation of customs or identifications of the feasts. But it is also capable of referring to "certain 'Jews' in particular" whose exact identity depends upon context, a literary convention that is evident in Philo and Josephus.[42] When the evangelist has established the context, he often designates the various actors as "the Jews," but when possible ambiguity lurks, he is typically careful to identify the group in question more explicitly as the rulers, Pharisees, chief priests, and so forth.[43] This does not mean the Jews in question are always different subsets of the people. They are indeed very often those centered in Jerusalem, in positions of authority, and devoted to the law, but this has to be determined on a passage-by-passage basis. Thus, to Ruth Sheridan's assertion that "there is no subset of Jews implied in the term οἱ Ἰουδαῖοι—the text reads not 'some Jews' but '*the* Jews,'" I must reply with a rejoinder.[44] The text may not *read* "some Jews" but in many passages it assuredly *means* "some Jews" just as it does in Josephus or Philo.[45]

The Jews of the Fourth Gospel are usually (though not always) Judeans, as Malcolm Lowe and others before him had reasoned.[46] They are frequently the Jewish authorities in Jerusalem, as has long been recognized.[47] They are often a scrupulously Torah-observant contingent among the larger populace, *pace* Motyer.[48] These identifications are all correct in their own measure, in concert but not alone. If we have to select one answer, we should take a cue from the seasoned college student. When in doubt, the safest wager is on "all of the above."[49]

To return to Schram's distinction, none of these referents constitutes the root sense of Ἰουδαῖος in the Gospel. For the evangelist, the Jews are a people, descended from Abraham, the recipients of God's revelation through Moses and the prophets. They are in the same taxonomical order as Samaritans, Romans, and Greeks.[50] Even if the Jews are the authorities in the majority of passages, "Jews" has not therefore become synonymous with "the Jewish authorities." Or if most in the story are unreceptive or outright hostile to Jesus, we cannot therefore conclude that "Jews" now means those who are so disposed. An author or speaker, to be sure, may reorient the sense of a word through performance, but had the evangelist been attempting to redefine the term, we would expect the Jews of the Gospel to form a unified front. As it stands, their unreceptivity and antagonism are punctuated with exceptions: a sympathetic, if ambivalent, Nicodemus, the friends of Mary and Martha in ch. 11, and the many Jews who believe in Jesus in 11:45 and 12:11. Consequently, it seems to me most consistent to take the divergences in the characterization of the Jews as the result of changing referents, not as the evangelist's failed attempt to foist a new meaning upon the term "Jew."[51] It is my contention that this is perfectly natural in terms of ancient literary convention.

CONCLUSION: ROLES IN RETROSPECT

I have spent some time on the identification of the Johannine Jews because the expansion and contraction of the referents of the term allow us to make a modification to Ashton's question about the role of the Jews in the Gospel. If the precise subset of Jews changes depending on context, the characterization in one passage not necessarily carrying over to others, then we ought to ask not about their role, under the assumption that a univocal answer awaits, but about their roles.[52] That is, despite the pronounced motif of opposition and unbelief, we do not have to erase the division among the Jews of the narrative to make room for a blanketing, undifferentiated *massa damnata*.[53] The evangelist did not select the more capacious term οἱ Ἰουδαῖοι for the purpose of stereotyping all Jews as unbelievers.

Yet if we cannot assign one role to the Johannine Jews, if we cannot make them out to be a single character, we can nevertheless place them within the Gospel's total conception of the God-world relationship. Here we may take a cue from Udo Schnelle. "Above all," he writes, "they [the Jews] represent the two possible patterns of behavior with respect to the revelation of God in Jesus Christ: belief and unbelief."[54] They, like the world that is in darkness but remains an object of God's love, reside on both poles of the evangelist's dualistic system.[55] The crisis of belief and unbelief confronts the Jews just as it does the world as a whole.

A cut straight through the middle, however, would be out of sync with the evangelist's more pessimistic outlook. The division between those who believe and those who do not is not into symmetrical halves. The persistent feeling that the Jews in John are Jesus's opponents is to that extent valid. What fraction belongs to the realm of belief in the author's mind is impossible to say. It is small, no doubt. But there are believers, and if they are few among the Word's own, it is not that they are more numerous anywhere else. The world did not recognize him, Jew or Gentile. The Jews come under the microscope because this is a story about Jesus, a Jew who ministered among his own people. If the evangelist had written his own Acts of the Apostles, non-Jews, I assume, would have fared no better. There is no hint of Gentile triumphalism insofar as all humanity comes under indictment. Human beings love darkness instead of light because their deeds are evil (John 3:19). The world cannot accept the Spirit because it does not know him (14:17). The disciples will experience hatred from the world just as Jesus did from some of the Jews (15:18).[56] As Peder Borgen states: "God's Son, as the commissioned agent, caused a division between recognition/belief and rejection/disbelief within the Jewish people, and this dual reaction represented what was to happen everywhere."[57]

The Johannine Jews reflect the twin possibilities of belief and unbelief which confront all people of all times, but not in equal proportion. Their composite response to Jesus is a microcosm of the human response. This means unbelief on the part of most, but accompanying what might seem like categorical assertions of absolute rejection ("The world did not know him;" "His own did not receive him") is John's paradoxical qualification that some did receive him. The spectrum runs from unbelief, apostasy, curiosity, sympathy, and secret belief to true faith. As Jesus tells his disciples in the Farewell Discourse, "Remember the word that I said to you, 'Servants are not greater than their master.' If they persecuted me, they will persecute you; if they kept my word, they will keep yours also" (15:20). If we collapse the Johannine dialectic of division within the Jewish people in order to cast them as Jesus's monochrome enemies, we destroy the Gospel's deliberate tension.

NOTES

1. Ashton, "Identity and Function," 40–41.
2. Among others, C. J. A. Hickling ("Attitudes to Judaism in the Fourth Gospel," in *Évangile de Jean: Sources, rédaction, théologie*, ed. Marinus de Jonge, BETL 44 [Gembloux: Ducolot, 1977], 347–54) argues that the evangelist let stand a milder stance toward the Jews which he inherited from the tradition, even as the attitude of the community hardened over time. However, one then wonders why the evangelist would not have reworked that material more fully to align it with his own views. In any case, I shall argue that we need not posit an inconsistent or unthorough editor to account for the Gospel's diverse statements about the Jews.
3. The very term "the Jews," in fact, has been taken as a clue to the Gospel's literary development. At the extreme is the proposal of J. C. O'Neill that almost all occurrences of the term "the Jews" in the Gospel of John are scribal glosses; see idem, "The Jews in the Fourth Gospel," *IBS* 18 (1996): 58–75. More moderate and better known is the hypothesis of Urban C. von Wahlde, "The Terms for Religious Authorities in the Fourth Gospel: A Key to Literary-Strata?" *JBL* 98 (1979): 231–53. Von Wahlde distinguishes positive and neutral references to the Jews from those he deems hostile. The latter, he argues, always refer to the authorities (except possibly in 6:41 and 52) and belong to a later stage of the Gospel's composition.
4. Ashton, "Identity and Function," 49: "It is *a priori* unlikely (and certainly not to be assumed) that an intelligent author will incorporate into his own finished work a dictum with whose general tenor he is in radical disagreement."
5. The problem that John 11 presents for the traditional two-level reading is exposed by Reinhartz, "The Johannine Community and Its Jewish Neighbors."
6. Scholars have sometimes sought to classify positive, negative, and neutral connotations of the term "the Jews" in the Gospel of John. Often this is briefly noted, but a full list appears in Lars Kierspel, *The Jews and the World in the Fourth Gospel: Parallelism, Function, and Context*, WUNT 2/220 (Tübingen: Mohr Siebeck, 2006), 63–75. Similarly, Cirafesi observes the variety in John's use of *Ioudaios*, stating that the term is not stable, consistent, or evenly distributed in the Gospel, with two-thirds of the references appearing in non-polemical contexts (*John Within Judaism*, 96–97).
7. So Bultmann, *Gospel of John*, 86; Erich Grässer, "Die antijüdische Polemik im Johannesevangelium," *NTS* 11 (1964): 77, n. 10. Robert T. Fortna ("Theological Use of Locale in the Fourth Gospel," *AThR* 3 [1974]: 90) remarks that "the phrase *hoi Ioudaioi* obliterates virtually all distinctions within first century Palestinian society by speaking of the Jews in an external, monolithic way."
8. Bultmann, *Gospel of John*, 86–87. Already in 1840, Diac. Fischer ("Ueber den Ausdruck οἱ Ἰουδαῖοι im Evangelium Johannis: Ein Beitrag zur Charakteristik desselben," *Tübinger Zeitschrift für Theologie* 2 [1840]: 96–133) had articulated something like the view Bultmann would later take. According to Fischer, the Jews in the Gospel are in their entirety incapable of believing. Their role in the story is to exemplify unbelief and unreceptivity to Jesus, in order to bring out the glory of the Word made flesh through sharp and persistent contrast.

9. Culpepper, "Gospel of John and the Jews," 284.

10. Ibid., 276.

11. Robert Kysar, "Anti-Semitism and the Gospel of John," in *Anti-Semitism and Early Christianity: Issues of Polemic and Faith*, ed. Craig A. Evans and Donald A. Hagner (Minneapolis: Fortress, 1993), 26–27.

12. Reinhartz, "'Jews' and Jews," 220; eadem, "Forging a New Identity," 132–33. Others who charge the evangelist with stereotyping or who locate the Johannine Jews on the negative end of his dualistic thought include Eldon Jay Epp, "Anti-Semitism and the Popularity of the Fourth Gospel in Christianity," *CCAR Journal* 22 (1975): 43; Janis E. Leibig, "John and 'the Jews': Theological Antisemitism in the Fourth Gospel," *JES* 20 (1983): 212–16; Günther Baumbach, "Antijudaismus im neuen Testament: Fragestellung und Lösungsmöglichkeit," *Kairós* 25 (1983): 74; Wilhelm Pratscher, "Die Juden im Johannesevangelium," *BL* 59 (1986): 179; Felix Porsch, "'Ihr habt den Teufel zum Vater' (Joh 8,44): Antijudaismus im Johannesevangelium?" *BK* 44 (1989): 55; Brumlik, "Das judenfeindliche Evangelium," 7–9; Tina Pippin, "'For Fear of the Jews': Lying and Truth-Telling in Translating the Gospel of John," *Semeia* 76 (1996): 81–97; Ruth Sheridan, "Issues in the Translation of οἱ Ἰουδαῖοι in the Fourth Gospel," *JBL* 132 (2013): 671–95, especially 691–92.

This stream of interpretation has deep roots in the critical study of the Gospel, especially in Germany. See Fischer, "Ueber den Ausdruck." Fischer was followed in this respect by F. C. Baur, Franz Overbeck, and Wilhelm Heitmüller, among other early advocates of the position.

13. Reinhartz, *Cast Out*, 77. The tension also surfaces among scholars who caution against exaggerating the negative characterization of the Johannine Jews. Gerry Wheaton, for instance, critiques the positions of Culpepper and Reinhartz as overly severe. At the same time, he states that the evangelist's use of the term Ἰουδαῖοι has an "undeniably homogenizing effect," with the negative occurrences coloring the reader's perception of them. See Gerry Wheaton, *The Role of Jewish Feasts in John's Gospel*, SNTSMS 162 (Cambridge: Cambridge University Press, 2015), 49–52, at 49.

14. Mostly out of sight but nonetheless striking in this respect is Ashton's change of mind between the first and second editions of *Understanding the Fourth Gospel*. In 1991 (*Understanding*, 1st ed., 135), he responded to Bultmann's evaluation of the Jews' role in the Gospel with a hearty "Amen": "That the role of the Jews is as Bultmann describes it is surely beyond serious dispute." But by 2007 (*Understanding*, 2nd ed., 69), the imprimatur had been more or less rescinded. Bultmann's interpretation, though perhaps reasonable from the standpoint of a later Christian faith, is ultimately an imposition on the text: "It is not exegesis but eisegesis."

15. Susan Hylen (*Imperfect Believers: Ambiguous Characters in the Gospel of John* [Louisville, KY: Westminster John Knox, 2009]) has thus argued that the Jews in the Gospel of John are an ambiguous character. Ruben Zimmermann ("'The Jews': Unreliable Figures or Unreliable Narration?" in *Character Studies in the Fourth Gospel: Narrative Approaches to Seventy Figures in John*, ed. Steven A. Hunt, D. Francois Tolmie, and Ruben Zimmermann [Grand Rapids: Eerdmans, 2016], 71–109) attributes the ambiguity to an unreliable narrator. Below, I will suggest another way to approach the tension in the characterization of the Jews in the Fourth Gospel.

16. This is a fact that I would contend Reinhartz does not give sufficient weight in *Cast Out of the Covenant*. She writes, for example, (*Cast Out*, xx) that "with the exception of John 4:9, the Gospel does not refer to Jesus or his close disciples as *Ioudaioi*." However, it is clear that the Gospel presents the Jews as Jesus's own people. See also the response of Andrew Byers, "Review of *Cast Out of the Covenant: Jews and Anti-Judaism in the Gospel of John*, by Adele Reinhartz," *RBL* (2020): 348–54.

17. Similarly, Udo Schnelle, "Die Juden im Johannesevangelium," in *Gedenkt an das Wort: Festschrift für Werner Vogler zum 65. Geburtstag*, ed. Christoph Kähler, Martina Böhm, and Christfried Böttrich (Leipzig: Evangelische Verlagsanstalt, 1999), 229–30; D. François Tolmie, "The Ἰουδαῖοι in the Fourth Gospel: A Narratological Perspective," in *Theology and Christology in the Fourth Gospel: Essays by the Members of the SNTS Johannine Writings Seminar*, ed. Gilbert van Belle, J. G. Van der Watt, and P. J. Maritz, BETL 184 (Leuven: Leuven University Press, 2005), 396–97; Cirafesi, *John Within Judaism*, 95–97. Sigfred Pedersen ("Anti-Judaism in John's Gospel: John 8," in *New Readings in John: Literary and Theological Perspectives: Essays from the Scandinavian Conference on the Fourth Gospel in Aarhus*, JSNTSup 182 [Sheffield: Sheffield Academic, 1999], 190) remarks that "they [the Jews] do not generally appear in John as representatives of the Christ-rejecting world, but as part of the struggle with 'this world.'"

18. Although in what follows I do not adopt the specific terminology or methods of theoretical narratology, it is in one sense a "form of historical narrative criticism," as Cornelis Bennema ("A Theory of Character in the Fourth Gospel with Reference to Ancient and Modern Literature," *BibInt* 17 [2009]: 401) describes it. That is, I am concerned with how the evangelist characterizes the Jews but not to the exclusion of outside sources of information, since as a class of people, the Jews are not figments of the evangelist's imagination, even if their characterization should turn out to be unfair or distorted. More generally, because the Gospel refers to people and places known through other means, to take a wholly text-immanent approach is to select the wrong tool for the job, as Petri Merenlahti and Raimo Hakola caution in "Reconceiving Narrative Criticism."

19. Terry Leonard Schram, "The Use of *Ioudaios* in the Fourth Gospel: An Application of Some Linguistic Insights to a New Testament Problem" (ThD. diss., University of Utrecht, 1974), 28–33. Schram borrows his terminology from the field of linguistics, whereas Ashton takes his start from the German philosopher Gottlob Frege, who differentiated between *Sinn* as the object to which a term refers and *Bedeutung* as the manner in which the term refers to that object. Although I arrived at them independently, many of the arguments of this section run parallel to Stanley Porter, "Jesus, 'the Jews,' and John's Gospel," in *John, His Gospel, and Jesus: In Pursuit of the Johannine Voice* (Grand Rapids: Eerdmans, 2015), 149–73.

20. Schram, "Use of *Ioudaios*," 32.

21. As detailed in the Introduction; similarly, Judith Lieu ("'Parting of the Ways,'" 109) remarks: "Whatever the fuzziness at the edges, the use of the term Ἰουδαῖος without apology in both pagan literature and Jewish inscriptions implies a sufficiently coherent perception from outside and from within."

22. Dunn, "Question of Anti-semitism," 184.

23. Schram ("Use of *Ioudaios*," 226–27) does indeed speak of generic and specific references. The primary difference is that "sense" for Schram is more abstract, the meaning of a word as it is available for making references to objects or classes of objects that exist in the real world.

24. Caesarea Maritima: *J.W.* 2.287, 289, 291; Jotapata: 3.113, 114, 130, 142, 149, 150, 151, 157, 161, 165, 167, 170, 189, 191, 207, 211, 218, 239, 270, 276, 277, 279, 320, 355; Tiberias: 3.452; Tarichea: 3.471, 475, 479, 480, 488, 495, 530, 530; Gamala 4.36, 43, 75; Jerusalem: frequently throughout bks. 5 and 6 of *Jewish War*; Antioch: 7.49, 57, 62; Macheraus: 7.200, 206.

25. As, for instance, the fifty ambassadors from Judea sent to Rome to bring charges against Archelaus on behalf of their disgruntled compatriots (*J.W.* 2.80-92), are referred to in *J.W.* 2.92 simply as Ἰουδαῖοι.

26. Indeed, according to Josephus, it was civil strife and not the Romans which brought upon the city and the temple such terrible disasters. The moderate priests and aristocracy were not able to steer the ship of the state to a more profitable course because of the violence of the insurrectionists, who themselves were broken into several competing factions.

27. See Steve Mason, *Flavius Josephus on the Pharisees: A Compositional-Critical Study*, StPB 39 (Leiden: Brill, 1991), 57–81; Tessa Rajak, *Josephus, The Historian and His Society*, 2nd ed. (London: Duckworth, 2002), 78–103; also Sören Swoboda (*Tod und Sterben im Krieg bei Josephus: Die Intention von* Bellum *und* Antiquitates *im Kontext griechisch-römischer Historiographie*, TSAJ 158 [Tübingen: Mohr Siebeck, 2014]), who argues that Josephus utilizes scenes of death and calamity to show the depth of Jewish suffering and to rehabilitate the image of the Jewish people.

Mason states elsewhere ("Josephus's *Judean War*," in *A Companion to Josephus*, ed. Honora Howell Chapman and Zuleika Rodgers [Chichester: Wiley-Blackwell, 2016], 16–17), that many, having abandoned the older theory that Josephus wrote *Jewish War* as a piece of imperial propaganda, now hold that his chief motivation in writing was to absolve the Jewish people for their role in the war. Mason, for his part, is reluctant to elevate this theme to a purpose statement given Josephus's multiple sets of concerns.

28. As Paul Spilsbury has shown (*The Image of the Jew in Flavius Josephus' Paraphrase of the Bible*, TSAJ 69 [Tübingen: Mohr Siebeck, 1998]), Josephus certainly does intend to project a positive image of the Jewish people. They are peaceable, noble, and virtuous. The portrayal that Spilsbury detects in *Jewish Antiquities* largely holds true for Josephus's other works. Similarly, Mason ("Josephus's *Judean War*," 26–27) notes that in *Jewish War,* Josephus distinguishes between the poor political choices of some Jews and the Jewish national-ethnic character. As a people, they are courageous, daring, and contemptuous of death. The overarching point here is that Josephus's narrative is not controlled by the overall image of his people, as if he had to make all those he names "Jews/the Jews" fit it perfectly. Some of those so designated are bad Jews in his eyes. So also Graham Harvey, *The True Israel: Uses of the Names Jew, Hebrew, and Israel in Ancient Jewish and Early Christian Literature*, AGJU 35 (Leiden: Brill, 1996), 129.

29. Fortna, "Theological Use of Locale," 84: "But the chief role they [the Samaritans] have is to point up the contrast with the Jews, their long-standing enemies, and the lack of faith in Judea." Similarly, Wayne A. Meeks, "Galilee and Judea in the Fourth Gospel," *JBL* 85 (1966): 165-66.

30. Chapter 9, in fact, has proven especially amenable to organization into dramatic form. See Hans Windisch, "John's Narrative Style," in *The Gospel of John as Literature: An Anthology of Twentieth-Century Perspectives*, ed. Mark W. G. Stibbe, NTTS 17 (Leiden: Brill, 1993), 25-64, first published in German in 1923; also famously Martyn in *History and Theology*.

31. Against the suggestion of Bernier (*Aposynagōgos and the Historical Jesus*, 71) that the evangelist switches from "Pharisees" to "Jews" at this point because v. 18 introduces a broader coalition of Jewish interrogators. Nor is the switch indicative of a secondary source for vv. 18-23. With Bultmann (*Gospel of John*, 335, n. 1), I attribute the alternation to the evangelist's editorial activity, or rather his storytelling style, since the move to "the Jews" after context has been established is part of the author's regular procedure.

32. The passage is described as a "text of terror" by Jeffrey S. Rogers ("Texts of Terror and the Essence of Scripture: Encountering the Jesus of John 8: A Sermon on John 8:31-59," *RevExp* 103 [2006]: 205-12), borrowed from Phyllis Trible, *Texts of Terror: Literary-Feminist Readings of Biblical Narratives*, OBT 13 (Philadelphia: Fortress, 1984). Of the opinion that it is likely the most anti-Jewish statement in the NT is Jürgen Becker, *Das Evangelium nach Johannes*, ÖTK 4 (Gütersloh: Mohn, 1979), 1:304.

33. Günter Reim ("Joh. 8.44—Gotteskinder/Teufelskinder: Wie antijudaistisch ist 'die wohl antijudaistischste Äusserung des NT'?" *NTS* 30 [1984]: 619) recalls having seen a photograph from the Nazi era of a sign at the entrance to a village with words drawn from John 8:44: "The father of the Jews is the devil." The photograph to which Reim refers has been reproduced in Martin Broszat and Elke Fröhlich, eds., *Bayern in der NS-Zeit II: Herrschaft und Gesellschaft im Konflikt* (Munich: Oldenbourg, 1979), 306. The phrase also appears as the title on the first page of an anti-Semitic children's picture book published in 1936: Elvira Bauer, *Trau keinem Fuchs auf grüner Heid und keinem Jud auf seinem Eid* (Nuremberg: Stürmer, 1936). They are sober reminders of the terrifying history of interpretation of passages such as John 8:31-59 but also of the solemnity of the exegetical task.

34. Thus, for example, John 11:44 reports Lazarus's exit from the tomb as follows: "The dead man came out, his hands and feet bound with strips of cloth, and his face wrapped in a cloth (ἐξῆλθεν ὁ τεθνηκὼς δεδεμένος τοὺς πόδας καὶ τὰς χεῖρας κειρίαις)." The first perfect participle τεθνηκώς (which the NRSV translates as "the dead man") denotes a former state while δεδεμένος ("bound") has a proper perfect meaning. As for the verb πιστεύω, the perfect participle occurs in Acts (15:5; 18:27; 19:18; 21:20) with the sense of present belief, but in the Shepherd of Hermas (Vis. 3.7.1), the same form indicates apostasy—people who had formerly believed but do so no longer. See Terry Griffith, "'The Jews Who Had Believed in Him' (John 8:31) and the Motif of Apostasy in the Gospel of John," in *Gospel of John and Christian Theology*, 184-85.

35. So James Swetnam, "The Meaning of πεπιστευκότας in John 8.31," *Bib* 61 (1980): 106–9; K. L. McKay, "On the Perfect and Other Aspects in New Testament Greek," *NovT* 23 (1981): 312; Sigfred Pedersen, "Anti-Judaism in John's Gospel," 184–92; Griffith, "Motif of Apostasy," 185–86.

36. Griffith, "Motif of Apostasy," 186–87. Patrick Chatelion Counet ("No Anti-Judaism in the Fourth Gospel: A Deconstruction of Readings of John 8," in *One Text, A Thousand Methods: Studies in Memory of Sjef van Tilborg*, ed. Patrick Chatelion Counet and Ulrich Berges, BibInt 71 [Leiden: Brill, 2005], 203–4) also identifies the problem of apostasy as a shared theme across these passages, though he does not equate the Jews of 8:31 with those of 6:60-71.

37. Here we have another example of the Gospel's self-allusiveness, its quality of referring back to events and persons from earlier in the story. For example, the fact that the disciples are not arrested with Jesus (18:9) is said to fulfill Jesus's words in 6:39. In 18:14, Caiaphas is identified by allusion to the events of 11:49-50. In 19:39, it is specified that Nicodemus is the one who came to Jesus by night (3:2). There are also proleptic statements. Judas's betrayal is hinted at already in 6:64. Mary is described as the one who anointed Jesus and wiped his feet with her hair (11:2), even though this does not happen until 12:3. Even if "the Jews who had believed in him" of 8:31 are not the defectors of 6:60-71, the evangelist has hinted at things to come in 2:23-25. From very early on in his public ministry, Jesus knows that some of those who believe in him are not themselves worthy of trust.

38. Klaus Wengst (*Bedrängte Gemeinde und verherrlichter Christus: Ein Versuch über das Johannesevangelium*, 3rd ed. [Munich: Kaiser, 1990], 126–27) reads John 8:31-59 as a two-level drama, in which a falling away of members of the Johannine community is read back into Jesus's life. More common is the view that the Jews of 8:31-59 represent Jewish believers of the evangelist's day whose faith is deficient, rather than those who have already apostatized. So Brown, *Community,* 76–81; Henk Jan de Jonge, "'The Jews' in the Gospel of John," in *Anti-Judaism and the Fourth Gospel*, 128–32; Matthias Rissi, "'Die Juden' im Johannesevangelium," *ANRW* 26.3 (1996): 2099–141.

39. This is all the more so for those, such as Ashton, who assign ch. 11 to a late stage in the Gospel's development. More generally, Tolmie ("Ἰουδαῖοι in the Fourth Gospel," 397) remarks that although the negative characterization of the Jews receives the most emphasis, this does not nullify the response of those who believe.

40. Similarly Reim, "Wie antijudaistisch?" 623: "Jesus does not speak generally of the Jews' filiation from the devil but only in opposition to a determined group, who would like to stone him" (translation mine). Mark Stibbe, *John's Gospel*, New Testament Readings (London: Routledge, 1994), 124–25: "Admittedly, the narrator does describe the antagonists as hoi Ioudaioi in 8.48, 52, and 57. But this is shorthand for broader designation offered in 8.31, 'the Jews who had believed in him.'" So also Chatelion Counet, "No Anti-Judaism," 207.

41. Wendy E. S. North, "'The Jews' in John's Gospel: Observations and Inferences," in *Judaism, Jewish Identities and the Gospel Tradition: Essays in Honour of Maurice Casey*, ed. James G. Crossley (London: Equinox, 2010), 213. Similarly, Wheaton, *Role of Jewish Feasts*, 42–43: "The best approach to the data of the Fourth

Gospel is to acknowledge the lack of uniformity of reference across the narrative as a whole, and even within individual contexts, and to allow the reference of any given use to be decided by careful examination of the narrative context in which it appears." This, I hope to have shown, is amply supported by the usage of the term and related terms in other ancient Jewish authors.

42. Sjef van Tilborg ("Jezus temidden van de joden van het Loofhuttenfeest in Johannes 8," in *Jaarboek 2001—Theologie in Exegese*, ed. H. J. M. Schoot [Utrecht: Thomas Institut Utrecht, 2002], 66) contends that "the Jews" in the Fourth Gospel are "the Jews, who according to this story, are present at this narrative place and in this narrative time." Translation from the Dutch by Chatelion Counet, "No Anti-Judaism," 198. Similarly, Porter, "Jesus, 'the Jews,' and John's Gospel," 161.

43. North, "'Jews' in John's Gospel," 214.

44. Sheridan, "Issues in the Translation of οἱ Ἰουδαῖοι," 692.

45. See also Porter's observations ("Jesus, 'the Jews,' and John's Gospel," 160–61) on the Greek definite article.

46. Lowe, "Who Were the Ἰουδαῖοι?" Before Lowe: Brooke Foss Westcott, *The Gospel according to St. John* (London: Murray, 1908), 1:xvii; Geoffrey J. Cuming, "The Jews in the Fourth Gospel," *ExpTim* 60 (1949): 292.

47. Fischer ("Ueber den Ausdruck," 98–99) identifies "the Jews" in part with the Sanhedrin, a view he also ascribes to Wilhelm M. L. de Wette. In another early article, Johannes Belser ("Der Ausdruck οἱ Ἰουδαῖοι im Johannesevangelium," *TQ* 84 [1902]: 175–76) speaks of multiple meanings of "the Jews" standing side by side: the Jewish people, Judeans, and the Jewish authorities in particular.

48. Motyer, *Your Father the Devil?* 54–56.

49. This is in some respects an extension of what Belser had seen in 1902 and what Lowe had suggested in 1976 ("Who Were the Ἰουδαῖοι?" 107–8). Except whereas they speak of different meanings of the term "the Jews," I would speak of multiple referents. It is worth noting that Belser ("Ausdruck," 176) considered it a consensus position of the time that "the Jews" in the Fourth Gospel is a polyvalent term.

50. Similarly, Porter, "Jesus, 'the Jews,' and John's Gospel," 159, and Philip F. Esler, "From *Ioudaioi* to Children of God: The Development of a Non-Ethnic Group Identity in the Gospel of John," in *In Other Words: Essays on Social Science Methods and the New Testament in Honor of Jerome H. Neyrey*, ed. Anselm C. Hagedorn, Zeba A. Crook, and Eric Clark Stewart (Sheffield: Sheffield Phoenix, 2007), 118–24. The prophecy of Caiaphas about Jesus's death for the people (11:50-52) and Pilate's sarcastic reply to Jesus, "Am I a Jew? Your own nation and the chief priests have handed you over to me" (18:35) make this clear. It is the ἔθνος of the Jews to which Jesus belongs and on whose behalf he dies.

51. As Schram states ("Use of *Ioudaios*," 20), although those named "the Jews" are often depicted in opposition to Jesus, "this is not yet to show any negative connotation in the term *IOUDAIOS*, any emotional response to the term itself rather than to the referents of the term."

52. In a similar way, it seems to me problematic to treat the Jews in the Fourth Gospel as a single character, as Culpepper does in *Anatomy of the Fourth Gospel*, 126. They are one group only in the sense that all so named are members of the Jewish

people. I do not consider it a limitation, as Culpepper does, that we must always be asking precisely who the referents of "the Jews" are in each passage, any more than it would be a limitation in Philo or Josephus.

53. Similarly Grässer, "Die antijüdische Polemik," 77.

54. Schnelle, "Die Juden," 227 (translation mine).

55. Ibid., 228.

56. As Kierspel (*Jews and the World*, 155–78) has shown, the concept of "the world" in the Gospel of John cannot be narrowed to the Jewish people but encompasses the whole stage of humanity. Kierspel concludes: "It is the author's intention to say that the kind of opposition which Jesus faced from the Jews is not unique to his experience, but will always happen to all of his followers at any place. Creating this 'universal outlook' about Jesus' mission and opposition is the main contribution of the term κόσμος" (178).

57. Peder Borgen, *The Gospel of John: More Light from Philo, Paul, and Archaeology*, NovTSup 154 (Leiden: Brill, 2014), 95.

Chapter 3

Mistaking the Word's Own for an Alien People

The Gospel's Dialectic of Division and Jewish Otherness

As Jesus's public ministry reaches its completion in John 12, the narrative pace of the Gospel slows to a crawl. For the next five chapters, the master, knowing that the time of his glorification is at hand, comforts and prepares his closest followers for the events to follow and for life after his departure. Shortly after their final meal together and after Judas has made his exit, Jesus announces to the disciples, "Little children, I am with you only a little longer. You will look for me; and as I said to the Jews so now I say to you, 'Where I am going, you cannot come'" (13:33). How is it that Jesus, a Jew, speaks to the Jewish apostles as if they were not themselves Ἰουδαῖοι? This becomes all the more peculiar when, two chapters later, he refers to a Christologically interpreted passage in the Psalms as written in "their law" (15:25).

It was the purpose of the last chapter to show that the frequency of the expression οἱ Ἰουδαῖοι does not serve to stereotype all Jews as unbelievers. The nomenclature, rather, is shorthand for whatever Jewish contingent is acting at that point in the narrative, whether the Jewish mourners in Bethany, the Pharisees, the chief priests, or some other subset of the people. The regular expansion and contraction of the referents of "the Jews" follows a literary pattern present in Josephus and Philo. Thus, although the strongest note of the Gospel of John is on widespread unbelief, this is not at the expense of more favorable Jewish responses. But these passages from the Farewell Discourse, and the handful of others like them, would seem to pull once more in the other direction.[1] Does not the evangelist "other" the Jews, so that the dialectic of faith and unbelief collapses in on itself? Or to put it in the Gospel's own terms, if believers are in the world but not of the world (17:11-14), are Jewish followers of Jesus *among* the Jews but not *of* them?[2] Earlier I had occasion to quote Bultmann's lapidary remarks about the Johannine Jews as symbols of unbelief. An attentive reader, especially one familiar with Bultmann's iconic commentary, may have noticed the ellipsis in the middle of the quoted text. The omission was not meant to prejudice the results of that chapter, but I would be remiss to leave it unattended to altogether, for once again Bultmann gets to the heart of the matter:

> The Jews are spoken of as an alien people, not merely from the point of view of the Greek readers, but also, and indeed only properly, from the stand-point of faith; for Jesus himself speaks to them as a stranger and correspondingly, those in whom the stirrings of faith or of the search for Jesus are to be found are distinguished from the "Jews," even if they are themselves Jews. In this connection therefore even the Baptist does not appear to belong to the "Jews."[3]

Reinhartz echoes Bultmann in this respect, remarking that

> in John's rhetoric of binary opposition, anyone who becomes a follower, whether Jew or pagan, is no longer identified a *Ioudaios* because for John the *Ioudaioi* are those who reject the Gospel's claims about Jesus, belief, eternal life, and covenantal relationship with God.[4]

There are indeed some strange turns of phrase that appear to put Jesus and the disciples at some remove from the Ἰουδαῖοι: the crowds in Jerusalem not speaking "for fear of the Jews" (7:13) when all in the narrative are presumably Jewish, Jesus's references to the Torah as "your law" (8:17; 10:34), and so forth.[5] I made the case in ch. 1 that the model of a religious schism in which former Jews now abandoned that identity fits uneasily with the evangelist's more assertive posture, but now those features of the Gospel which have fed the impression of detachment must be considered directly.

"MANY LEFT THE JEWS"?

The first thing to be observed is that nowhere is it explicitly said that an ethnically Jewish believer's identity is erased in Christ. Neither the evangelist in his own voice nor the Johannine Jesus makes a pronouncement or articulates a general principle to that effect. Believers, it is true, experience an identity transformation, an event that the Gospel envisions with a panoply of metaphors. They are given the right to become children of God (1:12). They are born from above (3:3), born of the Spirit (3:5), and children of the light (12:36). They worship the Father in Spirit and in truth (4:23). They are sheep kept safe by the Good Shepherd (10:1-18). But never is it stated that this acquired standing supersedes the individual's ethnic identity.[6] When, in the high-priestly prayer of John 17, Jesus tells the Father (it would seem for the benefit of his followers rather than for his own sake) that the disciples are not of the world (v. 16), κόσμος stands in for a principle of ungodliness. Its meaning has transitioned from the stage of human activity into an abstracted life stance defined by opposition to the Creator.[7] So although the disciples have been granted a transfer of origins from the earthly to the heavenly realm, it is not as though they have become ontologically non-human. Thus, although the promised adoption as sons and daughters of God for those who believe, or the imagery of one flock under one shepherd, could be construed as creating an all-consuming meta-identity, it could also be reasonably interpreted as establishing a nested hierarchy.[8] There are Jewish children of God and Gentile children of God. There is one flock which embraces both the *ecclesia ex circumcisione* and the *ecclesia ex gentibus*, at the same time unified and distinct.[9]

The closest the Gospel comes to a forthright denial of the ethnic state of Jewish believers in which they were called is perhaps John 12:11. For the evangelist, it is the raising of Lazarus from the dead, and not the cleansing of the temple as in the Synoptic Gospels, that triggers the official decision of the Sanhedrin to have Jesus arrested and killed. It also proves to be a major catalyst of Jewish belief, first among those present and then among the general population as the word spreads. By all appearances, 12:11 is one of the relatively few notices of Jewish reception of Jesus. On account of Lazarus, "many of the Jews were deserting and were believing in Jesus (πολλοὶ δι' αὐτὸν ὑπῆγον τῶν Ἰουδαίων καὶ ἐπίστευον εἰς τὸν Ἰησοῦν)." The syntax of the verse, however, leaves room for ambiguity, since the genitive "of the Jews (τῶν Ἰουδαίων)" follows the verb (ὑπῆγον) and not the subject "many (πολλοί)." According to Meeks, "this verse could be translated, 'Many *left the Jews* and believed in Jesus.'"[10]

The fact that English translations are virtually unanimous in taking τῶν Ἰουδαίων as a partitive genitive in relation to πολλοί steers us away from this rendering. A perusal of the LSJ shows that when transitive, ὑπάγω takes a direct object in the accusative. To express it rather woodenly, and with due awareness of the etymological fallacy, one brings someone or something under something else.[11] It is as an intransitive verb that ὑπάγω accrues connotations of self-withdrawal or departure. If ὑπῆγον in John 12:11 bears the meaning of "were going out," presumably Jerusalem is the point of departure, since according to 11:55-56 many pilgrims had congregated there from the countryside in anticipation of the festival. The NRSV's "were deserting" suggests more a movement in the social sphere than relocation of place.[12] It might even be that ὑπάγω serves as the active counterpart to being made ἀποσυναγωγός. Many of the Jews willingly cut themselves off from the public assembly. They withdrew, having resolved to pay the price for their faith.[13]

As a highly inflected language, Greek, more than English, lends itself to the figure of speech known as hyperbaton, the separation of elements that belong together. Grammatically, there is no impediment to the consensus translation. The syntax of 12:11, moreover, parallels the summary of Samaritan belief in 4:39: "From that city many of the Samaritans believed in him on account of the woman's word (Ἐκ δὲ τῆς πόλεως ἐκείνης πολλοὶ ἐπίστευσαν εἰς αὐτὸν τῶν Σαμαριτῶν διὰ τὸν λόγον τῆς γυναικός)." Even though the main verb and its oblique object (ἐπίστευσαν εἰς αὐτόν) intervene between πολλοί and τῶν Σαμαριτῶν, together they form the subject of the sentence: "many of the Samaritans."[14] The success with which Jesus meets among the Samaritans of Sychar in ch. 4 replays itself now among a portion of the Jewish populace in Judea. There are indeed some Jews who come to believe in Jesus.[15]

A MANUFACTURED XENOPHOBIA?

Without any express statement in the Gospel itself, the conclusion that John intentionally sets Jesus, and by association Johannine Christ followers, apart from the Jewish people and their religious institutions and customs (and turns them into foreigners, so to speak) has been arrived at by inference. The process of inference typically runs along two interrelated tracks. First, the Gospel's seeming ambivalence toward central Jewish institutions and its relative silence on matters of Jewish ritual observance that feature often enough in the Synoptic Gospels have often been felt to be the product of a supercessionist theology.[16] Jesus fulfills in himself the meaning of Jewish festivals and religious customs, and indeed the law of Moses *tout court*, and thereby makes them obsolete.[17] Thus Jesus does not say "our law" but "your law" and "their law." The ancestors of the Jews of John 6 are not "our fathers" but "your fathers." And practices like Sabbath observance and temple worship, though not denigrated, are nowhere affirmed as divine ordinances with enduring validity. Second, as we have seen, are statements about οἱ Ἰουδαῖοι in which other Jewish figures appear to be excluded from the collective to which they naturally belong.

The First Track of Inference: The Fourth Gospel and the Law

The relationship between Jesus and Moses (and the law given through him), if not as pervasive a theme as others, nevertheless exercised the thought of the evangelist, for he broaches the subject already in the prologue: "The law indeed was given through Moses; grace and truth came through Jesus Christ" (1:17). Unfortunately for exegetes, the statement is terse to the point of ambiguity. Is the comparison antithetic, such that the law is abolished with the coming of Christ?[18] Or is it synthetic, the Torah still valued as a God-given grace, even if relativized by Jesus's earthly advent?[19] Despite its occasional reference to this greatest of Jewish heroes and the law given through him, the body of the Gospel does little to clarify matters.[20] Jesus, no doubt, has pride of place far above all the other figures of Israel's past, but what would this have meant for the daily life of the evangelist or those under his pastoral care?

One thing is certain: the evangelist was no Marcion. He was not ready to dispense with Israel's Scriptures and God, as if these only served to shackle the church to the principles of this world.[21] For John, the law of Moses and the sacred writings are, if nothing else, witnesses to the Word, and so their testimony goes unheeded to one's own detriment. Although he has most assuredly reappraised their significance in some measure, he has not tossed them away entirely as the detritus of past revelation. Scripture cannot be broken (10:35).

And yet, if John has little in common theologically with the ship owner from "icy and inhospitable Pontus," as Tertullian scorned Marcion's native land (*Marc.* 1.1), that by no means ensures that he or the original recipients of the Gospel were Torah-observant. Maurice Casey has made the case that in practice, the Johannine Christians had given up many of "the identity factors of Second Temple Judaism" and had in the process taken on a Gentile self-identification.[22] The law is presented as the possession of an outside group, circumcision and purity regulations as alien customs. The Sabbath is explicitly abrogated (5:18), the festivals replaced. Scripture is accepted in its capacity as witness, but its injunctions are otherwise ignored. According to Casey's reconstruction, the expulsion of Johannine believers in Jesus from the synagogue accelerated their assimilation to the customs of the ethnically non-Jewish members already part of the community. They had become Gentiles.[23]

This train of thought, however, pushes us into a methodological cul-de-sac, or rather into several of them. First, there is the possible disjunction between the evangelist's ethnic self-identification and that of the Gospel's intended recipients. That is, we may be dealing with a Jewish author who is writing for Gentiles with varying degrees of familiarity with Jewish life and history, just as Josephus addresses himself to Greeks and Romans. If so, the explanations of Jewish customs, the identification of the festivals as "of the Jews," and the Gospel's lack of concern about Jewish ritual practice might say more about the ethnic makeup of the intended audience than about the evangelist.[24]

The gap between practice and self-identification forces us into a second impasse. It cannot be assumed that divergence in behavior or practice from group norms, even dramatic departures, will entail a corresponding sense of having exited the social entity in question. Doubtless, there were some Jews in antiquity who were lax with respect to Torah, who occasionally went to the market on a Saturday to sell their goods, or who had a taste for non-kosher meat. As we have seen in ch. 1, there were some who went much further, reproached by other Jews as apostates. Although for the most part we do not have access to these individuals' own testimonies, it might be suspected that some of them rejected the derisive tag and continued to think of themselves as Jews.[25] As Paula Fredriksen reminds us, "Then as now, there was never a single universal standard of Jewish practice against which to measure all the various other enactments and interpretations of Jewish tradition."[26]

If we have any first-hand accounts from an accused apostate, it is through the letters of the apostle Paul. Paul's writings reveal conflict with synagogue authorities and fellow Jews (1 Thess 2:14-16; 2 Cor 11:21-29; Rom 3:5-8), and the book of Acts suggests controversy over Paul's Jewish bona fides, with some alleging that he had abandoned the Torah and was encouraging other Jews to do the same (Acts 21:20-25). It has long been supposed that after Paul's encounter with the risen Christ, he no longer regarded himself as bound to the Torah. What mattered now was a new creation, detached from ethnic particulars such as circumcision and dietary laws.[27]

It is not possible, or necessary within the parameters of this study, to engage all of the literature on Paul's relationship to the Torah. Paula Fredriksen and Mark Nanos, among other representatives of what has come to be known as the "Paul within Judaism" perspective, have made a sustained case that Paul not only continued to identify as a Jew and practice Torah but that he upheld its enduring and normative force for the community of Jewish believers.[28] What Paul objects to, says Fredriksen, is not the Torah *per se* but the requirement of full conversion for Gentile believers, who though required by Paul to Judaize in some respects (worship of the God of Israel, avoidance of sexual immorality, etc.), were nevertheless to remain Gentiles in order to fulfill the prophets' eschatological vision of the turning of the nations to the God of Israel.[29]

What I would like to say here is that despite some of the salutary correctives of the "Paul within Judaism" movement, there is still good reason to think that at least intellectually Paul had detached faithfulness to Israel's God from life under the Sinaitic covenant.[30] While Paul writes primarily to Gentiles, the statements he makes about the Torah are not only in reference to Gentiles.[31] He speaks in the first person of dying to the law (Gal 2:19). He says that he himself is not under the law, though he becomes like those under the law to win them for Christ (1 Cor 9:20).[32] He writes that *all* who rely on the works of the law are under a curse (Gal 3:10) and that Christ redeemed "us" from the curse of the law, referring to himself and other Jewish believers (Gal 3:13-14; 4:3-5).[33] Paul describes the covenant at Sinai as a ministry of death engraved on letters of stone (2 Cor 3:7). Believers have been released from the Torah in order to serve in the new way of the Spirit and not in the old way of the written code (Rom 7:6). The old covenant is a ministry of condemnation whose glory was temporary, while the glory of the new covenant lasts forever (2 Cor 3:8-11).[34] The Torah's provisional nature within God's redemptive plan for humanity also forms the theme of Gal 3. While the law is not opposed to the promises of God, it cannot make one righteous. Rather, it was a guardian until Christ came: "Now that this faith has come, we are no longer under a guardian" (Gal 3:25). God's commands in the Torah are holy, righteous, and good, but they enliven sin, bringing condemnation and death (Rom 7:7-20). The law is powerless to make a person righteous because it is weakened by the flesh (Rom 8:3).

Taken together, it is hard to read these passages as exclusively about the law's negative effects on Gentiles. According to Paul, Jesus's life, death, and resurrection brought about a more fundamental change in the relationship between God and God's people. It had initiated a new covenant, not of the letter but of the Spirit.[35] Yet for all of Paul's reservations about the Torah, the apostle never set aside his own identity as a Jew.[36] By the measure of many of his contemporaries, Paul may have been a sinner or apostate. But in his own mind, he remained a Ἰουδαῖος, an Israelite according to both spirit and flesh. Thus, even were it certain that John or the members of the Johannine community no longer kept the Sabbath, or purity regulations, or some other statutes of the Torah, these are not infallible indices of their ethnic self-identification. And if the "Paul within Judaism" perspective is correct, and the preceding observations do not hold, then it is best to remain agnostic. Though a Johannine abandonment of certain Jewish practices *might* have meant a rejection of their Jewish identity, it cannot be assumed.

A third methodological dead end arises from the very fact that the Gospel is a story about Jesus. He is the one who speaks about the Torah as "your law/their law," who works on the Sabbath just as his Father is working, and who refers to Abraham as "your father." Surely the evangelist believed what he wrote about Jesus. But by reading the narrative as if this stranger from heaven were a transparent mouthpiece for a preacher in the community or its corporate voice, we ignore the Gospel's character as an interpretation of past events.[37] There is, no doubt, a sort of mimesis expected of the disciples. They are to love one another as Jesus has loved them (13:34). Jesus sends them into the world, just as the Father sent him (20:21). They will do even greater works than Jesus because, having ascended to the Father, he will send another Paraclete, the promised Spirit of Truth (14:12). Yet however we might conceive the operation of the Paraclete in a hypothetical community, presumably those so inspired did not make their utterances *in persona Christi* but with the prophetic, "Thus says the Lord."[38] Jesus, in other words, is not the spokesperson for the Johannine community in the sense that all of his words are their own.[39] He stands both within and above the community, both Lord and friend, straddling the line between heaven and earth. As the Word made flesh, his voice is unique.

It is possible that "your law" or "your fathers" in the mouth of Jesus corresponds to the *ad hominem* rhetorical situation within the narrative, "your" putting the onus on the hearers to act according to a standard they themselves would recognize.[40] The convention occurs relatively frequently in the book of Deuteronomy and again occasionally in Joshua.[41] Addressing the assembled Israelites, Moses consistently speaks with second-person plural pronouns: "Your ancestors went down to Egypt seventy persons; and now the Lord your God has made you as numerous as the stars in heaven" (Deut 10:22). Here "your" is not exclusive, as if Moses had some other God or the people's ancestors were not also his own, but intensifies the speech.[42] The statements in the Fourth Gospel are likely tinged with more irony than those in Deuteronomy—"your law" having the force of "the law as you (mis)interpret it"—but even then, they could serve more as an admonishment for Jesus's opponents to recognize the true meaning of that which they claim as their prized possession and the arbiter of truth than as a repudiation of the Torah.[43] Or we could take the suggestion of Cirafesi that Jesus speaks of "your law" in recognition of the Samaritan claim to Moses and the Torah. Jesus thus does not distance himself from the law but affirms its possession by other members of the Israelite family.[44]

Nevertheless, it seems to me that when Jesus speaks of "your law" or "your fathers," he does so as the one sent by the Father from above, simultaneously a Jewish man and bread from heaven. Here the paradox of the eternal Word becoming flesh is at its sharpest. As Hugo Odeberg remarked in 1929:

> It is indefensible to take into account only *one* of the following facts, *vis.* (1) that J[esus] doubtlessly speaks of the Tora as containing spiritual words, as belonging to the Spiritual World, hence cannot possibly reject it, (2) that he never says "our Tora," but several times "your Tora." The explanations seems to be: J[esus] declares himself expressly, in both contexts (5:30-47 and here, in both passages referring to the Holy Writ) to be a Celestial Being, the Son of his Father. *God never says "our Law" but either "my Law" or "your Law." J[esus] stands in the same relation to the Tora as his Father.*[45]

As one who is over the people, the all-powerful suzerain in the covenant with Israel, God says "Abraham your father" (Isa 51:2), "your festivals" (Isa 1:14; Amos 5:21), and "your ancestors" (Jer 7:22; Zech 1:4-5), and although Jesus depends entirely on the Father and so does not speak on his own (5:19), he too is the one from above who is above all. The Jews are his own people, and yet he pre-existed them. John holds on to both propositions.

Thus, when Jesus breaks the Sabbath, he does so as one who makes himself equal with God (5:18), enjoying the divine prerogatives of giving life and executing judgment.[46] It is a display of his divine status. There is nothing in John 5 and 9, where Jesus's Sabbath healings raise the ire of the authorities, equivalent to Mark's aside to readers that Jesus had declared all foods clean (7:19), no generalizations about Sabbath observance among the Christian community. Hakola states that "it is not very likely that the Johannine Christians would have continued to keep the Sabbath themselves while accepting without further ado that their Lord habitually broke it or even abrogated it."[47] The deduction is not a non-sequitur, but at the same time, it minimizes the difference between Jesus and all others.[48] Would ethnically Jewish members of the Johannine community have thought these particular deeds of Jesus open for or even demanding imitation? Or would they see in them an authority that belonged exclusively to the Son of God, actions that were meant to inspire faith in Jesus more than guide their own behavior?

In the end, the path to reconstructing the evangelist's or Johannine community's religious practice, I would argue, is obstructed at too many points for us to say much about it with confidence. It does not necessarily follow from the Gospel that believers in Jesus are to cease from observing the rituals commanded in the Torah. On the other hand, Cirafesi's argument that the Gospel assumes, or even promotes, the continuing practice of the Torah by Jesus's followers also pushes us beyond the limits of our evidence. It requires reading the Torah into passages which have more natural and immediate referents.[49] Cirafesi, for example, follows Daniel Boyarin's reading of the prologue. According to Boyarin, there is no Incarnation before 1:14. The references to Jesus's rejection refer rather to Israel's failure to understand and accept God's Word/Wisdom. The people failed to understand the Torah, so God took on flesh to do fully what Moses was only able to do partially—bring the gift of divine revelation.[50] It is questionable, however, whether the prologue is meant to be strictly chronological, given that it moves quickly from "the beginning" in 1:1 to the testimony of John the Baptist in v. 6. Boyarin takes vv. 6-8 as a proleptic transition from a Genesis midrash in vv. 1-5 to a Wisdom aretalogy in vv. 7-13.[51] But the theme of rejection in vv. 9-13 is perfectly consonant with the story told about Jesus in the pages of the Gospel. The rejection of God's Wisdom may certainly lie in the background of John 1:9-13, but it is a foreshadowing of the rejection of the earthly Jesus that belongs in the foreground.

Jesus, moreover, is not presented as the interpreter of Torah but as the exegete, so to speak, of God. The prologue ends with the apophatic statement that, "No one has ever seen God. It is the only Son, himself God, who is close to the Father's heart, who has made him known." The verb ἐξηγήσατο in v. 18b ("made known," as the NRSV renders it) lacks a direct object, which nearly all translations supply with "him," that is, God. Cirafesi suggests that the implied object might also be an "it," namely the Torah.[52] What Israel lacked was an interpreter able to maximize the revelatory potential of the Torah, a need which Jesus now fills.[53] However, the standard translation and interpretation has better grammatical support—since "God" is the direct object of 18a—and anticipates the thematic development within the rest of the Gospel. Jesus's revelation of the Father constitutes one of the text's most prominent motifs. It is expressed in a myriad of ways. Jesus does and says exactly what the Father has shown him (John 5:19-30; 7:16-18; 8:14-20, 54-56; 12:49-50). Whoever has seen Jesus has seen the Father (14:9-14). Jesus reveals the name of the Father to the disciples (17:6). No one has seen God, but Jesus has made God known.

Similarly, Cirafesi asserts that the references to Jesus as rabbi cannot mean anything other than that he is a teacher of Torah or of Scripture more generally.[54] Yet when we look at the content of Jesus's teaching in the Fourth Gospel, it is strikingly and relentlessly Christocentric. It revolves around Jesus's identity as the one sent by God, his unique relationship to the Father, his authority to give eternal life, and the work which the Father has given him to do. There is nothing resembling the Sermon on the Mount from Matthew's Gospel or the teaching on divorce recorded in Mark 10. While Jesus occasionally engages in halakhic disputes, particularly concerning the Sabbath, these become vehicles for the proclamation of Jesus's identity as God's Son (John 5) and light of the world (John 9). Jesus, to be sure, appeals to the Torah as a witness and defense in several exchanges (5:45-57; 8:14-17), but is that a sufficient indicator of ritual behavior?[55] That is not to say that a putative Johannine community could not have kept the Torah. It is to say, rather, that the Gospel is not readily transparent to inferences about the quotidian religious practice of Johannine Christ followers.

The Second Track of Inference: Jews over against "the Jews"

As is clear by now, the true weight of the controversy centers upon the term οἱ Ἰουδαῖοι itself. Does the evangelist place those who are Jews by birth outside of that ἔθνος in a sort of manufactured xenophobia? It should be noted that those who are seemingly contrasted with the Jews are not always believers. The lame man of ch. 5, the divided crowds of ch. 7, and the blind man's parents of ch. 9 are all set over against "the Jews," but none of them is said to have put their faith in Jesus. Indeed, even Caiaphas, for whom the evangelist hardly has any sympathy, is said to be "the one who advised the Jews (ὁ συμβουλεύσας τοῖς Ἰουδαίοις)" to hand Jesus over to the procurator so that the rest of the nation might be spared from Roman aggression (18:14). The evangelist, we may reasonably surmise, did not try to put distance between

Caiaphas and the Jews, as if the man who engineered Jesus's demise was a crypto-Christian, or at any rate, something other than an ethnic Jew.

How, then, do we explain the juxtaposition between various figures in the Gospel and those named the Jews? One of the primary contributions of this chapter is to once more show how ancient literary convention gives context to Johannine usage. It is not uncommon in ancient Jewish/Israelite texts for an individual to be set off literarily from the social body to which he or she belongs without a distancing intent. This literary convention is again evident in Josephus's writings, in which Jewish figures, including the author himself, are from time to time juxtaposed with "the Jews."[56] When Vespasian arrives in Galilee, the Jewish forces in the region scatter. Josephus reports (in the third person) that seeing he lacked a sufficient army to contend with the Romans and that the spirits of the Jews (τὰ φρονήματα τῶν Ἰουδίαιων) were dejected, he retreated for a time to Tiberias (*J.W.* 3.130). Later in bk. 5 of *Jewish War*, Josephus recounts having been knocked unconscious by a stone from the wall of Jerusalem while trying to persuade the rebels to surrender to the Romans. Upon this, he writes, "the Jews made a rush for the body" (*J.W.* 5.541).[57] It can be said with confidence that Josephus does not thereby put a wedge between himself and his Jewish identity, since shortly after this he appeals to the people of Jerusalem as a fellow Ἰουδαῖος: "Remember, too, that I who exhort you am your countryman, that I who make this promise am a Jew . . . For never may I live to become so abject a captive as to abjure my race or to forget the traditions of my forefathers" (*J.W.* 6.96-110).

Josephus's vehement affirmation of his Jewish credentials in the face of indictments of betrayal converges thematically with the portrayal of the apostle Paul in the Acts of the Apostles. If the most severe accusations of anti-Jewish bias have been leveled against the Fourth Gospel, the book of Acts stands in the courtroom as the second defendant, and to this point I have kept it at arm's length.[58] But whatever we make of Luke's attitude toward Jews and Judaism, one of his tendencies is to characterize the protagonists of the narrative as devout Jews, scrupulously adhering to the law of their fathers. Twice (21:39; 22:3) he has Paul avow that he is a Jewish man, trained in and faithful to the Torah, despite malicious rumors to the contrary. Paul addresses the Jewish crowd in Jerusalem and the Sanhedrin as brothers and fathers (22:1, 3; 23:1, also the Jews of Rome in 28:17). The Jewish people are his people, their ancestors his ancestors (24:17; 28:17). Thus, in those instances in which Paul acts over against those named "the Jews" or vice versa (14:45, 50; 17:5; 18:6, 19; 22:30; 23:12; 24:9; 26:2, 4), any impression of the Jews' otherness is a mirage.[59]

The evangelist was likely familiar with this literary convention, since it abounds in the narrative portions of the Pentateuch and, to a lesser extent, in Joshua and Judges, where the authors distinguish Moses, Aaron, Joshua, and other Israelite leaders from the children of Israel. "Moses spoke to the Israelites" is a common refrain in Exodus, Numbers, and Deuteronomy. During the desert wanderings, those designated as "the children of Israel" repeatedly grumble against Moses and Aaron (Exod 16:2-3; Num 14:2), even attempting to stone them. Joshua likewise is said to speak to "the Israelites" (Josh 3:9; 4:21). They do as he commands (4:8). He circumcises them (5:3). According to Jdg 2:6, Joshua "dismissed the Israelites" to go and take possession of their assigned inheritance. Later in Judges, the Israelites send Ehud to Eglon, the king of Moab (3:15), come to Deborah to have their disputes adjudicated (4:5), request Gideon to rule over them (8:22), and ask the Levite whose concubine is abused and murdered to recount the sordid affair (20:3-4).

This characteristic of biblical storytelling produces scenes in which tribal subunits also serve as principal actors alongside "the Israelites." The Reubenites, Gadites, and half-tribe of Manasseh of Josh 22 belong to Israel, brothers of those settled on the west side of the Jordan (1:14; 22:3), and yet it is "the Israelites" who send Phineas son of Eleazar to interrogate them about the altar which they have built at the river's edge (vv. 9, 11, 13, and 32). And when the nation erupts in civil strife in Jdg 20, the warring parties are named "the Israelites" and "the Benjamites," even as the narrator of the story knows that all involved in the conflict are kin (v. 14). The people, to be sure, are often portrayed as inconstant and unfaithful, and in that respect are set apart from their leaders. But this should not be interpreted as the conceit of an author trying to make the Israelites an alien people.[60]

So, in the Fourth Gospel when Jesus speaks to οἱ Ἰουδαῖοι, or when they are said to undertake some action in relation to him, or when John the Baptist, the lame man, or the blind man's parents are distinguished from "the Jews," it may be something much less pernicious than an "othering" of the Jews: an effect of literary convention. This would account for the fact that it is not only Jesus and those who believe in him who are presented as undertaking some action in relation to the Jews but also figures like Caiaphas who reside on the negative side of the evangelist's dialectic of faith and unbelief.

THE REMAINING *CRUCES*

Having bracketed out such passages, we are left with a much smaller pool of *cruces interpretum*. Two of these belong to the dialogues between Jesus and the disciples. It has been thoroughly reiterated that the Jesus of the Fourth Gospel is and remains a Ἰουδαῖος. But what about his inner circle of disciples, whose ethnic identities are nowhere made explicit? As the Twelve only figure as minor characters, Peter and the unnamed beloved disciple being the most prominent of the group, it should come as no surprise that the evangelist makes few direct statements about their origins and biographical profile. Philip and the pair of brothers, Andrew and Peter, hail from the town of Bethsaida in Galilee, Nathanael from Cana to the southwest. A few others are named but appear and disappear as if they had hardly set foot on the stage.

It might be supposed that they too are assumed to be Jewish were it not for John 11:8 and 13:33, since in these verses they speak, and Jesus speaks to them, in contradistinction to the Jews. According to 11:8, the disciples try to dissuade Jesus from returning to Judea: "A short while ago the Jews tried to stone you, and yet you are going back there?" And 13:33, as already observed, contrasts the "you" whom Jesus addresses with "the Jews." Reinhartz concludes that

> the disciples themselves—the role models for audience identification—are never referred to as *Ioudaioi*. This point in itself rhetorically implies that the disciples are not *Ioudaioi* and, therefore, that there must be another category that covers those who engage in Jewish behaviors and yet do not belong to the category of *Ioudaioi* as such.[61]

Yet we must take care not to exaggerate the idiosyncrasy of Johannine usage, since the convention observed above extends into direct discourse. The author of Esther narrates a message from Mordecai to his orphaned cousin, now ascended to royalty, in the following words:

> Do not think that because you are in the king's house you alone of all the Jews will escape. For if you remain silent at this time, relief and deliverance for the Jews will arise from another place, but you and your father's family will perish (4:13-14).

Esther, in turn, petitions Mordecai to "gather together all the Jews who are in Susa, and fast for me" (v. 15).[62] Josephus recounts in his autobiography that "the Jews" pressured Gentile dignitaries from the court of Agrippa II to undergo circumcision, a measure which the general opposed as contrary to God's will and the nation's strategic interest (*Life* 113). Again, near the end of *Life*, he boasts of the favors which Titus and Vespasian bestowed upon him, recalling their protection against continual threats:

> I was often in danger of death, both from the Jews, who were keen to have me at their mercy, for the sake of revenge, and from the Romans who imagined that whenever they suffered defeat, this resulted from my betrayal (*Life* 416).

It could be that for John, the Twelve do not in fact belong to the Jews, in which case, their ethnic status would still have to be determined, but in light of these examples, this seems unlikely.

The third crux is the statement in John 7:12-13 that no one among the crowds present in Jerusalem for the Feast of Tabernacles said anything publicly about Jesus "for fear of the Jews." The subject of 7:13 is not a named individual or subset of the people as in the previous examples but an indefinite "no one" (οὐδείς). It sounds as if the Jews stand over the crowds as an authoritative body, and so it must be asked whether this stretches the convention beyond what it reasonably can bear. The antithesis of Jew and Christian, or of Jew and potential Christian, which breaks down in many of the examples presented above, also breaks down in this case. For although some in the crowd have determined that Jesus is a good man, others retort that he deceives the people.

It would be expedient to identify the Jews in this passage with the upper crust of Jerusalem society, the religious and political elite who have already cast their vote against Jesus, as the case appears to be. The Jews before whom the masses acquiesce in v. 13 appear in context to be the same as those in 7:1 who are seeking to take Jesus's life. John 7:1, in turn, alludes to 5:18, where the threat to Jesus is stated in nearly identical terms.[63] But then we are faced with the problem of a subset of a group bearing the name of the whole *in contrast* to the larger collective, a usage which, as far as I can tell, would be unique to the Fourth Gospel among ancient texts.[64]

The Jews of 7:12-13, of course, are also Judeans in the strict sense, and it could be that the tension revolves around geography. The Jews of the adjacent regions of Palestine and those of the diaspora, away from the seat of power in Jerusalem, hesitate to make any public pronouncement for fear of the reaction of their more politically influential compatriots in Judea. On the other hand, as Ashton notes,

> although there is plenty of evidence in contemporary writing (above all Josephus) for the use of the term οἱ Ἰουδαῖοι to refer to the people of Judaea, it is nowhere used to *distinguish* them from Jews of the diaspora or of other parts of Palestine.[65]

Had the evangelist meant the inhabitants of Judea as opposed to other Jews, we would expect some qualification such as we find in the opening letter of 2 Maccabees (1:1-9) where "the Jews who live in Jerusalem and in the countryside of Judea (οἱ ἐν Ἱεροσολύμοις Ἰουδαῖοι καὶ οἱ ἐν τῇ χώρᾳ τῆς Ἰουδαίας)" send greetings to their compatriots in Egypt.

Perhaps here we are, after all, at the mercy of Johannine eccentricity, struggling to rein in usage that does not perfectly conform to what we know from elsewhere. Yet the present indecision should not overshadow the question that John 7:12-13 prompts: Are all the characters of the narrative world of the Fourth Gospel in fact Jews? There are the Greeks in 12:20-21 whose request to see Jesus marks the advent of Jesus's hour. Are there others, and if so, how does that affect our understanding of Johannine terminology? I will take up that question in the next chapter.

CONCLUSION

At first glance, the Fourth Gospel might seem to inhabit a world of its own, its presentation of Jesus far removed from the earth-bound sage of the Synoptic Gospels.[66] The distinctiveness of its Christology in comparison with the whole deposit of early Christian tradition remains an unsettled matter.[67] On the other hand, I hope to have shown that the evangelist's handling of the term Ἰουδαῖος has much in common with other ancient works. If the total presentation is uniquely Johannine, many of the turns of phrase involving "the Jews" are not. The evangelist does not write in an idiolect that must be deciphered on the basis of the Gospel alone.

Although John has a decidedly critical edge, the juxtaposition of Jesus and the Jews, or John the Baptist and the Jews, or the lame man and the Jews bespeaks more of literary convention than a process of separation. The Jews as a whole are not alienated from the standpoint of Christian faith. I would suggest, therefore, that these Johannine locutions do not unravel the dialectic of division, that motif of widespread unbelief relieved by small pockets of sympathizers and believers. John, at the crossroads of experience and tradition, portrays the rejection of Jesus by his own, but he does not essentialize Jewish unreceptivity. The line between belief and unbelief still cuts through the Jews of the narrative.

The focus of chs. 2 and 3 has been exegesis, informed as it must be by historical and literary context. How does the evangelist characterize the Jews? What role do they play in the Gospel? Now I must turn, as Ashton advises, to the order of explanation. Why does John portray them in this way? Why does he opt so often for "the Jews" when other terms were available?

NOTES

1. Culpepper (*Anatomy*, 128–29), for instance, suggests that such phrases contribute to the creation of a stereotype of the Jews as unbelievers. Brown (*Community*, 41), taking these passages as a window into the situation of the Johannine community, concludes that "the Jesus who speaks of 'the Jews' (13:33) and of what is written in 'their Law' (15:25; see 10:34) is speaking the language of the Johannine Christian for whom the Law is no longer his own but is the hallmark of another religion."

2. Or as Meeks pointedly asks ("'Am I a Jew?'" 163): "Could Pilate's question ['Am I a Jew?'] have been put in the mouth of the author himself? Or, for that matter, of his central character, Jesus?" Similarly Reinhartz, "'Jews' and Jews," 224.

3. Bultmann, *Gospel of John*, 86–87; idem, *Theology of the New Testament*, trans. Kendrick Grobel (London: SCM, 1955), 2:5. Along similar lines, Hoskyns, *Fourth Gospel*, 173; Fortna, "Theological Use of Locale," 90–92; Robert G. Bratcher, "'The Jews' in the Gospel of John," *BT* 26 (1975): 403–8.

4. Reinhartz, *Cast Out*, 84.

5. Although I shall argue that the distancing effect of such expressions can be exaggerated, Brown (*Community*, 41) hits upon their apparent strangeness: "But to have the Jewish parents of the blind man in Jerusalem described as being 'afraid of the Jews' (9:22) is just as awkward as having an American living in Washington, DC, described as being afraid of 'the Americans.'"

6. See Byers, *John and the Others,* 61–64; Cirafesi, *John Within Judaism*, 95–126.

7. That is, "world" in this verse begins to slide toward the sense it bears in 1 John 2:15-17, where the anonymous author of the letter warns the congregation against love of the world and the things in the world, the world not referring to "humanity but to 'the distasteful cosmic trinity' of the lust of the flesh, the lust of the eyes, and the pride of life" (Kierspel, *Jews and the World*, 160). The transition is noted also by Stanley B. Marrow, "Κόσμος in John," *CBQ* 64 (2002): 90–102.

8. Byers (*John and the Others*, 63), for example, argues that while the evangelist relativizes ethnicity so that it no longer has any value for soteriology and ecclesiology, he does not thereby nullify it entirely. Race still exists as a category of human experience, but it is no longer a determinant of one's membership in the people of God. Similarly, while Cirafesi (*John Within Judaism*, 122–23) views the Johannine concept of "the children of God" as a cosmic broadening of covenantal belonging that is transethnic, he states that this does not imply the erasure of discrete ethnic identities within Jesus's singular flock. See also Penwell, *Jesus the Samaritan*, 95–104.

That the evangelist was attempting to erase former identities and replace (rather than supplement) them with allegiance to Christ is the view of Reinhartz ("Forging a New Identity," 128) and Esler ("From Ioudaioi to Children of God"), among others. This is one of the central theses of Reinhartz's *Cast Out of the Covenant*. She states (*Cast Out*, 43), for example, that "John's powerful rhetoric of affiliation is matched by an equally strong rhetoric of disaffiliation that marks the boundary between the children of God and those who claim falsely (in John's view) to be the children of God, that is, the *Ioudaioi* . . . And through a rhetoric of vituperation, the Gospel constructs a profound chasm—or a high wall—between his compliant audience and those who reject his claims. No member of God's family can be a *Ioudaios*; no *Ioudaios* can be a child of God."

9. I have borrowed the language of the *ecclesia ex circumcisione* and *ecclesia ex gentibus* from the fifth-century mosaic of the Santa Sabina basilica in Rome. For present purposes, it need not be determined whether the artist(s) envisioned this as a

meta-identity (the *ex* implying a former state) or as a differentiated unity. The point, rather, is that the metaphors with which the evangelist plays are open to a conceptualization of the Christian community which retains ethnic difference within the greater body.

10. Meeks, "'Am I a Jew?'" 183.

11. LSJ, s.v. "ὑπάγω," 1850.

12. So Hoskyns, *Fourth Gospel*, 416–17: "It was because of Lazarus, the author notes, that many of the Jews withdrew (i.e. from their obedience to the Jewish authorities, cf. vi. 67) and began to believe on Jesus."

13. Or to put it more colloquially, they quit before they could get fired.

14. The first hand of Codex Sinaiticus omits εἰς αὐτόν, but this appears to have been a scribal error. NA[28] only provides a negative apparatus, since the printed reading is secure.

15. Indeed, neither John 4:39 nor 12:11 intimates that the faith of these Samaritan and Jewish believers is inadequate or that their ethnic affiliation is thereby dissolved. The plain sense of John 12:11, therefore, is that the Jews who believe belong among the "all who received him" of the prologue (1:12).

16. The contours of the current debate are laid out by Reimund Bieringer, Didier Pollefeyt, and Frederique Vandecasteele-Vanneuville in their introduction to *Anti-Judaism and the Fourth Gospel* ("Wrestling with Johannine Anti-Judaism," 25–28).

17. So Brown, *The Gospel according to John*, 2 vols., AB 29-29A (Garden City, NY: Doubleday, 1966–1970), 1:104; Dunn, *Partings*, 93–95; Culpepper, "Anti-Judaism as a Theological Problem," 69–72; Maurice Casey, *From Jewish Prophet to Gentile God: The Origins and Development of New Testament Christology* (Louisville: Westminster John Knox, 1991), 29–31. Against this, see Marianne Meye Thompson, *The God of the Gospel of John* (Grand Rapids: Eerdmans, 2001), 218–24. Thompson contends that it would be more appropriate to speak of Jewish festivals anticipating the events of Jesus's life, without the evangelist stripping the feasts or institutions of their original significance. She remarks in relation to Passover: "Jesus does not 'supersede' or replace the action of God through Passover; rather, Passover clarifies and illumines the nature of Jesus's own work" (219).

18. As Ashton, for example, understands it and makes programmatic for *The Gospel of John and Christian Origins*. According to Ashton, the evangelist consciously intended to supplant Moses with a new religion: "This statement, bleak, blunt, uncompromising, illustrates more clearly than any other in the whole of the New Testament the incompatibility of Christianity and Judaism. It announces a new religion" (3).

19. So Brown (*Gospel of John*, 1:17), concludes that "there is no suggestion in John that when the Law was given through Moses, it was not a magnificent act of God's love." Similarly, Johannes Beutler, *Judaism and the Jews in the Gospel of John*, StudBib 30 (Rome: Pontifical Biblical Institute, 2006), 40; Jörg Augenstein, "Jesus und das Gesetz im Johannesevangelium," *Kirche und Israel* 14 (1999): 161–79.

20. Severino Pancaro (*The Law in the Fourth Gospel: The Torah and the Gospel, Moses and Jesus, Judaism and Christianity according to John*, NovTSup 42 [Leiden:

Brill, 1975], 519) concludes that the law of Moses is "looked upon as associated in some special way with the Jews" but that at the same time the evangelist "attributes great importance to the Law." Thus, John's attitude toward Torah "is hardly that of one who considers the Law no longer relevant."

21. The question of Marcion's attitude toward Israel's God and Scriptures has been taken up again in Sebastian Moll, *The Arch-Heretic Marcion*, WUNT 250 (Tübingen: Mohr Siebeck, 2010), 47–106. See also Judith Lieu, *Marcion and the Making of a Heretic: God and Scripture in the Second Century* (Cambridge: Cambridge University Press, 2015).

22. Casey (*Jewish Prophet to Gentile God*, 12–20) settles on eight "identity factors" of Second Temple Judaism: ethnicity, Scripture, monotheism, circumcision, Sabbath observance, dietary laws, purity laws, and major festivals. Casey scores the Johannine community a 1.5 out of 7 or 8 on this scale. Dunn (review of *From Jewish Prophet to Gentile God*, by Maurice Casey, *JTS* NS 44 [1993]: 304) questions whether these categories imply too much fixity, the border between Jew and Gentile being more nebulous than Casey allows. The larger problems, I will suggest below, are how well such a scale gauges self-identification and to what extent the Gospel is transparent to the religious practices of its intended recipients.

23. Hakola (*Identity Matters*), though not quite as direct about the Gentile self-identification of the Johannine community, also moves in this direction, concurring with Casey that the Johannine Christians had abandoned traditional Jewish practices like circumcision and Sabbath observance.

24. I will consider this in greater detail in ch. 4. For the moment, it may be said that although with Martyn's *magnum opus* opinion began to turn toward an audience of ethnically Jewish believers in Jesus, there have been and remain many who subscribe to a more heterogeneous intended readership.

25. And that even if others concluded that they had sloughed off their Jewish identity. Casey (*Jewish Prophet to Gentile God*, 12), too, recognizes that a group or individual's self-identity and the perception of others need not coincide, but he does not follow that fact through with respect to the Fourth Gospel. This is, of course, an argument from silence, but so too is the position that all of those considered apostates by some segment of their peers would have conceded the charge. We must always be wary when what we hear about a group is only what its opponents have to say. For a case study, see Alan Appelbaum, "On the Apostasy of Tiberius Julius Alexander," *JAJ* (2023): 47–76.

26. Paula Fredriksen, *Paul: The Pagans' Apostle* (New Haven: Yale University Press, 2017), 111. Similarly, Cirafesi, "Rethinking John and the 'Synagogue,'" 685–86; Christine Hayes, "Paul Within Judaism." Fredriksen does not thereby imply that Jews in antiquity lacked a shared culture. However, expressions of Jewish identity could and did vary. Fredriksen (ibid., 45–49) also surveys the epigraphic evidence for Jewish participation in what otherwise might be regarded as non-Jewish institutions and religious practices.

27. It is safe to say, I believe, that this has been the prevailing paradigm in the history of interpretation, both religious and academic. See Fredriksen, *Paul, the Pagans' Apostle*, 110.

28. See, for example, Fredriksen, *Paul, the Pagans' Apostle*; Nanos, *Reading Paul within Judaism* (Eugene, OR: Cascade, 2017); Mark D. Nanos and Magnus Zetterholm, eds., *Paul within Judaism: Restoring the First-Century Context to the Apostle* (Minneapolis: Fortress, 2015); Matthew Thiessen, *A Jewish Paul: The Messiah's Herald to the Gentiles* (Grand Rapids: Baker, 2023); Pamela Eisenbaum, *Paul Was Not a Christian: The Original Message of a Misunderstood Apostle* (New York: HarperCollins, 2009). Other studies which resonate with some of the characteristic emphases of the "Paul within Judaism" school include David J. Rudolph, *A Jew to the Jews: Jewish Contours of Pauline Flexibility in 1 Corinthians 9:19-23*, WUNT 2/304 (Tübingen: Mohr Siebeck, 2011); John Gager, *Reinventing Paul* (Oxford: Oxford University Press, 2000); Peter J. Tomson, *Paul and the Jewish Law: Halakha in the Letters of the Apostle to the Gentiles*, CRINTS Sec. 3, Jewish Traditions in Early Christian Literature 1 (Assen: Van Gorcum; Minneapolis: Fortress, 1990); Lloyd Gaston, *Paul and the Torah* (Vancouver: University of British Columbia Press, 1987). For a broader examination of the "within Judaism" approach, see Karin Hedner Zetterholm and Anders Runesson, eds., *Within Judaism? Interpretive Trajectories in Judaism, Christianity, and Islam from the First to the Twenty-First Century* (Lanham, MD: Lexington Books/Fortress Academic, 2023).

29. Fredriksen, *Paul: The Pagans' Apostle*, 107–30.

30. John M. G. Barclay (*Jews in the Mediterranean Diaspora*, 385) speaks similarly of Paul's sense of freedom with respect to the Torah's injunctions, a liberty which other Jews would have seen as "deeply corrosive to the Jewish way of life." Though I do not agree with them in all respects, Steve Mason and Paul Foster's critiques of the "Paul within Judaism" perspective are salient to the following discussion. See Mason, "Paul Without Judaism: Historical Method over Perspective," in *Paul and Matthew among Jews and Gentiles: Essays in Honour of Terrence L. Donaldson*, ed. Ronald Charles, LNTS 628 (London: Bloomsbury, 2021), 9–40; Foster, "An Apostle Too Radical for the Radical Perspective on Paul," *ExpTim* 133 (2021): 1–11.

I say intellectually detached because the day-to-day mechanics of Paul's missionary practice elude us. It would seem to me that among all-Gentile congregations, he would have had no trouble dropping many traditional Jewish customs. That is the most straightforward reading of 1 Cor 9. Paul felt free to adapt his lifestyle to particular mission fields.

31. So also, Foster, "An Apostle Too Radical," 4–5.

32. Nanos (*Reading Corinthians and Philippians within Judaism* [Eugene, OR: Cascade, 2017], 52–92) argues that 1 Cor 9:19-23 does not concern Paul's behavioral adaptability but his rhetorical adaptability. Paul adapts his speech to different audiences as he tries to persuade them of the truth of the Gospel, reasoning from their own cultural premises. Paul, however, speaks of becoming a slave to all people, which is more indicative of adaptation in behavior than merely tailoring speech according to the audience. Nor does rhetorical adaptability account for Paul's statement that he himself is not under the law.

33. See also Foster, "An Apostle Too Radical," 4–5. Gentiles cannot be in view when Paul speaks of the redemption of those under the law, since they were by nature not under its purview, and Paul chides the Galatians precisely for wanting to

be under the law, which implies that they had not been under its authority formerly (4:21). Paul, moreover, describes being under the Torah as a state of slavery, which he applies to the earthly city of Jerusalem, now in slavery with her children (4:25).

34. Ludvig Nyman ("New Perspectives on the Old Covenant: 2 Corinthians 3 and *Paul within Judaism*," *Neot* 54 [2020]: 351–71) has observed the paucity of engagement with 2 Cor 3 in much of the "Paul within Judaism" literature. It is clear in this passage that the fading glory of the Torah is not only in reference to Gentiles. Paul writes that Moses veiled his face to prevent the Israelites from seeing the end of what was passing away (v. 13). According to Paul, that veil is still metaphorically preventing the Israelites in his day from seeing the temporary nature of the covenant at Sinai. See also Mason, "Paul Without Judaism," 20.

35. See, for example, Brant Pitre, Michael P. Barber, and John A. Kincaid, *Paul, A New Covenant Jew: Rethinking Pauline Theology* (Grand Rapids: Eerdmans, 2019). That is not to say that Paul preached a "law-free" message. He continues to speak of the law of God/law of Christ/law of the Spirit (1 Cor 9:21; Gal 6:2; Rom 8:2). This law, however, does not find its expression in a written code. While its content overlaps with various laws and principles from the Torah, it is not coterminous with the covenant at Sinai.

36. I assume here the arguments of ch. 1.

37. As Counet ("No Anti-Judaism," 206–7) remarks with respect to John 8:17: "It is Jesus who speaks to the Ἰουδαῖοι about 'your law'; it is not the evangelist speaking to Jews in a synagogue in Ephesos."

38. Some have, in fact hypothesized that the Paraclete was modeled on prophets in the Johannine community. See M. Eugene Boring, "The Influence of Christian Prophecy on the Johannine Portrayal of the Paraclete and Jesus," *NTS* 25 (1978): 113–23. Nevertheless, as the profile of the Holy Spirit/Paraclete in John matches that of Jesus in so many respects, it seems most apt to speak of a mutuality between believers and the Spirit that also respects the distance between them. So George Johnston, *The Spirit-Paraclete in the Gospel of John*, SNTSMS 12 (Cambridge: Cambridge University Press, 1970), 147. Something comparable to a Christian prophet speaking *in persona Christi* is suggested by Barnabas Lindars (*Behind the Fourth Gospel*, Studies in Creative Criticism 3 [London: SPCK, 1971], 43–60). Lindars proposes that much of the discourse material of the Fourth Gospel began life as separate homilies that were meant to deepen the faith of the Christian community.

39. That is, even if the Gospel reflects the historical situation of a community painfully breaking away from the synagogue and its Jewish heritage, it does so only in a general way. Martyn's version of the two-level drama is more decidedly allegorical. In John 9, for example, Jesus stands in for a preacher in the Johannine community, the blind man for a convert, and so forth. Martyn (*History and Theology*, 85) recognizes that he may be pressing the point too far. Few have maintained such a close correspondence between individual characters and groups in the Gospel and specific persons and events in a late first-century setting, though Brown's doubling of characters in *Community* comes close.

40. So Jörg Augenstein, "'Euer Gesetz': Ein Pronomen und die johanneische Haltung zum Gesetz," *ZNW* 88 (1997): 311–13; also Beutler, *Judaism and the Jews*, 40.

Similarly, Chatelion Counet ("No Anti-Judaism," 206) compares Jesus's reference to "your law" in John 8:17 to the prophet's statement in Isa. 59:2: "Your iniquities have been barriers between you and your God."

41. Augenstein, "'Euer Gesetz,'" 312–13.

42. Thus Moses also speaks of "the LORD my God" (Deut 4:5) and "the LORD our God" (5:2) despite the frequency of the second-person pronoun in such expressions.

43. So already Marie-Joseph Lagrange, *Évangile selon Saint Jean* (Paris: Gabalda, 1925), 234; Keener, *Gospel of John*, 1:225. According to Pancaro (*Law in the Fourth Gospel*, 528), it is the misunderstanding of the law of Moses, not the law in itself, which is the object of the evangelist's attack. See also, Cirafesi, *John Within Judaism*, 142–44.

44. Cirafesi, *John Within Judaism*, 143. As I will argue in ch. 4, I do find it plausible that the evangelist's awareness of the ethnic diversity of first-century Palestine has partially conditioned some of the seemingly odd turns of phrase in the Gospel.

45. Hugo Odeberg, *The Fourth Gospel: Interpreted in Its Relation to Contemporaneous Religious Currents in Palestine and the Hellenistic-Oriental World* (Uppsala: Almqvist & Wiksells, 1929), 292; similarly Hartwig Thyen, "Über die johanneischen Gebrauch von Ἰουδαῖος und Ἰουδαῖοι," in idem, *Studien zum Corpus Iohanneum*, WUNT 214 (Tübingen: Mohr Siebeck, 2007), 654–55; Per Jarle Bekken, *The Lawsuit Motif in John's Gospel from New Perspectives: Jesus Christ, Crucified Criminal and Emperor of the World*, NovTSup 158 (Leiden: Brill, 2015), 141.

46. See also, Cirafesi, *John Within Judaism*, 180–82. There is, of course a paradox here, as John 5:18 says that by claiming God as Father, Jesus is asserting equality with God, while other passages imply the Son's subordination to the Father. Thus, Jesus tells the disciples during the Farewell Discourse that "the Father is greater than I" (14:28). The evangelist lets the tension stand; the Word is both God and with God (1:1).

47. Hakola, *Identity Matters*, 144.

48. Similarly, Pancaro (*Law in the Fourth Gospel*, 530) commenting on the Sabbath healing in John 5, says the evangelist is not primarily interested in the relationship between Jesus's followers and Torah but rather "the authority and position of Jesus with respect to the Law."

49. Besides the passages considered below, Cirafesi also reads a reference to the Torah into John 6:45 with the following gloss: "John assumes that 'everyone who has heard and learned from the Father,' that is everyone who keeps the law, will likewise come to Jesus" (*John Within Judaism*, 139). Jesus here may allude to the function of Scripture as a witness to Jesus, as in John 5:39-40 and 45-47, or the import may be that whoever hears and obeys Jesus has in fact been taught by God since the Son speaks exactly and only what the Father has commanded him. See also ibid., 104–8 in relation to the exchange between Jesus and the Jews in John 8.

50. Ibid., 133–36.

51. Boyarin, *Border Lines*, 100.

52. Cirafesi, *John Within Judaism*, 136.

53. Ibid., 137. Wheaton (*Role of Jewish Feasts*, 14–24, at 23) offers an alternative account of John 1:17-18. According to Wheaton, while the evangelist affirms the giving of the Torah as a grace from God, it was a prophetic grace that prepared for the revelation of salvific grace through Jesus. Thus, there is both continuity and discontinuity between Jesus and Moses.

54. Cirafesi, *John Within Judaism*, 137.

55. As John Van Maaren notes in his review of *John Within Judaism*, the argument that the evangelist's "children of God" are presumed to keep the Torah relies on narrative hints. The type of evidence available in the Gospel, however, limits our ability to extrapolate from those hints with certainty (p. 365). At times, Cirafesi takes a more cautious stance. For example, with respect to purity rituals, he says (*John Within Judaism*, 145–46) that John gives no explicit value judgment on their observance and shows a "lack of evaluative clarity."

56. As for example, Simon son of Mattathias in *J.W.* 1.50; Alexander Jannaeus and his queen in *J.W.* 1.107; Agrippa II and the people of Jerusalem in *J.W.* 2.342. See Dunn, "Question of Anti-semitism," 184.

57. Josephus and "the Jews" are also the actors in *J.W.* 3.136, 142-143; *Life* 113, 416.

58. According to Dunn's calculation ("Question of Anti-semitism," 182), John and Acts make up over 75% of the total usage of "Jew/Jews" in the NT. In describing the book of Acts as "the second defendant," I recognize that other NT writings have their moments of infamy. One thinks above all of the self-imprecation that Matt 27:25 puts in the mouths of the people of Jerusalem ("Let his blood be upon us and upon our children") or the "synagogue of Satan" of Rev 2:9 and 3:9. However, whereas Matthew and Revelation are naturally situated within a Jewish context (that is, the language is still that of intra-Jewish controversy), the author of Luke-Acts has often been seen as attacking the Jews from the outside as a non-Jew with a triumphalist mindset. See Andrew J. Overman, *Matthew's Gospel and Formative Judaism: The Social World of the Matthean Community* (Minneapolis: Fortress, 1990); Anthony J. Saldarini, *Matthew's Christian-Jewish Community*, CSHJ (Chicago: University of Chicago Press, 1994). The view that Luke writes against the Jews as a non-Jew has been put forward most forcefully by Jack T. Sanders, *The Jews in Luke-Acts* (Philadelphia: Fortress, 1987); idem, "The Jewish People in Luke-Acts," in *Luke-Acts and the Jewish People: Eight Critical Perspectives*, ed. Joseph B. Tyson (Minneapolis: Augsburg, 1988), 51–75. Joseph B. Tyson ("Jews and Judaism in Luke-Acts: Reading as a Godfearer," *NTS* 41 [1995]: 19–38) contends that by the end of Acts, the Jews are "firmly defined as unbelievers." The counterargument has been made by Joshua Paul Smith, *Luke Was Not a Christian: Reading the Third Gospel and Acts Within Judaism*, BibInt 218 (Leiden: Brill, 2024).

59. So also Dunn ("Questions of Anti-semitism," 184): "So too Paul's apparent readiness to distinguish himself from 'the Jews' in the latter stages of Acts should not be given exaggerated significance as though he thereby distanced himself from and disowned his own Jewishness." We find another example of this literary phenomenon in Acts 18, where Apollos, identified in v. 24 as a Jew from Alexandria, is said to have "powerfully refuted the Jews in public" (v. 28).

60. Similarly, Ezra 5:1; 9:20, 23; Jer 40:12; 1 Macc 14:33-41. First Macc 14 records the decree of the Jewish people and their leaders commemorating all of Simon's achievements for the Jewish people. According to v. 41, "the Jews and their priests decided that Simon should be their leader and high priest forever, until a trustworthy prophet should arise."

61. Reinhartz, *Cast Out*, 84–85.

62. Nehemiah also speaks of "Jews" in first-person speech (Neh 1:2; 2:16; 4:12; 5:17; 13:23), though he is Jewish himself.

63. According to 5:18, because Jesus claimed God as his Father (besides healing on the Sabbath), "the Jews tried all the more to kill him (μᾶλλον ἐζήτουν αὐτὸν οἱ Ἰουδαῖοι ἀποκτεῖναι)." In 7:1, Jesus delays a trip to Judea because "the Jews were seeking to kill him (ἐζήτουν αὐτὸν οἱ Ἰουδαῖοι ἀποκτεῖναι)."

64. Although it is potentially significant that the evangelist does not say that the *crowds* feared the Jews, but no one individually dared to speak up.

65. Ashton, *Understanding*, 66–67.

66. The problem is brought to a head by Ashton, *Understanding*, 141–42. The Johannine Christ, he writes, "does not belong to this world at all" but is a "preexistent divine being, whose real home is in heaven." In contrast to the very human Jesus of the Synoptic Gospels, the Jesus of the Fourth Gospel is "master of his fate, captain of his soul," supremely confident from beginning to end. Whether this exaggerates matters or not (and this depends on one's understanding of the Christology of the Synoptic Gospels), Ashton masterfully encapsulates one of the central questions of Christian origins.

67. And that for two reasons: (1) At least a handful of scholars judge the Synoptic Gospels to have a high Christology. Richard Bauckham (*Jesus and the God of Israel: God Crucified and Other Studies on the New Testament's Christology of Divine Identity* [Grand Rapids: Eerdmans, 2008], 18–30), for example, finds a Christology of divine identity throughout the NT. See also Simon J. Gathercole, *The Pre-existent Son: Recovering the Christologies of Matthew, Mark, and Luke* (Grand Rapids: Eerdmans, 2006). And (2) a fair assessment of Johannine themes, such as Jesus's preexistence, must take the rest of the NT, and above all Paul's letters, into consideration. The problem, important as it is, cannot be entered into here.

Chapter 4

Why "the Jews"?
Considerations of Setting and Audience

Deeply disturbed by the rising tide of anti-semitism in Europe in the interwar period, Anglican clergyman James Parkes sounded a clarion call for the Christian community to reevaluate its relationship with Judaism and disavow its anti-Jewish prejudice. Parkes's magnum opus, *The Conflict of the Church and the Synagogue*, published five years before the start of the Second World War, was one of the first Christian attempts to trace the origins of anti-Judaism in the church.[1] According to Parkes, while Christianity began as a Jewish sect, it broke decisively from Judaism sometime between the destruction of the temple in 70 CE and the mid-second century. Instrumental in the split was the promulgation and dissemination of the "Blessing of the Heretics," composed by the rabbinical authorities in Yavneh between 80 and 90 CE.[2] The Gospel of John, Parkes says, belongs to this period as evidenced by "its complete lack of distinction between parties, and its condemnation of 'the Jews' as a whole for actions which the synoptists had more specifically ascribed to the Pharisees or some other party."[3]

The arguments of the previous two chapters mitigate the severity of Parkes's judgment, but contained within it is an important observation. The Synoptic Gospels are also set in first-century Palestine. They follow a similar outline of Jesus's public ministry, death, and resurrection as the Gospel of John. They too recount stories of confrontation and dispute. Yet, they rarely speak of "the Jews." To say that the Gospel of John does not stereotype the Jews or make faith in Jesus and Jewish identity mutually exclusive is not sufficient. Some account must be given of why the fourth evangelist, alone among the Gospel authors, does not content himself with Synoptic-like terms for Jesus's opponents, especially when these were readily available to him.

Why would a self-consciously Jewish author so strongly prefer "the Jews" over more restrictive nomenclature?

In ch. 1, I surveyed several attempts to untie this Gordian knot. These proposals typically fall into two categories: historical and rhetorical/literary. Some, like Daniel Boyarin and Christopher Blumhofer, correlate the Johannine language about the *Ioudaioi* with purported historical developments in the post-exilic period. Boyarin frames these developments in terms of Jewish sectarianism, arguing that the *Yehudim* (Hebrew: יהודים, Aramaic: יהודיא) were an elite religious body that traced its origins to the returnees from the Babylonian exile. The "people of the land," those who had not gone into exile, were excluded from the company of the *Yehudim*, who regarded them as second-class citizens despite their Israelite lineage.[4] The author of the Fourth Gospel and his community, concludes Boyarin, belonged to this outgroup. They were not and never had been *Yehudim*.[5] While not offering an explicit historical reconstruction, Blumhofer also discerns a disjuncture in Second Temple Jewish literature between the name "Jew" as signifying a particular confessional-historical community and "Israel" as the idealized people of God. The Gospel of John, it is argued, belongs to a group that identified itself with Israel but not with the *Ioudaioi* or their vision for Israel's future. The evangelist would be Jewish by modern standards but not by his own.

The second set of solutions, as we've seen, appeals to Johannine irony. As an ethnic Jew, the evangelist nevertheless attempts to rhetorically undermine the self-assuredness of those he calls *Ioudaioi*. John ironically grants their self-ascribed status as arbiters of Jewish identity only to destabilize it. Or he targets their belief that Jewish ethnicity is a prerequisite for membership in the people of God by using that label against them. "The Jews" in the Gospel of John thus means something like "those who purport to be the guardians of Jewish identity" or "those who pride themselves on their Jewish genealogy as the necessary condition for salvation."

As I suggested in ch. 1, both of these approaches leave themselves open to serious objections. Consequently, neither has gained significant traction as a compelling substitute for the religious-schism model. In the next two chapters, then, I will offer an alternative answer to the "virtually irresolvable" question posed above: Why would a self-consciously Jewish author so strongly prefer "the Jews" over other nomenclature? I will consider several of the factors which may have conditioned the evangelist's choice of terminology, building toward a synthetic account of the Gospel's presentation of the Jews as a function of its scriptural imagination. The present chapter will devote itself to two of those factors: (1) the author's probable knowledge of the demographics of first-century Palestine and (2) the Gospel's intended audience.

ETHNIC DIVERSITY IN FIRST-CENTURY PALESTINE

A rich store of ancient texts written by and about Jews has been passed down to us. By an odd turn of history, much of it was preserved by Christians, reworked or reinterpreted to meet their own theological and apologetic needs.[6] For all the historical gaps that remain, these writings open a fairly broad window onto ancient Judea and Jewish life in the diaspora. One consequence of this is that when scholars write about first-century Palestine, it is Jewish history, culture, and society that loom large. The imbalance in written sources, however, could easily distort the cultural vibrancy of the region.[7] To the south of the territory of Judea resided the Idumeans, who had been partially incorporated into the Judean state during the Hasmonean period; to the north were the Samaritans, the Jews' bitter rivals. The Nabateans and other Arab tribes lived to the east and southeast. In addition to the Idumeans, Nabateans, and Samaritans who abutted the territory of Judea, strings of Greek-style *poleis* dotted the Mediterranean coast and the Decapolis. Sebaste in Samaria and Scythopolis in the Jezreel Valley (reckoned as part of the Decapolis) also had non-Jewish majorities.[8] The Phoenicians lived to the north and west of Galilee and the Itureans to the north, centered in the Beqaa Valley.[9]

Judea's neighbors, it is true, languish in relative obscurity.[10] The last word about the Idumeans, who had encroached as far north as Hebron, comes from Josephus.[11] The remains of Petra testify to the flourishing of Nabatean culture in this period, but the Nabateans have left us only inscriptions, coinage, and a few documents. The Samaritans have preserved their religious traditions to the present, but what we know of their practice in the first century is filtered through Josephus and the NT. Other peoples in the vicinity of Judea had already disappeared from the historical record by the first century CE. Without the requisite written sources, not much can be said about the self-identities of these peoples, but the archaeological and written materials that have survived are suggestive of cultural spheres which overlapped in some ways but had not coalesced.[12]

Over time, many (but not all) of these ethnic identities were lost or supplanted, but that process was far from complete in the time of Jesus or the fourth evangelist several decades later. The Idumeans, for example, appear to have held on to their ancestral traditions for some time despite their recent incorporation into the Judean state. Although Josephus reports in *Jewish Antiquities* that John Hyrcanus forcibly converted the Idumeans, making them undergo circumcision and submit to the customs of the Jews so that they became Ἰουδαῖοι (*Ant.* 13.257-258), the assimilation must have been only partial.[13] Strains of nationalist sentiment persisted long after the Hasmonean period. And at least a segment of the Jewish populace resented Herod the Great as an interloper, a foreign oppressor rather than a native dynast.[14] Costobar, one of Herod's closest associates, was a priest of the god Qos, who, like an Idumean Maccabee, wanted to return the country to its native traditions (*Ant.* 15.252-258). This attitude among the aristocracy, I suspect, had broader support at the grassroots level.[15]

Indeed, the narrative of *Jewish War* does not give the impression that the Idumeans had become Jews at all.[16] There Josephus paints them as a violent and unstable *ethnos*, delighting in revolutionary change. Hyrcanus's annexation of Idumean territory is scarcely mentioned, nor is anything said of compulsory conversion to the Jewish way of life. Politically, the Idumeans are presented as allies of the Jewish state during the revolt against Rome, coming to the defense of Jerusalem during the siege, but even then their presence in the capital is more hindrance than help.[17] Josephus's statement a few decades later that they became Jews thus comes across as accommodation to an audience less familiar with pre-revolt Judea, for whom the difference between Jews and Idumeans may have been of minor concern.

Some of the Jews' ancient neighbors, moreover, have preserved their ethnic bonds through the intervening centuries, as Jewish-Samaritan relations illustrate. The feud between the two, so deeply entrenched in Christian consciousness through the Gospel narratives, is far from the sum of Samaritan history. A small community, in fact, still worships on Mount Gerizim, self-identifying as non-Jewish Israelites.[18] Whereas today they teeter on the verge of extinction, numbering only in the hundreds, in the first century, they were significant regional players.

Greater Judea, then, was not monolithically Jewish, and it was surrounded by non-Jewish populations.[19] It must also be remembered that Jerusalem, the mother-city of the Jewish people, was itself a hub for commerce and pilgrimage. It could not rival the cosmopolitan ambience of Rome, Alexandria, Antioch, or Ephesus, but Hasmonean and Herodian investment in the city—socially, politically, and economically—had transformed it from a small Jewish settlement in the Persian period to a bustling city by the time of Roman occupation.[20] Its leaders cultivated regional and international contacts. Under direct Roman administration, the Antonia Fortress at the northwest corner of the temple enclosure housed auxiliary troops, most of whom were likely drawn from the local non-Jewish population.[21] And Herod the Great's building projects, particularly the extensive renovation and enlargement of the temple precincts, had made Jerusalem something of a tourist destination. The ancient Samaritans, it is probably safe to say, did not participate in the festivals of their political enemies in a city they viewed as an illegitimate cultic site.[22] Yet in light of the ethnic diversity of the region and the economic and religious importance of Jerusalem, it is not unreasonable to suppose that the Jewish capital hosted some permanent non-Jewish residents, along with foreign visitors when swollen with crowds during the annual festivals.[23] Indeed, according to the testimony of Josephus, these celebrations drew many non-Jews to the city (*J.W.* 6.427-428). There were enough non-Jews, at least, that Jewish priestly officials thought it necessary to post warning inscriptions, written in Greek, that prohibited Gentiles past a certain point on the temple grounds.[24] In that context, distinguishing between the Jewish majority and others of non-Jewish extraction might prove necessary.

The Fourth Evangelist and the *Ethnē* of Palestine

Given that the Gospel of John is set primarily in Galilee and Judea and revolves structurally around Jesus's pilgrimages to Jerusalem, it is natural that most of the characters who appear in its pages are Jews. But was the fourth evangelist aware, nonetheless, of the region's ethnic diversity? Several observations suggest that he was. Since these non-Jewish figures are on the periphery of the evangelist's field of vision, it is unlikely that cognizance of their presence in Palestine will have been the prime driver for preferring "the Jews" over more restrictive terms, but it may, nonetheless, comprise one piece of the puzzle and furnish context for some of the Gospel's *cruces interpretum*.

First, John, more than the Synoptic Gospels, shows familiarity with the people and places of Palestine and with Jerusalem in particular.[25] Where we are able to check them against the archaeological record, Johannine toponyms and geographical details have proven accurate. Whatever symbolic associations they have accrued in the Gospel, they are not inventions at the service of theology. Perhaps the most striking example of this is afforded by the Pool of Bethesda, which is mentioned in John 5:2 as the site of one of Jesus's healings. John locates the pool by the Sheep Gate, stating that many disabled people would congregate in its five porticoes. Remains of the pool, or rather pools, have been found near St. Anne's Church in the Old City of Jerusalem.[26]

Second, although the Idumeans, Nabateans, and related groups are absent from any of the Gospel accounts, the fourth evangelist does show a marked interest in the Samaritans. Because of their prominence in John 4, it has been suggested that Samaritan converts had joined the Johannine community early in its history and contributed to its developing theology.[27] Proposed traces of Samaritan influence in the Gospel are ambiguous, often dependent on sources centuries later than the Gospel of John. Yet if we should hesitate to speak in terms of influence, we need not doubt the evangelist's knowledge about the Samaritans. Among the NT writings, the Gospel of John alone notes the Samaritans' worship on Mount Gerizim and their self-understanding as descendants of the patriarch Jacob.[28] If the evangelist was not aware of the full ethnic diversity of first-century Palestine, he was at the very least interested in the Jews' rivals to the north.

Jesus's stay with the Samaritans of Sychar in John 4 is followed by another cordial reception, this time by the Galileans. According to John 4:45, the Γαλιλαῖοι welcome Jesus when he arrives in the region, having seen all the signs he had performed in Jerusalem during the Passover festival, for they too had been there. If for some time the construct of a first-century "Galilee of the gentiles" had wide currency, today the model of a predominantly Jewish Galilee is nearly axiomatic, enjoying strong support from both the archaeological and the written record.[29] It might therefore be assumed that the Galileans of John 4 are the Jewish inhabitants of Galilee. It is at least worth considering, however, whether the fourth evangelist makes a distinction between the Γαλιλαῖοι and the Ἰουδαῖοι who live in Galilee. I have made the argument elsewhere that the Jewish historian Josephus—our best source for the demographics of Palestine during this period—differentiates between οἱ Γαλιλαῖοι (the Galileans) and the Jewish inhabitants of Galilee.[30] That is, when Josephus refers to the Γαλιλαῖοι he has in mind an independent ἔθνος related to but distinct from the Jews.[31] If that thesis holds (and admittedly, it must remain tentative), perhaps John takes a similar view of the Γαλιλαῖοι.

Since the appellation Γαλιλαῖοι in John 4:45 is a *hapax* in the Gospel, the only test of the hypothesis—that in the evangelist's eyes they are something other than Ἰουδαῖοι—is its compatibility with the Gospel's narrative trajectory. Under this assumption, Jesus is welcomed in ch. 4 not by the Jews of Galilee but by an autochthonous population of which he is not a member.[32] This would pair with the missionary success among the Samaritans of Sychar to form an important development in the Gospel's plot. As Jesus begins to encounter opposition from his own people—the Jews—he finds refuge with others. That is not to say that Judea symbolizes the realm of unbelief and Samaria and Galilee the inverse.[33] There is both belief in Judea (11:45; 12:11) and lack of faith in Galilee (6:60-66).[34] Jesus's movement from Judea to Galilee better corresponds to a polarity of threat and safety at the Gospel's story level than to one of unbelief and faith at the level of theological allegory.

The Galileans' amiability, moreover, is not tantamount to a profession of faith.[35] The only people of Galilee explicitly said to believe are the disciples (2:11) and the royal official whose son lay sick at Capernaum (4:53). The Galileans, on the other hand, "welcome" (δέχομαι) Jesus rather than "receive" (λαμβάνω) him or "believe" (πιστεύω) in him, and so John 4:45 does not conform to the Prologue's terminology for faith in Jesus: "to all who received him, who believed in his name" (1:12). What the stories of ch. 4 convey, however, is that the threat to Jesus is concentrated in the Jewish heartland among "his own." From then on, the narrative oscillates between Jesus's short-term and conflict-ridden visits to Judea, which for their temporal brevity occupy most of chs. 5–12, and his more extended stays in the outlying areas, where he enjoys relative security. Galilee, while not necessarily the place of belief and discipleship in contrast to the hard spiritual soil of Judea, does become a place of refuge for Jesus.

Even if this interpretation of the Γαλιλαῖοι in the Gospel of John proves mistaken, we are able to say with some certainty that the fourth evangelist shows awareness that the Palestine of his day was not populated exclusively by Jews. He knows of the Samaritans. He also knows of Greeks who come to Jerusalem to celebrate the Passover (12:20-22). And if among the festival crowds there are some non-Jews (Greeks, Γαλιλαῖοι, or others) over whom stand the Ἰουδαῖοι, then it would not be so jarring to speak of their "fear of the Jews" (7:13). In a multi-ethnic context, the ethnonym Ἰουδαῖοι would help differentiate the actors, just as someone might refer without confusion to "the English" when recounting events that also involved people of Welsh and Scottish heritage.

THE GOSPEL AUDIENCE

Although as a methodological principle I have not assumed a specific communal situation in which the Gospel of John originated or to which it addressed itself, any account of the evangelist's preference for the term οἱ Ἰουδαῖοι will also depend in part on how we envision the Gospel's intended audience. That the Gospel was composed with a Gentile or mixed Jewish-Gentile readership in mind cannot be rejected out of hand. The Fourth Gospel certainly contains a great deal of material that would be most fully appreciated by those acquainted not only with the Scriptures but also with first-century Judean society and religion. Jesus's invitation at the Feast of Tabernacles to all those who are spiritually thirsty to come and drink (7:37-38) and the self-declaration of 8:12 ("I am the light of the world"), for example, take on the greatest significance when interpreted against the background of contemporary festal practice unknown from the biblical account alone. The lighting of candles in the temple precincts and the drawing of water from the Pool of Siloam—or some liturgical or exegetical precursor to these rites—become the themes of Jesus's public teaching.[36]

On the other hand, the explanation of some Jewish customs and the labeling of many of the feasts as "of the Jews" seem to serve as an orientation for readers not intimately familiar with Jewish life and worship.[37] A community of diaspora Jews might have needed some help with Aramaic terms like Messiah and Rabbi or with customs unique to their compatriots in Judea, but no Jewish Christ followers would have to be told that Passover or Tabernacles was a feast of the Jews, just as it would be superfluous for an American to write to fellow citizens about the Thanksgiving feast of the Americans.[38]

There are several layers to this problem that forestall its definitive resolution. First, if we were to pursue a consistent two-level reading of the Fourth Gospel, we would have to follow Brown and make room for the presence of Samaritans and Gentiles in the Johannine community.[39] If the healing of the blind man in ch. 9 reflects the activities of a preacher in the Johannine community at the end of the first century, why methodologically should we ignore the Samaritan believers in 4:39-42, the "other sheep not of this fold" of 10:16, or the Greeks of 12:20-21? Then, too, we must explain why in the Farewell Discourse and the Johannine epistles "the Jews" mostly fade into the background, replaced by "the world." Did the Johannine community now face opposition from the Gentile powers?[40]

There is, however, an even more fundamental problem. Even if it is valid to read the Gospel on two historical levels and the expulsion refers to events toward the end of the first century, it cannot be safely assumed that John writes for those who personally endured the trauma.[41] For the sake of argument, let us presume that Johannine believers were in fact expelled from a local synagogue around 85 CE and that the conflict between Jesus and the Jews in the Gospel is patently anachronistic, reflecting the evangelist's own situation more than what Martyn called the story's *einmalig* level.[42] The Gospel would necessarily post-date this event, but by how long?[43] It is certainly conceivable that from the time of expulsion to the completion and circulation of the Gospel a few years or more had passed. Let us imagine that in the meantime the evangelist had moved on, as some preachers are wont to do, and was now active in the life of another congregation. Thus, the Gospel might reflect experiences projected onto the life of Jesus yet not mirror those of the reading community. In brief, it cannot be taken for granted that the home in which the evangelist grew up, so to speak, was the home in which the Gospel came to reside.[44]

Second, although a thorough knowledge of first-century Jewish life and thought will deepen the reader's understanding, this fact is not determinative for the ethnic makeup of the intended audience. Nuances will be lost to the less perceptive reader, but anyone conversant with the rudiments of the OT and the basic contours of Jesus's life and ministry should be able to track the Gospel's important themes and message.[45] The evangelist has provided enough guidance to the reader by means of the prologue and the frequent narrative asides, and has enunciated the central theme of Jesus's revelation so clearly and so persistently that one will not be lost even if he or she is not in a position to appreciate the minutiae of the story.[46] A reader ignorant of rabbinic exegesis of Ps 82, or even of the sheep and shepherd imagery of the OT, for instance, will still grasp the thrust of what Jesus is saying in John

10:1-39, since the metaphor, as so many in the Fourth Gospel, is drawn from everyday life.

Third, because the evangelist had access to traditions, eyewitness or otherwise, we must not approach all of the details of the narrative as if they were free inventions. So when one of Jesus's sayings presupposes some subtle allusion to Jewish belief, custom, or line of biblical interpretation, it may be because it reaches back into the Jesus tradition, even as it is recast in the distinctive voice of the evangelist.[47] The author, not wanting to write a hefty commentary, will have limited himself to explanations of more elemental matters, just as the Gospel of Mark occasionally explains Jewish customs but fails to comment on terms like "Son of Man" or to elucidate the Jewish context of the Sabbath controversies. Or perhaps the evangelist foresaw a readership beyond the immediate circle of readers and hearers and therefore made some concessions for those who did not have the opportunity to hear his teaching personally.[48]

We need not multiply hypotheses to see that a touch of disciplined historical imagination can quickly escort us from an audience of ethnically Jewish Christ followers to one that is ethnically mixed or predominantly Gentile in character. We can reasonably infer that the intended readers of the Gospel knew Greek and were acquainted with the basic outline of Jesus's life, as they are presumed to know of Peter, Mary of Bethany, and a few others.[49] The physical realities of ancient book production, moreover, require a sympathetic audience if the text is to be preserved and copied for posterity. Otherwise, one runs the risk of consigning all of his or her efforts to oblivion, as by and large happened to the myriad writings of those adjudged heretics when they fell into the hands of men like Irenaeus and Tertullian. The Gospel's stated purpose of inspiring or sustaining faith in Jesus (John 20:31) points to an author who was not just writing for personal consumption but for the sake of others.[50] That he would have willingly handed over the finished Gospel to the unreceptive seems improbable.[51] Taken together, these facts strongly favor an intended Christian readership. But beyond this, little is known with confidence about those to whom the Gospel was first delivered.[52]

An audience that included Gentiles, therefore, is far from unreasonable and would help account for what has come off as a lack of nuance in the Gospel's presentation of the Jews.[53] The evangelist does not incriminate all Jews of Jesus's time or stereotype them, but he may move to the designation οἱ Ἰουδαῖοι as quickly as he does to accommodate readers and auditors who were at some remove culturally and temporally from the Pharisees, chief priests, and other religious and political factions of Palestine in the late 20s and early 30s. At the very least, the possibility ought to remain open given the lack of consensus and the absence of any external confirmation of the Gospel's destination.

CONCLUSION

The arguments of this chapter are necessarily partial. I present them as possible influences on the evangelist's language about the Jews, not as determinative causes. Writing about a multi-ethnic Palestine in the 30s for perhaps a non-Jewish audience toward the close of the first century, the evangelist may have gravitated toward "the Jews" as a well-recognized ethnonym much as Josephus does in *Jewish Antiquities*. It would be hard to argue, however, that these factors alone explain the Gospel's language about "the Jews," since in the Gospel of John it is not only the frequency of the term "the Jews" but also the intensity of the polemic that requires explanation. I will explore the confluence of these two features in the final chapter.

NOTES

1. James Parkes, *The Conflict of the Church and the Synagogue: A Study in the Origins of Antisemitism* (London: Soncino Press, 1934).
2. Ibid., 77–79.
3. Ibid., IX.
4. Boyarin, "*Ioudaioi* in John," 222–34. Boyarin develops this proposal on the basis of Shemaryahu Talmon's "The Emergence of Jewish Sectarianism in the Early Second Temple Period," in *Ancient Israelite Religion: Essays in Honor of Frank Moore Cross*, ed. Patrick D. Miller, Paul D. Hanson, and S. Dean McBride (Philadelphia: Fortress, 1987), 587–616. In support of Boyarin, see also Calvin J. Roetzel, "*Ioudaioi* and Paul," in *The New Testament and Early Christian Literature in Greco-Roman Context: Studies in Honor of David E. Aune*, ed. John Fotopoulos, NovTSup 122 (Leiden: Brill, 2006), 3–15. Boyarin's approach has much in common with that of John Ashton in idem, *Understanding*, 67–99. In their respective judgments, the Jews of the Fourth Gospel must be a discreet religious group to which the evangelist and his community stand in opposition.
5. Boyarin, "*Ioudaioi* in John," 234–39. Against this, Ashton (*Understanding*, 74) questions how, if Boyarin is correct, the Johannine believers could have been expelled from the synagogue as 9:22 seems to imply. I would add that Boyarin does not address the Gospel's presentation of Jesus as a Ἰουδαῖος and the Jews as his own people. Thus, it seems to me strained to identify Jesus and his disciples, who according to Boyarin function as representatives of the Johannine community, as non-Ἰουδαῖοι Israelites.
6. Samuel Sandmel (*OTP* 1:xi) describes this state of affairs as "the strangest quirk of fate respecting literature that I know of." If "odd" is too strong, given the emergence of the Christian faith from a Jewish matrix, it is still noteworthy that these texts were preserved in a non-Jewish context.
7. Compare also Steve Mason, *A History of the Jewish War: A.D. 66-74* (Cambridge: Cambridge University Press, 2016), 226–38.

8. See Mordechai Aviam and Peter Richardson, "Appendix A: Josephus' Galilee in Archaeological Perspective," in *Life of Josephus: Translation and Commentary*, vol. 9 of *Flavius Josephus: Translation and Commentary*, ed. Steve Mason (Leiden: Brill, 2001), 179–81 for an overview of the Decapolis and coastal cities; also Mark A. Chancey, *The Myth of a Gentile Galilee: The Population of Galilee and New Testament Studies*, SNTSMS 118 (Cambridge: Cambridge University Press, 2002), 130–55.

9. In addition to Kasher's remarks on the Itureans, see E. A. Myers, *The Ituraeans and the Roman Near East: Reassessing the Sources* (Cambridge: Cambridge University Press, 2010).

10. The most thorough study of Judea's southern and eastern neighbors is Aryeh Kasher, *Jews, Idumaeans, and Ancient Arabs: Relations of the Jews in Eretz-Israel with the Nations of the Frontier and the Desert during the Hellenistic and Roman Era (322 BCE–70 CE)*, TSAJ 18 (Tübingen: Mohr Siebeck, 1988). Of necessity, Kasher relies heavily on Josephus for the events and movements of the centuries under consideration. The Samaritans have generated more scholarly interest. See the recent works of Reinhard Pummer, *The Samaritans: A Profile* (Grand Rapids: Eerdmans, 2016); Gary N. Knoppers, *Jews and Samaritans: The Origins and History of Their Early Relations* (Oxford: Oxford University Press, 2013); as well as the collection of essays in Menachem Mor and Friedrich V. Reiterer, eds., *Samaritans: Past and Present: Current Studies*, SJ 53 (Berlin: de Gruyter, 2010). On Samaritan self-identification and labeling, see Penwell, *Jesus the Samaritan*, 58–80.

11. There is also evidence of an Idumean presence in Egypt. See Uriel Rappaport, "Les Iduméens en Égypte," *RevPhil* 43 (1969): 73–82.

12. So, for example, while remains of many Greek and Roman temples have been unearthed around the periphery of Galilee, there is no evidence that any stood within its borders in the first century CE. The remains of a temple in Sepphoris have been dated to the second century CE. The numismatic data that suggest the presence of a Roman sanctuary in Tiberias also date to that period. These archaeological findings cohere with Josephus's delineation of the borders of Galilee in *J.W.* 3.35-40. See Mordechai Aviam, *Jews, Pagans and Christians in the Galilee: 25 Years of Archaeological Excavations and Surveys Hellenistic to Byzantine Periods* (Rochester, NY: University of Rochester Press, 2004), 9–21.

13. Many questions have been raised about the historicity of Josephus's account and the precise nature of the Idumeans' "conversion." With others, Seth Schwartz ("Conversion to Judaism in the Second Temple Period: A Functionalist Approach," in *Studies in Josephus and the Varieties of Ancient Judaism: Louis H. Feldman Jubilee*, ed. Shaye J. D. Cohen and Joshua J. Schwartz, Ancient Judaism and Early Christianity 67 [Leiden: Brill, 2007], 232–33) suggests that this conversion should be thought of in terms of a model of fictive kinship and partial religious accommodation that was, however, "gradual, not immediate, and perhaps never complete" (232).

14. See Matthew Thiessen, *Contesting Conversion: Genealogy, Circumcision, and Identity in Ancient Judaism and Christianity* (Oxford: Oxford University Press, 2011), 96–103. Cohen (*Beginnings of Jewishness*, 18) remarks that for some Jews, Idumeans like Herod would always be outsiders. Josephus provides a glimpse of

this in an exchange between Antigonus, son of Aristobulus and Herod before the walls of Jerusalem (*Ant.* 14.403). In the hearing of the Roman authorities, Antigonus impugns Herod's credentials as king of Judea because of his Idumean ancestry. The gloss "half-Jew" for "Idumean," I suggest, is supplied by Josephus for the aid of his readers. Idumeans were "half-Jews" because they had adopted some Jewish customs but were not Jewish by descent. This is not, of course, to say that all Jews, much less Herod himself, saw matters in this way. See again, Cohen, *Beginnings of Jewishness*, 13–24.

15. With Richard A. Horsley, "The Expansion of Hasmonean Rule in Idumea and Galilee: Toward a Historical Sociology," in *Second Temple Studies III: Studies in Politics, Class, and Material Culture*, ed. Philip R. Davies and John M. Halligan, JSOTSup 340 (Sheffield: Sheffield Academic, 2002), 145–46 and Cohen, *Beginnings of Jewishness*, 111–12, against the suggestion of Kasher (*Jews, Idumaeans, and Ancient Arabs*, 62–63) that Costobar and others like him comprised a small group of atavists. In any case, the main line of evidence that assimilation between Jews and Idumeans was incomplete by the first century CE is how Josephus speaks of them in *Jewish War*.

16. Similarly, Joshua D. Garroway, *Paul's Gentile-Jews: Neither Jew nor Gentile, but Both* (New York: Palgrave Macmillan, 2012), 28, though Garroway wishes to emphasize Josephus's ambiguity. See also Alan Appelbaum, "'The Idumaeans' in Josephus' *The Jewish War*," *JSJ* 40 (2009): 1–22. Appelbaum makes a sustained case that the Idumeans of *Jewish War* are not Jews from the territory of Idumea but a people of their own and that Josephus stereotypes them as aggressive and turbulent.

17. Since, according to Josephus, they aligned themselves with the Zealots and wrought havoc in Jerusalem before coming to their senses (*J.W.* 4.305-333).

18. See Pummer, *Samaritans*, 289–304. An insider's perspective may be gleaned from http://www.israelite-samaritans.com, a website maintained by members of the Samaritan community.

19. By greater Judea, I mean the province as Greek and Roman authors often spoke of it, inclusive of Judea proper, Samaria, and Galilee. See, for example, Strabo, *Geogr.* 16.2.2 and 16.2.21. In Jesus's time, the Roman province of Judea included Samaria, while the administration of Galilee was in the hands of Herod Antipas. After the death of Agrippa I in 44 CE, all three regions were under the authority of the Roman procurator until the time of the Jewish revolt against Rome (though Agrippa II was gifted the cities of Tiberias and Tarichea). When the evangelist refers to Judea (3:22; 4:3, 54; 7:1; 11:7), he means Judea proper.

20. As well summarized by Steve Mason, *Orientation to the History of Roman Judaea* (Eugene, OR: Cascade, 2016), 252–88.

21. See Steve Mason, *Judean War 2*, vol. 1b of *Flavius Josephus: Translation and Commentary*, ed. Steve Mason (Leiden: Brill, 2008), 185, n. 1401.

22. Certainly not *en masse*, even if some happened to find themselves in the Jewish capital.

23. Similarly, Lester L. Grabbe, "Ethnic Groups in Jerusalem," in *Jerusalem in Ancient History and Tradition*, ed. Thomas L. Thompson, JSOTSup 381 (London: T&T Clark, 2003), 160–63. Other pieces of evidence for the pilgrimage of non-Jews

to Jerusalem are collected by Samuel Safrai, "Relations between the Diaspora and the Land of Israel," in *The Jewish People in the First Century: Historical Geography, Political History, Social, Cultural and Religious Life and Institutions*, ed. S. Safrai and M. Stern in co-operation with D. Flusser and W.C. van Unnik (Leiden: Brill, 1974), 184–215, at 199–200.

24. The temple warning inscriptions are mentioned by Josephus in *J.W.* 5.194. Two copies of the inscription are extant, though the second is fragmentary. See Hannah M. Cotton et al., eds. *Corpus Inscriptionum Iudaeae/Palastinae*, vol. 1, *Jerusalem*, pt. 1, *1-704* (Berlin, 2010), 42–45.

25. Certainly, the author of John makes a concerted effort to give that impression. Richard Bauckham ("Historiographical Characteristics of the Gospel of John," *NTS* 53 [2007]: 17–36) has argued that because of its chronological and geographical detail, the Gospel of John would have appeared to first-century readers more like historiography than the Synoptic Gospels. On the accuracy of the Fourth Gospel's geographical references, see, for example, James H. Charlesworth, "The Historical Jesus in the Fourth Gospel: A Paradigm Shift," *JSHJ* 8 (2010): 3–46, at 40–43. Urban C. von Wahlde, in particular, has detailed John's acquaintance with Palestinian topography in idem, "Archaeology and John's Gospel," in *Jesus and Archaeology*, ed. James H. Charlesworth (Grand Rapids: Eerdmans, 2006), 523–86; idem, "The Gospel of John and Archaeology," in *The Oxford Handbook of Johannine Studies*, ed. Judith M. Lieu and Martinus C. de Boer (Oxford: Oxford University Press, 2018), 101–20.

26. See again Urban C. von Wahlde, "The Pool(s) of Bethesda and the Healing in John 5: A Reappraisal of Research and of the Johannine Text," *RB* 116 (2009): 111–36; idem, "The Puzzling Pool of Bethesda: Where Jesus Cured the Crippled Man," *BAR* 27 (2011): 40–47.

27. See, for example, Raymond Brown, *Community*, 36–40; John Bowman, "Samaritan Studies," *BJRL* 40 (1958): 298–327; Edwin Freed, "Samaritan Influence in the Gospel of John," *CBQ* 30 (1968): 580–87.

28. Or more precisely, that the Samaritans worship on a mountain in the vicinity of Sychar. John does not name it Mount Gerizim, though this is surely intended. The Samaritans' high regard for Mount Gerizim is corroborated by Josephus (*J.W.* 3.307) and by two inscriptions discovered on the island of Delos in 1979 dedicated by "the Israelites who bring first-fruit offerings to Holy Argarizein." Inscriptions published by Philippe Bruneau, "'Les Israélites de Délos' et la juiverie délienne," *BCH* 106 (1982): 465–504. The Samaritans also feature in the Gospel of Luke (9:51-56; 10:25-37) and the book of Acts (8:4-25), but quite briefly and without much attention to their beliefs and practices.

29. The evidence is brought together by Jonathan L. Reed, *Archaeology and the Galilean Jesus: A Re-examination of the Evidence* (Harrisburg, PA: Trinity International, 2000); Chancey, *Myth of a Gentile Galilee*.

30. Nathan Thiel, "The Use of the Term 'Galileans' in the Writings of Flavius Josephus Revisited," *JQR* 110 (2020): 221–44. I argue that Γαλιλαῖος in Josephus's writings does not function as a general term for a native or resident of Galilee. It is not coterminous with our word "Galilean," just as the designation Ἰουδαῖος is not

coterminous with the English word "Judean." To put it sharply, not all geographic Galileans were Γαλιλαῖοι in the same way that not all inhabitants of, say, modern China are ethnically Chinese or all the inhabitants of Turkey ethnically Turkish. As I say there, it is by no means my intention to revive the outdated model of a Gentile-dominated first-century Galilee, nor, of course, to lend credence to a racially motivated cleavage of Jesus from his Jewish context. Reconstructions of first-century Galilee have often become vehicles for more expansive claims about the relationship between Jesus and his social environment and thus also between Christianity and Judaism, as Roland Deines shows in "Galilee and the Historical Jesus in Recent Research," in *Life, Culture, and Society*, ed. David A. Fiensy and James Riley Strange, vol. 1 of *Galilee in the Late Second Temple and Mishnaic Periods* (Minneapolis: Fortress, 2014), 11–50.

31. Josephus is not the only ancient author to mention Γαλιλαῖοι. The name appears in the Gospels (Mark 14:70; Luke 13:1-3; 22:59; 23:6) and Acts (1:11; 2:7; 5:37), where it denotes an inhabitant of the region of Galilee. In his *De prosodia catholica*, the second century CE grammarian Aelius Herodianus glosses Γαλιλαῖος as an ἔθνος of Judea; text in August Lentz, ed., *Grammatici Graeci* (Leipzig: Teubner, 1867), 3:1:130. Other references to the Galileans in Greek are later and/or derivative from the NT accounts. Among other sources, Tacitus reports a fracas between the *natio Galilaeorum* and the Samaritans (*Ann.* 12.54). Tacitus, it seems, understands both the Galileans and Samaritans as subdivisions of the Jewish *gens*. Josephus gives an alternative version of these events in *J.W.* 2.232-244. There is also a cryptic reference to מיאללגה in a letter of Simon bar Kosiba to one of his subordinates; Hebrew text in J. T. Milik, "Textes hébreux et araméens," in *Les grottes de Murabba'ât*, ed. P. Benoit, J. T. Milik, and R. de Vaux, DJD 2 (Oxford: Clarendon, 1961), 1:159-61.

32. The syntax of John 4:45c implies that the Galileans had attended the festival with some other group. As 2:13 explicitly describes the Passover as "of the Jews," the nearest antecedents are the Ἰουδαῖοι. If that is indeed the intended pairing, we would not expect the term Γαλιλαῖοι to bear a strictly geographical meaning (Galilean Jews in contrast to Judean Jews). As we've seen, this would be like referring to expatriate Americans in Paris as "the French" *in contrast* with "the Americans" back home.

33. Proponents of a symbolic reading include R. H. Lightfoot, *Locality and Doctrine in the Gospels* (London: Hodder & Stoughton, 1938), 89–105, 143–58; Meeks, "Galilee and Judea"; Fortna, "Theological Use of Locale," 83–89.

34. With Brown, *Community*, 39–40: "The fact that in Galilee the royal official and his whole household come to faith (4:53) is not really more significant than the fact that in Jerusalem the blind man comes to faith (9:35-39)."

35. I thus side against Meeks ("Galilee and Judea," 165) and Jouette M. Bassler ("The Galileans: A Neglected Factor in Johannine Community Research," *CBQ* 43 [1981]: 243–57) who attach the symbolism to people (Judeans vs. Galileans) rather than to territory (Judea vs. Galilee). If the Γαλιλαῖοι are indeed symbols of belief, it is surprising that they do not have a more prominent role in the Gospel. As Fortna ("Theological Use of Locale," 88–89) observes, Galilean faith "is never shown as a widespread thing," though he too insists on a geographic symbolism that contrasts Judea with Galilee.

36. On the relation between Jesus's speeches and first-century temple ritual, see Gale A. Yee, *Jewish Feasts and the Gospel of John*, Zacchaeus Studies: New Testament (Wilmington, DE: Glazier, 1989), 70–82; Dorit Felsch, *Die Feste im Johannesevangelium*, WUNT 2/308 (Tübingen: Mohr Siebeck, 2011), 171–218; Wheaton, *Role of Jewish Feasts*, 127–58. It must be acknowledged that the sources for the lighting of the candles and water-drawing ceremony post-date the composition of the Fourth Gospel, since they are first recorded in tractate Sukkah of the Mishnah (compiled ca. 200 CE). Nevertheless, the convergence between the Mishnah and the Gospel of John on this point suggests that these rabbinic traditions about Tabernacles reach back into the first century. For a slightly more cautious approach, see Brian D. Johnson, "The Jewish Feasts and Questions of Historicity in John 5-12," in *Aspects of Historicity in the Fourth Gospel*, 122–23.

37. So, Culpepper, *Anatomy*, 221–22; Brown, *Community*, 55; Hengel, *Johannine Question*, 119–24; Jörg Frey, "Das Bild 'der Juden' im Johannesevangelium und die Geschichte der johanneischen Gemeinde," in *Israel und seine Heilstraditionen im Johannesevangelium: Festgabe für Johannes Beutler SJ zum 70. Geburtstag*, ed. Michael Labahn, Klaus Scholtissek, and Angelika Strotmann (Paderborn: Schöningh, 2004), 40.

38. "Rabbi" is not unknown from the late antique Greek inscriptions that Shaye J. D. Cohen ("Epigraphical Rabbis," *JQR* 72 [1981]: 1–17) has cataloged, but it is hard to determine the extent of its popular usage among Greek-speaking Jews.

Both Brown (*Gospel according to John*, 1:114) and Martyn ("A Gentile Mission that Replaced an Earlier Jewish Mission?" in *Exploring the Gospel of John: In Honor of D. Moody Smith*, ed. R. Alan Culpepper and C. Clifton Black [Louisville: Westminster John Knox, 1996], 126) maintain that the modifier "of the Jews" may reflect the Johannine community's painfully conscious sense of the Jews' otherness: "The feasts are *theirs*, and thus ours no longer." C. K. Barrett (*The Gospel according to St. John* [Philadelphia: Westminster, 1978], 197) suggests that the specification may owe itself in part to the evangelist's knowledge of a Christian Passover. If there is an intended point of contrast, however, the nearest referents are the Samaritans who shared many religious traditions with their Jewish neighbors despite the well-known animosity between the two groups.

39. Brown, *Community*, 35–40 (Samaritans), 55–58 (Gentiles). Similarly, David Rensberger, *Johannine Faith and Liberating Community* (Philadelphia: Westminster, 1988), 145; Reinhartz, "Forging a New Identity," 126–34.

40. So François Vouga, *Le cadre historique et l'intention théologique de Jean* (Paris: Beauchesne, 1977), 97–111; Frey, "Bild 'der Juden,'" 49. Kierspel (*Jews and the World*, 177–213) develops this line of argumentation more fully. Frey ("Bild 'der Juden,'" 41–42), though, cautions against a straight chronological reading from a situation of Jewish opposition to Gentile opposition because, in his judgment, the various historical levels in John are so intertwined as to make a precise separation impossible (53).

41. Bauckham ("For Whom Were the Gospels Written?" 15–16) makes the more general distinction between the communities *in which* the Gospels were written and those *for which* they were written; the two, as Bauckham observes, have often been conflated.

42. As Ashton (*Understanding*, 33; *John and Christian Origins*, 75–79) takes as a cue to the essential correctness of Martyn's hypothesis whatever other assaults may be leveled against it; also D. Moody Smith, "Contribution of J. Louis Martyn."

43. Similarly, Frey, "Bild 'der Juden,'" 40: "How long ago the definitive split occurred and whether later there was still contact and dispute is difficult to say" (translation mine).

44. In other words, the perspective that "a Gospel is the creation of the community in which it is celebrated," as Tomson ("'Jews' in the Gospel of John," 176) puts it, must not be assumed uncritically. An author, as Richard A. Burridge ("About People, by People, for People: Gospel Genre and Audiences," in *Gospels for All Christians*, 126) says, may "move around, collecting ideas and developing their understanding. Their ideas get refined by wider experience and by the collection of source material." The point is well made by Richard Bauckham, "Is There Patristic Counter-Evidence? A Response to Margaret Mitchell," in *The Audience of the Gospels: The Origin and Function of the Gospels in Early Christianity*, ed. Edward W. Klink III, LNTS 353 (London: T&T Clark, 2010), 105–6.

45. Bauckham has argued that John, far from being a sectarian Gospel hermetically sealed to outsiders, is, in fact, the one most accessible to the Christian novice and non-Christian alike. See idem, "The Audience of the Fourth Gospel," in *Jesus in Johannine Tradition*, ed. Robert T. Fortna and Tom Thatcher (Louisville: Westminster John Knox, 2001), 101–11; slightly modified in idem, *Jesus and the Eyewitnesses: The Gospels as Eyewitness Testimony* (Grand Rapids: Eerdmans, 2006), 113–26; on this, see also North, "'Jews,'" 207–8, who colorfully describes John as a "born pedant." Although Ashton (*Gospel of John and Christian Origins*, 81) is probably right to question the sweeping character of Bauckham's assertion, he too is well aware that "help is always at hand because the evangelist (like most authors) wants his intended readership to understand what he writes."

46. Gilbert Van Belle (*Les parenthèses dans l'Évangile de Jean*, SNTA 11 [Leuven: Leuven University Press, 1985], 206) comes to a similar conclusion about the Fourth Gospel's parenthetical remarks. The evangelist deliberately aids the reader, as exegetes of the Gospel have long noticed, a claim which Van Belle backs up with an impressive list of some 35 scholars.

47. That the evangelist was constrained in part by the tradition he received is plain enough from the overlap between the Fourth Gospel and the Synoptics, both in terms of the general contours of the narratives and with respect to particular events and sayings. Among the most thorough attempts to isolate traditional material in the Gospel of John is C. H. Dodd's classic, *Historical Tradition in the Fourth Gospel*.

48. Edward W. Klink III (*The Sheep of the Fold: The Audience and Origin of the Gospel of John*, SNTSMS 141 [Cambridge: Cambridge University Press, 2007], 172–77) has argued that the evangelist's perplexing handling of *Judaica,* simultaneously known and unknown to the readers, is suggestive of multiple sets of implied readers.

49. So Culpepper, *Anatomy*, 213–23; Klink, *Sheep*, 157–65.

50. And even if Barrett's (*Gospel according to St. John*, 135) sense that the evangelist wrote primarily to satisfy himself is true, there was still an intended audience

whom the author wanted to persuade or edify, even if his principal motivation in writing was personal.

51. Indeed, even if the Gospel was designed as a missionary tract, its purpose could hardly have been achieved without the mediation of those who were already believers.

52. J. A. T. Robinson's remarks in 1960 ("Destination and Purpose," 117) are as salient now as they were when he wrote over fifty years ago: "After all this time the question of the destination and purpose of the Gospel is as wide open as it ever was. Was it addressed to a Jewish or Gentile audience, or indeed to the inquiring individual whatever his background?" As Brodie (*Quest for Origins*, 146) observes: "In dealing with John, and in asking what social world he reflects, the difficulty is to find balance between the universal and the specific."

53. Notable scholars who incline toward a Gentile element in the intended audience include Brown, Culpepper, Hengel, and Reinhartz, among others.

Chapter 5

Like (Fore)fathers Like Sons

The Wandering Israelites and the Johannine Jews

Alongside John 8:44, Rev 2:9 is perhaps the most troubling statement about Jews in the NT. According to Jesus's word of comfort to the harassed Christian community in Smyrna, the Jews of that city are no Jews at all but a synagogue of Satan (συναγωγὴ τοῦ σατανᾶ; also Rev 3:9). By general consensus, the seer who put these words to page was an ethnically Jewish Christ follower.[1] In fact, although at first glance the attack may seem directed from the outside, its logic operates on the assumption that the name "Jew" is a mark of honor.[2] Those who follow Jesus are the true Jews. The pattern, like that in the Fourth Gospel with respect to Abraham, Moses, and the Scriptures, is appropriation or retention on the part of the author and denial to the author's opponents: "We are the real Jews; those who slander and persecute us have lost all right to that title."[3]

Internecine verbal swordsmanship, such as we see in the Book of Revelation, is plentiful in the Israelite/Jewish literary tradition. Associated most of all with the prophets' lashings of Israel and Judah for their chronic infidelity to the LORD and abuse of the poor and socially vulnerable, it is found throughout the books that would come to make up the Jewish canon and in many others that would not enjoy that fortune.[4] No epithet of opprobrium, it seems, is spared: the people are a sinful nation, the offspring of iniquity, rebels, murderers, thieves, and whores—and this in the first chapter of Isaiah alone! In the Dead Sea Scrolls, the enemies of the community are lambasted as the sons of Belial, sons of the pit, sons of darkness, greedy, wicked, haughty, deceitful, stiff-necked, and hard-hearted.[5] This type of rhetoric, so shrill to modern ears, verged on convention.[6] While we might rue the inclination toward objectification of opponents, it becomes immediately apparent that the ancients could and often did reserve their most damning criticism for compatriots and confreres.

It is not the intensity of John's polemic, then, that prevents us from reading it as the product of a self-consciously Jewish author, for it is not any more acerbic, and arguably less so, than some of the sectarian scrolls, or even some of the canonical prophets. Nor is it the frequency of the phrase οἱ Ἰουδαῖοι that makes the Fourth Gospel exceptional. For although in many Jewish writings the endonym "Israel" predominates, some Jews did indeed write to other Jews about "the Jews"—the authors of Ezra-Nehemiah, 2 Maccabees, and Esther, among other texts. A writer's preference for one term or the other is not a sure guide to his or her social location. To gauge from the extant papyri, numismatic evidence, and other windows into popular practice, many Jews were happy to be known as such in communication both with their kinsmen and with Gentiles.[7] The letter preserved in 2 Macc 1:1-9, for instance, shows very clearly that Jews did not necessarily avoid that title in internal communication. The authors of the festal letter refer to themselves as the Jews of Jerusalem and address the correspondence to the Jews who live in Egypt. In that vein, it is interesting to observe that whereas 1 Maccabees features "Israel" very frequently and mostly reserves "Jews" for communication involving Gentiles, in 1 Macc 13:41-42, the *people* are reported to have begun signing their contracts to the year of Simon, "high priest, commander, and leader of the Jews."

What is unique to the Gospel of John is that here intensity of polemic and frequency of phrase coincide. It is specifically "the Jews" who so often bear the brunt of the criticism. In chs. 2–3, I attempted to show that John neither stereotypes the Jews nor instantiates a dichotomy in which being Jewish and believing in Jesus are mutually exclusive, even as he makes clear that very few of Jesus's own embraced his message. In ch. 4, I considered how the Gospel's setting and audience may have contributed to the evangelist's preference for "the Jews" over other available terms. We are, nonetheless, still faced with a kind of *reductio ad absurdum*. Why would someone who thought of himself as a Jew and who was equipped with a handful of narrower terms for the Jewish parties involved in the story not only prefer the term οἱ Ἰουδαῖοι but also present them so critically?

Ultimately, then, a measured examination of the Gospel's narrative setting and original audience, though far from inconsequential, is only of partial explanatory value. It concerns the frequency of "the Jews" in John more than the intensity of the criticism. It does not adequately account for the evangelist's overarching theological framework, in which Jewish unbelief, though not universal, is indeed pervasive. We must still supply a compelling explanation for this side of the Gospel's presentation of the Jews—precisely the feature that has imbued Martyn's two-level reading with such vitality. In what follows, I will make the case that the fourth evangelist has modeled his criticism of those named "the Jews" after the scriptural narratives of the children of Israel. He has keyed Jesus's person, work, and rejection to seminal moments in Israel's history—above all the Sinai and desert wandering traditions—putting Jesus's contemporaries in the place of the rebellious Israelites who failed to trust God despite the powerful manifestations of God's glory in their midst. We best understand the evangelist, then, not as someone who had renounced membership in the Jewish people but as a self-consciously Jewish author whose imagination, interpretive impulses, and language about "the Jews" were profoundly shaped by Israel's Scriptures.

INTRA-ISRAELITE POLEMIC AS PRECEDENT FOR THE FOURTH GOSPEL

Naturally, many investigations of John's attitude toward the Jews have fastened upon the appellation οἱ Ἰουδαῖοι itself, but if we cast our net wider, some possible influences on the evangelist's presentation begin to emerge. Whereas many of the putative sources and influences to which scholars have turned to illuminate the Gospel's thought-world are now stashed deep in the archives (few commentators today are quick to reach for the Hermetica or the Mandean Ginza Rabbah, for example), one influence is beyond any reasonable dispute.[8] The evangelist knew Israel's Scriptures (some of them, at least), and he knew about many of the formative events of Israel's history: the exodus from Egypt, the desert wanderings, and the giving of the law at Sinai at the barest minimum. Jesus's discourses in particular evince intimate acquaintance with the Scriptures, the allusions occasionally bordering on the obscure: Moses's lifting up of the bronze serpent in the wilderness as a type of the crucifixion (John 3:14) and Jesus's appeal to Ps 82 ("I have said you are gods") as part of an *a fortiori* argument in defense of his right to be called the Son of God (John 10:34-36), to take two of the more abstruse examples.[9] The Jesus of Johannine tradition, little interested in messianic proof-texting, draws deep from the scriptural well.

Though its appropriation of Scripture is arguably less intricate, the narrative material shares the same theological sensibility, abounding in quotations and allusions to Israel's sacred writings and the seminal figures of her past.[10] One would be hard-pressed to come up with a more appropriate title for John than Andreas Obermann's *Schrifttheologe*.[11] John, as C. K. Barrett says, may have fewer direct quotations than the Synoptic Gospels, but he has a wide and comprehensive knowledge of the OT.[12] From the prologue's climactic statement that "the Word became flesh and tabernacled among us," as God dwelt amidst the Israelites in a portable sanctuary, to the people's grumblings in chs. 6–7, surely meant to recall the incessant murmuring of the Israelites in the desert, through the summary statement closing the Book of Signs that Isaiah had foreseen the people's hardness and predicted their unbelief (12:37-50), to the scriptural fulfillment formulas that dot the Book of Glory (13:18; 15:25; 19:24-25, 28), Jesus's life and the response to him are interpreted through a Christological reading of Scripture.[13] It is the outgrowth of the Johannine conviction, shared with all the NT authors, that the Scriptures, rightly read, testify to Jesus: "You search the scriptures because you think that in them you have eternal life; and it is they that testify on my behalf" (John 5:39).[14]

Searching the Scriptures, we discover that relatively little is said about "the Jews" under that name except in Esther, parts of Ezra-Nehemiah, and Jeremiah 40–44, though even then, they do not go entirely without censure.[15] The prophetic denunciation in Jer 44 (Jer 51 LXX) is said to concern "all the Jews living in the land of Egypt" (MT: אל כל־היהודים הישבים בארץ מצרים; LXX: ἅπασιν τοῖς Ιουδαίοις τοῖς κατοικοῦσιν ἐν γῇ Αἰγύπτῳ).[16] Because they have obstinately persisted in their worship of false gods, God has determined to wipe them out, leaving them no remnant in the land to which they have fled for refuge. Never again will the Jews living in Egypt invoke the LORD's name. In an inversion of the promises of restoration in Jer 29:11-14, God swears, "I am going to watch over them for harm and not for good; all the people of Judah who are in the land of Egypt shall perish by the sword and by famine, until not one is left" (44:27). That the divine threats are directed toward "the Jews" is not insignificant insofar as it is an extension of the prophetic critique of Israel and Judah. Nevertheless, this is an isolated example in a vast sea of literature. Despite the evangelist's scriptural expertise, it cannot safely be assumed that he knew the passage, much less that it shaped his discourse about the Jews.

In contrast to the paucity of material about "the Jews" in the OT, a great deal is said about Israel and Judah, much of it less than flattering. Starting with the prophets, we find not only scathing oracles against kings, priests, and nobility, but also sweeping indictments of Israel and Judah as national entities. Israel, according to the marital metaphor of Hosea (Hos 1–3) and Jeremiah (Jer 2–3), is an unfaithful bride, having run after deceptive courtesans who are impotent to deliver on their promises. She is a "stubborn heifer" (Hos 3:16), a "hard-hearted" people (Ezek 2:4; 3:7), who together have gone astray. The nation of Israel and the people of Judah are the LORD's vineyard, but when he looked for justice, there was only bloodshed, and when he sought righteousness, he heard only cries of distress from the oppressed (Isa 5:1-7). The Israelites, like their ancestors, have rebelled against the LORD, defiling themselves with detestable idols (Ezek 20:1-31).

The sectarians who produced the Damascus Document and the Rule of the Community (1QS) must have imbibed some of this prophetic spirit, for they too fault Israel for national apostasy.[17] The Damascus Document speaks of a time when God "hid his face from Israel and from his sanctuary" because the people had forsaken him (CD I, 3-4). Contemporary Israel apparently had not learned her lesson, for according to CD III, 13-14 they are like Hosea's stubborn heifer, misled by the "scoffer" and ignorant about the hidden matters "in which all Israel had gone astray." They have been caught in the demon Belial's snares, corrupted by wealth, fornication, and ritual defilement (CD IV, 13-18).[18] The Rule of the Community is not much more optimistic about Israel's spiritual state. As part of the rite of initiation into the community, the Levites are instructed to "rehearse the wicked acts of the children of Israel, all their guilty transgressions and sins committed during the dominion of Belial" (1QS I, 22-24), as a sort of antiphon to the priestly recitation of God's mercies which precede.

There is no doubt a distancing effect in these pronouncements, but to the extent that they create "others," this is done from within. That is, the broad-based accusations against Israel and Judah are leveled by those who consciously belong to Israel and Judah. Against the background of such texts, John's language about the Jews becomes less peculiar. The rancorous debate between Jesus and the Jews in John 8, in that respect, is not altogether different from the LORD's manifold complaints against the people of Israel in Isaiah or Hosea, as Stephen Motyer argues.[19] Yet we cannot rest here, in the first place, because the frequency of "Israel" and "Judah" in these prophetic indictments does not quite compare with the proliferation of "Jews" in the Fourth Gospel; second, because I have yet to demonstrate the evangelist's dependence upon any particular passage or set of themes, leaving us with the unsatisfactory proposition of a vague osmosis from the prophetic books to the Fourth Gospel.

Criticism of the Children of Israel in Exodus-2 Kings

The prophets and those who edited the books under their names were not alone in their disappointment with the people of Israel and Judah, past and present. If the author of Hebrews had it in mind to write a brief history of faith in the famous encomium of ch. 11, those responsible for the Pentateuch and Deuteronomistic History (Joshua-2 Kings) were deep in the project of writing a history of faithlessness. This is a rhetorical way to put it, of course, but the conscious hyperbole is not far from Scripture's own assessment. The story of the Israelites as told in Exodus-2 Kings is a tale of rebellion: the repeated grumbling against Moses and Aaron, the worship of the golden calf, the wailing to return to Egypt where things were better, the refusal to enter the promised land upon first offer, the repeated lapses into idolatry in the tumultuous period of the Judges, the disastrous split between Israel and Judah, and a slew of impious kings, all culminating in exile when the LORD could endure their sin no more.[20] Were one to chart Israel's moral progress, the peaks of covenantal fidelity would be dwarfed by the expansive valleys of disobedience. "It is a story," as Mary C. Callaway says, "told in the voice of a relentless critic rather than a proud heir."[21]

If I am in danger of one-sidedly amplifying this aspect of ancient Hebrew historiography, it should be remembered that this is the very impression which a number of biblical authors, reflecting on their people's past history and present spiritual condition, sought to convey. The Deuteronomist is perhaps the most consistently gloomy in this respect. Moses's charge against the Israelites in Deut 31:27 epitomizes the book's critical perspective: "For I know well how rebellious and stubborn you are. If you already have been so rebellious toward the Lord while I am still alive among you, how much more after my death!" Surveying the nation's history up to the exile of the Northern Kingdom, the author of 2 Kgs 17 concurred. The Israelites "were stubborn, as their ancestors had been, who did not believe in the Lord their God. They despised his statutes, and his covenant that he made with their ancestors, and the warnings that he gave them" (2 Kgs 17:14-15). Rehearsal of the people's sins, often in the *Sitz im Leben* of communal confession (Pss 78, 106; Ezra 9:6-15; Neh 9:6-37; Dan 9:1-19), becomes something of a standard form in post-exilic works, recalling and reinforcing the characterization of earlier texts. In the prayer of Ezra 9, to take an especially potent example, the priest and teacher of the Torah laments the people's sin of taking foreign wives. Their transgressions, he confesses, have risen higher than their heads, mounting up to the heavens (v. 6). From the days of their ancestors, their guilt has been great (v. 7). The community of Israel has forsaken the commandments of God and cannot even lift their faces in God's presence because of the weight of their guilt (v. 15).[22]

When the authors and editors of these texts criticize their forebears, they often do so in expansive terms. In the prophetic books, the charge is thus brought against the people collectively as "Israel," "the house of Israel," "the house of Judah," "the men of Judah," "the children of Israel and Judah," and so forth.[23] In the prose narratives of the Hebrew Bible, the accusation of covenantal infidelity is often leveled against "the children of Israel." Although we might attribute the philippic in a passage like 2 Kgs 17 in part to a southern parti pris against the northern kingdom of Israel, most of these critical moral evaluations of the Israelites come from the Pentateuch, Joshua, and Judges, where they encompass all twelve tribes. We need only remember the chorus of Judges that "the children of Israel did evil in the eyes of the LORD" (2:11; 3:7, 12; 4:1; 6:1; 10:6; 13:1).

What we encounter throughout the Hebrew Bible, then, are authors, editors, and compilers of tradition who will have undoubtedly numbered themselves among the descendants of the patriarch Israel, who are writing for fellow Israelites, but who for the most part characterize their people, past and present, as a faithless brood, the mass of covenantal shortcomings relieved by individual or generational exceptions. Familiarity with these texts may inure us to their charge of disobedience, so that we miss the strangeness of their invective. It would be like an American writing for compatriots about the sins which "the Americans" have committed—or a Jew writing for other Jews about the stubbornness of "the Jews." Here we begin to see how the evangelist's criticism of the Jews might be reasonably interpreted as the product of someone who still counted himself a member of the Jewish people. He presents Jesus's contemporaries like the Scriptures so often present the children of Israel.

Desert Wandering Traditions in the Fourth Gospel

The evangelist knew the Scriptures, Scriptures in which Israel is consistently presented as a wayward people, all too prone to break their end of the solemn agreement with God, and in which criticism of the children of Israel by other Israelites is in no short supply. In theory, he had a template for what he said about the Jews in Scripture's intramural criticism of the Israelites. But if we are to move beyond suggestion, it must be shown that John did indeed make use of these traditions with their motif of widespread unbelief.

It can be said with confidence that the Fourth Gospel alludes to the time of Israel's sojourn in the desert and, moreover, that the evangelist consciously invokes these stories to characterize both the Gospel's protagonist and its ancillary actors.[24] Mention has already been made of the lifting up of the snake in the wilderness (Num 21) as a type of Jesus's crucifixion. The purpose of the comparison is evident as part of the constellation of images associated with Jesus's death and glorification, but here the context of the source passage seems peripheral to the discourse. The image has been extracted for its own sake.

Elsewhere, the evocation of the wilderness stories contributes in central ways to the Gospel's narrative arc, beginning as one would expect with the prologue, which serves as a sort of "reader's guide" to the Gospel, as Adele Reinhartz puts it, and in whose light the rest of the Gospel is to be understood.[25] Although the vividness of the expression is sometimes masked by nondescript English translations, it can hardly be a coincidence that the sequel to the climactic, "And the Word became flesh" (1:14), is that "he tabernacled among us" (καὶ ἐσκήνωσεν ἐν ἡμῖν). The verb σκηνόω is cognate to σκηνή, the Greek word for "tent" and the same term used in the LXX for the edifice which the Israelites were instructed to build at Sinai and which accompanied them for the duration of their wanderings in the wilderness.[26]

Securing the allusion is the pairing of ἐσκήνωσεν with the author's claim in the second half of v. 14 to have beheld Jesus's glory (δόξα).[27] The tabernacle was to be God's dwelling place in the midst of the people, sanctified by his glory (Exod 29:43). Immediately after Moses finishes setting up the tabernacle and putting all its accoutrements in order, the cloud covers it, and the glory of the LORD fills it, signaling God's approval of the work (Exod 40:34-35). He has come to live among his people. At times of crisis, the glory of God descends upon the tabernacle to vindicate Aaron and Moses and quash the people's uprisings (Num 14:10; 16:19, 42; 20:6). As God's presence accompanies the Israelites in this temporal dwelling and as his glory manifests itself there, so too the Father's presence is mediated through the Son and the divine glory revealed through Jesus's signs and words.

It has been plausibly argued that vv. 14-18 play upon a related set of images drawn from Moses's encounter with the LORD on Sinai in Exod 33–34.[28] The latter, it will be recalled, recounts Moses's request to see God's glory. The LORD obliges his servant but on the condition that Moses will only catch a glimpse of the LORD's back as he passes by. After proclaiming his name before Moses, the LORD relays another set of commandments that Moses, in turn, is to teach the people. The Law, presumably encompassing all of the Pentateuchal legislation, is the express subject of John 1:17. Expanding upon the statement in v. 16 that from Jesus we have received grace upon grace (καὶ χάριν ἀντὶ χάριτος), the evangelist writes, "The law indeed was given through Moses; grace and truth came through Jesus Christ." The "we" of the prologue situate themselves in a position like that of Moses before God. Just as in Exod 34 Moses beholds God's glory, so too the anonymous bearers of the tradition have beheld the divine glory in Jesus, revealed, as we later learn, through the signs which he performs (2:11). Just as the LORD warns Moses in Exod 33:20 that no one may see his face and live, John 1:18 affirms that no one has ever seen God, even as the Son makes him known (similarly John 6:46; 14:7-9). And just as God by his very nature responds to Israel with an abundance of lovingkindness and covenant faithfulness (Hb: רב חסד ואמת; Exod 34:6), Jesus comes from the Father full of grace and truth (πλήρης χάριτος καὶ ἀληθείας, 1:14).[29]

The conjunction of motifs does not seem to be arbitrary. The evangelist, I would argue, has read the theophany to Moses at Sinai and God's presence with the people of Israel in the tabernacle as Christophanies, just as Justin Martyr and many church fathers later would.[30] The profession that no one has ever seen God presents a conundrum, since the OT records many divine apparitions, some of which the evangelist must have been aware of. Who was it, then, that appeared to the patriarchs, Moses, and the prophets? That it was the Word who spoke face to face with Moses in the tent of meeting and who proclaimed his name on the mountain is wholly consistent with the Gospel's Christology.[31]

In John 8, toward the end of an intense exchange, Jesus makes a stunning claim: Abraham rejoiced at the thought of seeing his day. In fact, the forefather of the Jewish people saw Jesus's day and was glad (8:56). The dialogue reaches its crescendo when Jesus invokes the divine name revealed to Moses in Exod 3: "Before Abraham was born, I am" (John 8:58).[32] Because the narrative drives toward Jesus's preexistence, Abraham's seeing and rejoicing seem to be regarded as a past event, experienced during his own lifetime.[33] If so, the appearances of God to Abraham in Genesis, or perhaps the appearance of the three visitors in Gen 18, in particular, supply the most obvious candidate for the encounter, as others have convincingly argued.[34]

Similarly, John 12:41 states without elaboration that the prophet Isaiah beheld Jesus's glory and spoke about him. Did Isaiah see the pre-incarnate Jesus or, guided along by the Spirit of God, did he predict the suffering and exaltation of Christ centuries in advance? Based on the biblical quotations in John 12:38 and 40, the answer to that in the Johannine imagination may well be both. The first quotation comes from Isa 53:1 and the suffering servant song. That John equated the servant with Jesus and read the passage from Isaiah as a prophecy of the Messiah's atoning death and resurrection hardly needs to be defended.[35] From a very early stage, the Christian community had taken that decisive interpretive step. The other quotation in John 12:40 is lifted from the scene in Isa 6, in which Isaiah beholds God in the temple. There is no equivocation about the identity of the figure in the vision. It is "the King, the LORD of hosts." For the evangelist, according to whom no one has seen God, this can be none other than an appearance of the Word, who is with God and is God, and who makes God known. Not only so, but Isa 6 and the suffering servant material of Isa 52–53 were already subject to inner-biblical interpretation. Isaiah sees God on his throne "high and lifted up" (6:1). The servant will be "exalted and lifted up and shall be very high" (52:13). John, it seems, has brought the two passages together with some assistance. Isaiah was a witness to the glory that Jesus had with the Father before the world began and the glory that he would paradoxically receive through his "lifting up" on the cross.

I believe that a compelling case can be made for reading the Gospel as an extended theophany of sorts, a balanced version of Ernst Käsemann's "God striding over the Earth" that does due justice to the fact that the Word did indeed become flesh, subject to human frailties and mortality, limited by time and space.[36] In a number of OT theophanies, the human recipients of the visitation do not at first recognize that it is God who stands before them.[37] In the Gospel of John, Jesus's divine identity remains partially clouded until after the resurrection when Thomas professes: "My Lord and my God!" (John 20:28).

Yet whatever we make of the theophanic traditions in the Gospel, it is clear that from the very start, the evangelist intends to relate the story of Jesus to the story of God's past dealings with his chosen people. God redeemed the Israelites from slavery in Egypt; Jesus comes to deliver his own from slavery to sin. It is also for this reason that Jesus's miracles bear their uniquely Johannine stamp as signs (σημεῖα), undoubtedly harkening back to God's commissioning of Moses, the exodus, and God's provision for the people of Israel during their long sojourn in the wilderness.[38] The signs granted to Moses authenticate the prophet's mission by revealing God's power and covenantal love for his harassed people. They display God's glory. Likewise, signs in the Fourth Gospel demonstrate that "God himself is at work in these acts of Jesus" and reveal Jesus's divine glory as the one sent from the Father.[39]

The association of Jesus with God's presence in the tabernacle and with the revelation of the divine name to Moses on Sinai anchors the evangelist's soaring estimation of Jesus's person and work in Scripture. The appropriation of wilderness traditions also serves the opposite purpose, namely, to ground the opposition to Jesus in those same Scriptures and to portray Jesus's adversaries as reenacting the unbelief of their forebears. To borrow from the discourse of collective memory, the evangelist has keyed the Gospel narrative to stories in the Torah. That is, he has paired the story of Jesus with "archetypal images or symbolically significant patterns from the past" in order to frame his (or his audience's) present experience and to imbue it with meanings attached to Israel's history.[40] The evangelist, we may say, evokes a cultural script in order to structure present experience in a process of analogic mapping between present and past. Although in a few biblical texts, Israel's sojourn in the wilderness evokes the image of a pristine beginning (e.g., Jer 2:2-3; Hos 2:15), it was more often remembered as a series of communal failures and divine mercy. The recitation of these failures in summary form in Pss 78, 106, and Neh 9 suggests an effort to make this way of remembering part of Jewish collective memory—the fashioning of a cultural script that associated the wilderness wanderings with the people's lack of trust in God despite the deliverance that he had won for them.[41]

The evangelist's keying of the lack of receptivity toward Jesus to these Pentateuchal narratives and their commemorations in later Jewish tradition becomes most transparent in the "Bread of Life" discourse in John 6:25-59. Both the temporal setting of the events of John 6 (according to 6:4 the Passover was near) and the content of the speech itself (the raining down of manna from heaven) recall the liberation from Egypt and Israel's hardships upon their exit. So when the crowd's innocent inquisitiveness turns to grumbling, now attributed to the Jews (6:41), one is undoubtedly intended to think of the complaints of the children of Israel to Moses in Exod 16 and of God's subsequent intervention in spite of their lack of faith.[42]

This characterization applies first and foremost to those in the immediate context, the Jewish crowds who had been with Jesus on the other side of the lake and who partook of the miraculous meal. At the same time, their response is not isolated, as we have seen, and so it is natural to ask whether the evangelist carries this line of thought farther or adopts it more comprehensively. We know that he interpreted the cold reception that Jesus received from his own people theologically. That is to say, it was God himself who blinded the people's eyes and hardened their hearts, as Isaiah had prophesied according to John 12:39-40. The summary of Jesus's public ministry resonates with the lament of the prologue that "he was in the world, and though the world was made through him, the world did not recognize him. He came to that which was his own, but his own did not receive him" (1:10-11). In the final verdict, they could not receive him.

Although John 12:37-50 draws most directly from Isaiah, it may also allude secondarily to a set of passages from Numbers and Deuteronomy. The grumbling of the Jews in John 6 is almost certainly meant to recall Exod 16. This, of course, is neither the first nor the only time that the children of Israel are said to murmur against God. The first report of popular discontent comes in Exod 15:22-24, right after the people cross the sea, and escalates in Exod 16:1-3 and 17:1-3. It is reprised once more in Num 11:1-3 and in 14:1-2, where the rebellion reaches murderous proportions. God himself is ready to wipe out the people and start over but relents at Moses's behest. The exegetical technique of word association, known in a more refined form from the rules of Hillel as *gezerah shavah* but practiced broadly by ancient Jewish interpreters, alongside the contextual similarities between the stories, make them prime candidates for a synoptic reading.[43] As we've seen, several psalmists (Pss 78 and 106) had already taken that step, stringing these stories together in condensed form as a reminder of Israel's history of rebellion.

Intriguing in this respect are the conceptual and verbal parallels between John 12:37 and Num 14:11.[44] The evangelist nowhere quotes from the story of the spies' exploration of Canaan, their discouraging report to the people, and the Israelites' subsequent mutiny against Moses and Aaron in Num 13–14, but the resemblances between this narrative and Exod 16 make John's acquaintance with it likely. Besides the similarity in narrative form established at the outset through the *Leitwort* "murmur" (Hb: לון, Gk: γογγύζω/ διαγογγύζω), both passages recount the people's disingenuous wish to have died in Egypt.[45] And in each pericope, God deems it necessary to act on his own behalf, manifesting his glory in the sight of all the people.[46] We may further note that in Num 14:18 Moses appeals to the proclamation of the divine attributes from Exod 34:6-7 to persuade God to forgive the people. If John 1:1-18 alludes to the events of Exod 33–34, as seems to be the case, this lends further support to the supposition that John knew the story in Num 13–14 as well.

As already mentioned, John 12:37-50 serves as a summary to the Book of Signs, capping it off with a sober acknowledgment of the people's lack of faith: "Even after Jesus had done all these signs in their presence, they still would not believe in him." The exasperation echoes God's impassioned reaction to the Israelites' refusal to enter Canaan. Having received the disheartening report from ten of the spies, the people raise their voices in despair (14:1-4). While the Israelites contemplate stoning Moses and Aaron (v. 10), the glory of the LORD appears at the tent of meeting. The LORD is incensed: "How long will this people despise me? And how long will they refuse to believe in me, in spite of all the signs that I have done among them" (v. 11)? Although the evangelist does not quote Num 14:11 verbatim, he matches each element except for the interrogative. Grouping the corresponding parts of the sentences together, we may compare them in Table 5.1. When we allow for the conversion of a first-person question into a third-person statement, John 12:37 comes quite close to Num 14:11 in both language and tone.[47]

One other passage is worth mentioning here. Brown has observed that John 12:37-50 is reminiscent of Moses's farewell address to the Israelites in Deut 29:1-4.[48] Conceptually, Deut 29:1-4 follows the same pattern as Num 14:11. Despite the LORD's powerful work on behalf of his people, they have not responded with commensurate fidelity. They have seen everything that God did for them in Egypt, the signs and great wonders, but "to this day the LORD has not given you a heart that understands, eyes that see, or ears that hear." The points of contact between John 12:37-41 and Deut 29:1-4 are threefold. First, of course, is the content of the summary itself. God has done miraculous works on behalf of his people, but to little effect on their attitudes toward him. Second, there are the shared verbal links with Isa 6:1-10, the trio of hearts, eyes, and ears (though John leaves out the last of these) that are not working as they should. Third, in Deut 29:1-4, as in Isa 6, the LORD is the agent—in

Table 5.1. John 12:37 Compared with Numbers 14:11. Created by the author

John 12:37	Num 14:11
τοσαῦτα σημεῖα	πᾶσιν τοῖς σημείοις
	בכל האתות
αὐτοῦ πεποιηκότος ἔμπροσθεν αὐτῶν	οἷς ἐποίησα ἐν αὐτοῖς
	אשר עשיתי בקרבו
οὐκ ἐπίστευον εἰς αὐτόν	οὐ πιστεύουσίν μοι
	לא־יאמינו בי

some mysterious sense the cause of the people's unbelief. *He* has not given them the ability to understand.

How far John 12:37 depends upon these passages, individually or together, need not be determined with absolute precision to see that the evangelist's summary follows a recurrent theme from Exodus to Deuteronomy.[49] God does signs and miracles, great deeds to rescue his people and to sustain them. With outstretched arm, he reveals himself to Israel. The signs are meant to elicit faith, but Israel disobeys and rebels time after time.[50] The divine kindness and provision are repaid with complaint and provocation. The Fourth Gospel, I suggest, recapitulates this narrative in broad strokes and has written Jesus and his Jewish contemporaries into it. Jesus dwells among the people as God travels with the children of Israel in the tabernacle. He reveals his glory through signs which are invitations to belief just as the LORD displays his glory in great signs and wonders. Sometimes the people respond in faith, but more often than not the miracles do not achieve their intended result. The contemporaries of Jesus are like their ancestors in the wilderness.[51] The characterization of the Jewish crowd in John 6 would seem to apply to the Johannine Jews in a more comprehensive way. The evangelist has keyed the events of Jesus's ministry to seminal moments in Israel's past so that these past narratives and images serve as "orienting symbols or templates for Johannine beliefs and commitments in the present."[52]

Children of Israel: Frequency of Expression and Intensity of Criticism

Do the affinities between the Johannine presentation of the Jews and the scriptural presentation of Israel extend to patterns in nomenclature? We cannot be dogmatic, but there are reasons to think that here too John owes a debt to the wilderness narratives. Although these stories refer to the people in a variety of ways, בני ישראל ("children of Israel" or "Israelites") is the designation of choice. Its use at times is extraordinarily dense, occurring in Exod 16, for instance, ten times in the span of thirty-six verses. In the sequel in Exodus 17:1-7, the people are referred to as the "children of Israel" twice more. In both scenes, the Israelites are portrayed as grumblers, without trust that God will provide food and water for them despite what he has done for them in Egypt and at the Red Sea. According to Moses's petition to God in 17:4, the people are on the verge of stoning him.

This frequency of use in the context of a generally disparaging evaluation of the people's behavior has a striking effect. That we typically reserve the name "Israelites" for the ancient people tends to dull the sting, but if for the sake of analogy we substitute "Jews" in these narratives for "children of

Israel," the sharp edge of the criticism is immediately felt. Thus modified, Exod 16:1-11 would read:

> The whole congregation of the Jews set out from Elim; and Israel came to the wilderness of Sin, which is between Elim and Sinai, on the fifteenth day of the second month after they had departed from the land of Egypt. The whole congregation of the Jews complained against Moses and Aaron in the wilderness. The Jews said to them, "If only we had died by the hand of the Lord in the land of Egypt, when we sat by the fleshpots and ate our fill of bread; for you have brought us out into this wilderness to kill this whole assembly with hunger."
>
> Then the Lord said to Moses, "I am going to rain bread from heaven for you . . ." So Moses and Aaron said to all the Jews, "In the evening you shall know that it was the Lord who brought you out of the land of Egypt, and in the morning you shall see the glory of the Lord, because he has heard your complaining against the Lord. For what are we, that you complain against us?"
>
> Then Moses said to Aaron, "Say to the whole congregation of the Jews, 'Draw near to the Lord, for he has heard your complaining.'" And as Aaron spoke to the whole congregation of the Jews, they looked towards the wilderness, and the glory of the Lord appeared in the cloud. The Lord spoke to Moses and said, "I have heard the complaining of the Jews; say to them, 'At twilight you shall eat meat, and in the morning you shall have your fill of bread; then you shall know that I am the Lord your God.'"

The criticism of the Israelites in Exod 16–17 is relatively mild when set next to a passage like Num 14, where the children of Israel are mentioned four times in vv. 1-11. If we again substitute "Jews" for "Israelites," we better sense the peculiarity of the rhetorical situation.

> Then all the congregation raised a loud cry, and the people wept that night. And all the Jews complained against Moses and Aaron; the whole congregation said to them, "Would that we had died in the land of Egypt! Or would that we had died in this wilderness!"
>
> Then Moses and Aaron fell on their faces before all the assembly of the congregation of the Jews. And Joshua son of Nun and Caleb son of Jephunneh, who were among those who had spied out the land, tore their clothes and said to all the congregation of the Jews, "The land that we went through as spies is an exceedingly good land. . . ." But the whole congregation threatened to stone them.
>
> Then the glory of the Lord appeared at the tent of meeting to all the Jews. And the Lord said to Moses, "How long will this people despise me? And how long

will they refuse to believe in me, in spite of all the signs that I have done among them? I will strike them with pestilence and disinherit them, and I will make of you a nation greater and mightier than they."

In several passages in the Book of Judges, we see a similar frequency in the use of the name "children of Israel." The phrase occurs six times and "Israel" four times within the first ten verses of Judges 6, for example.[53] It is an Israelite author, moreover, who intones throughout the book that "the children of Israel did evil in the eyes of the LORD" (2:11; 3:7, 12; 4:1; 6:1; 10:6; 13:1). In their original context, these are in-house, intergenerational jabs. Thus, Israel's Scriptures, and especially the desert wandering narratives, evince that same intersection of frequency of nomenclature with critical disapproval of the people's behavior that otherwise seems so distinct to the Fourth Gospel.

I have shown that the evangelist makes extensive use of the exodus and desert wandering traditions throughout the Book of Signs and that he casts the Jewish response to Jesus as a wilderness-rebellion redux. It is almost as if he lives within these tales; he speaks their vocabulary, filtered through an experience of the risen Christ and the abiding presence of the Paraclete. Passages like Exod 16–17 and Num 14, then, not only comprise part of the author's scriptural library, but their outlook has become his own. And in the case of Exod 16, he has very explicitly drawn an analogy between Jesus's Jewish contemporaries and the ancient Israelites' rebellion against God. The fourth evangelist may not stereotype all Jews as non-believers, but insofar as he lays the Gospel narrative over stories of national apostasy, we should not be surprised if he has also taken up their nomenclature and transposed it to a new setting. Patterns of speech which may seem foreign to us were not only familiar to the evangelist, but they were also embedded in narratives that are integral to the Gospel's framing of Jesus's ministry. John internalized and adapted their language as his own.

CONCLUSION

What I have tried to show in this chapter is how an author who thought of himself as Jewish could conceivably say the sorts of things that the evangelist says about the Ἰουδαῖοι. Why does he prefer that term over the others that were available to him? He writes, I have suggested, in conscious imitation of the Scriptures, troubled over what he perceives as a bewildering lack of faith on the part of most of Jesus's compatriots. In the eyes of the evangelist, many, probably most, of Jesus's contemporaries in Palestine were blind to the manifestation of God's glory through Jesus. Though the lack of faith was not universal, true believers were in the minority. This disregard for God's revelation was perplexing. It could only be explained as the inscrutable will of God. He had blinded their eyes and stopped up their ears. But it was not the first time Israel had hardened its heart. John retells Scripture, or rather, he has keyed the events of Jesus's ministry to Israel's story as he knew them from those Scriptures and from Jewish tradition.[54] The evangelist, like the tradents of Exodus-2 Kings, is a relentless critic, or nearly so. Such cutting theological assessment had long been part of Israel's counterintuitive way of telling its history.

NOTES

1. Already, for example, R. H. Charles, *A Critical and Exegetical Commentary on the Revelation of St. John*, ICC (Edinburgh: T&T Clark, 1920), 57; also Adela Yarbro Collins, *Crisis and Catharsis: The Power of the Apocalypse* (Philadelphia: Westminster, 1984), 46–48; Richard Bauckham, *The Theology of the Book of Revelation*, New Testament Theology (Cambridge: Cambridge University Press, 1993), 2; David E. Aune, *Revelation*, WBC 52a (Dallas, TX: Word, 1997), 1:l; Aune ("Revelation," *EDB* 1125) goes so far as to state that the "Jewish origin of the author is certain."

2. So also Mathias Rissi, "Das Judenproblem im Lichte der Johannesapokalypse," *TZ* 13 (1957): 242; D. Moody Smith, "Judaism and the Gospel of John," in *Jews and Christians: Exploring the Past, Present, and Future*, ed. J. H. Charlesworth (New York: Crossroad, 1990), 88–89; Jan Lambrecht, "'Synagogues of Satan' (Rev 2:9 and 3:9): Anti-Judaism in the Book of Revelation," in *Anti-Judaism and the Fourth Gospel*, 288; David Frankfurter, "Jews or Not? Reconstructing the 'Other' in Rev 2:9 and 3:9," *HTR* 94 (2001): 410.

3. Paul does something similar in Rom 2:28-29 and 9:6-9 with "Jew" and "Israel" respectively. In context, the point is that being a faithful Jew/Israelite requires more than birth status.

4. The relevant material from the HB is helpfully surveyed by Mary C. Callaway, "A Hammer That Breaks Rock in Pieces: Prophetic Critique in the Hebrew Bible," in *Anti-Semitism and Early Christianity: Issues of Polemic and Faith*, ed. Craig A. Evans and Donald A. Hagner (Minneapolis: Fortress, 1993), 21–38.

5. The Rule of the Community (1QS) supplies many of these, but derisive names and ill-wishes toward opponents, both Jewish and non-Jewish, are attested throughout the sectarian scrolls—those texts among the Dead Sea Scrolls which reflect the distinctive beliefs and practices of the Qumran community. The vocabulary, linguistic forms, and thought patterns of the sectarian texts are thoroughly probed by Devorah Dimant in "The Vocabulary of Qumran Sectarian Texts," in *Qumran und die Archäologie: Texte und Kontexte*, ed. Jörg Frey, Carsten Claussen, and Nadine Kessler, WUNT 278 (Tübingen: Mohr Siebeck, 2011), 347–95.

6. So, Luke T. Johnson, "The New Testament's Anti-Jewish Slander and the Conventions of Ancient Polemic," *JBL* 108 (1989): 419–41, although we should not,

therefore, downplay the seriousness of the charges volleyed back and forth between various competing groups.

7. See, Thiel, "'Israel' and 'Jew,'" 86–89. In fact, it might be argued that the numerical prominence of the term "Israel" in many of these texts is deceptive and that in practice "Jew" was the much more common self-designation both in Palestine and the Diaspora.

8. Readers today might be surprised by how heavily Bultmann leans upon the so-called Gnostic Redeemer myth in his commentary, or C. H. Dodd's frequent recourse to the Hermetica in *The Interpretation of the Fourth Gospel* (Cambridge: Cambridge University Press, 1953). As Barrett (*Gospel according to St. John*, 3) states: "For many years the prevailing critical opinion was that John was 'the gospel of the Hellenists'; it was written by a Greek thinker for Greeks." On the turning of the scholarly tide toward Jewish sources and backgrounds, see Meeks, "'Am I a Jew?'" 163–71.

9. The rabbinic tradition and the church fathers, to be sure, know of these passages, but unlike Ps 110 or Isa 6, they do not seem to have significantly influenced early Christian thinking about Jesus's messianic identity or served widely as apologetic arguments. On ancient Jewish interpretation of Num 21, see Jörg Frey, "'Wie Mose die Schlange in der Wüste erhöht hat . . .': Zur frühjüdischen Deutung der 'ehernen Schlange' und ihrer christologischen Rezeption in Johannes 3,14f," in *Schriftauslegung im antiken Judentum und im Urchristentum*, ed. Martin Hengel and Hermut Löhr, WUNT 73 (Tübingen: Mohr Siebeck, 1994), 153–205. On interpretation of Ps 82 in antiquity, both Jewish and Christian, see Carl Mosser, "The Earliest Patristic Interpretations of Psalm 82, Jewish Antecedents, and the Origin of Christian Deification," *JTS* NS 56 (2005): 30–74.

10. Studies of John's use of the OT are legion. Among others, C. K. Barrett, "The Old Testament in the Fourth Gospel," *JTS* 48 (1947): 155–69; M. C. Tenney, "The Old Testament and the Fourth Gospel," *BSac* 120 (1963): 300–8; E. D. Freed, *Old Testament Quotations in the Gospel of John*, NovTSup 11 (Leiden: Brill, 1965); Günter Reim, *Studien zum alttestamentlichen Hintergrund des Johannesevangeliums*, SNTSMS 22 (Cambridge: Cambridge University Press, 1974); D. A. Carson, "John and the Johannine Epistles," in *It is Written: Scripture Citing Scripture: Essays in Honour of Barnabas Lindars*, ed. D. A. Carson and H. G. M. Williamson (London: Cambridge University Press, 1998), 245–64; Anthony Tyrrell Hanson, *The Prophetic Gospel: A Study of John and the Old Testament* (Edinburgh: T&T Clark, 1991); Johannes Beutler, "The Use of 'Scripture' in the Gospel of John," in *Exploring the Gospel of John*, 147–62; Maarten J. J. Menken, "Observations on the Significance of the Old Testament in the Fourth Gospel," *Neot* 33 (1999): 125–43; Andreas J. Köstenberger, "John," in *Commentary on the New Testament Use of the Old Testament*, ed. G. K. Beale and D. A. Carson (Grand Rapids: Baker Academic, 2007), 415–512; Rekha M. Chettannu, "Scripture," in *How John Works: Storytelling in the Fourth Gospel*, ed. Douglas Estes and Ruth Sheridan, RBS 86 (Atlanta: SBL Press, 2016), 171–86; Thomas R. Hatina, ed., *Biblical Interpretation in Early Christian Gospels*, vol. 4: *The Gospel of John*, LNTS 613 (London: Bloomsbury, 2020). These

are in addition to a host of articles and monographs on John's use of specific passages, characters, or motifs from the OT.

11. Andreas Obermann, *Die christologische Erfüllung der Schrift im Johannesevangelium: Eine Untersuchung zur johanneischen Hermeneutik anhand der Schriftzitate*, WUNT 2/83 (Tübingen: Mohr Siebeck, 1996), 425. See also, Saeed Hamid-Khani, *Revelation and Concealment of Christ: A Theological Inquiry into the Elusive Language of the Fourth Gospel*, WUNT 2/120 (Tübingen: Mohr Siebeck, 2000), 132–56; Edward Gerber, *The Scriptural Tale in the Fourth Gospel: With Particular Reference to the Prologue and a Syncretic (Oral and Written) Poetics*, BibInt 147 (Leiden: Brill, 2016), 10–13, 32–63.

12. Barrett, "Old Testament in the Fourth Gospel," 155.

13. The general tenor of the present chapter thus has much in common with the arguments of Edward Gerber in *The Scriptural Tale in the Fourth Gospel*, though Gerber envisions a much more expansive retelling of Scripture in the Fourth Gospel than what I will present below. Nor does Gerber relate his findings to the question of the characterization of the Johannine Jews.

14. On the general topic of Christological interpretation of Scripture, see Donald Juel, *Messianic Exegesis: Christological Interpretation of the Old Testament in Early Christianity* (Waco, TX: Baylor University Press, 2017); Richard B. Hays, *Reading Backwards: Figural Christology and the Fourfold Gospel Witness* (Waco, TX: Baylor University Press, 2014); idem, *Echoes of Scripture in the Gospels* (Waco, TX: Baylor University Press, 2006). Studies on the use of the Jewish Scriptures in individual NT writings are too many to enumerate, but several surveys provide an orientation to the literature and interpretative issues. For example, Steve Moyise, *The Old Testament in the New: An Introduction* (London: T&T Clark, 2001); G. K. Beale and D. A. Carson, eds., *Commentary on the New Testament Use of the Old Testament* (Grand Rapids: Baker Academic, 2007); G. K. Beale, *Handbook on the New Testament Use of the Old Testament: Exegesis and Interpretation* (Grand Rapids: Baker Academic, 2012); David Allen and Steve Smith, eds., *Methodology in the Use of the Old Testament in the New: Context and Criteria*, LNTS 597 (London: T&T Clark, 2020).

15. "Jews" first appears in 2 Kgs 16:6 and 25:25. Also Jer 32:12; 34:9; 38:19; 41:3; 44:1; 52:28-30; Zech 8:23; Ezra 4:12, 23; 5:1, 5; 6:7, 8, 14; Neh 1:2; 2:16; 4:1, 2, 12; 5:17; 6:6; 13:23.

16. I give the reading of both the MT and the LXX because the textual forms underlying John's quotations are not always clear, and he may have quoted at times from memory. See, for example, Andrew Montanaro, "The Use of Memory in the Old Testament Quotations in John's Gospel," *NovT* 59 (2017): 147–70. Maarten J. J. Menken (*Old Testament Quotations in the Fourth Gospel: Studies in Textual Form*, CBET 15 [Kampen: Kok Pharos, 1996], 205–6) concludes that the LXX is the Bible of the fourth evangelist but that he also had occasional recourse to the Hebrew, a view he notes has been propounded by many others (206, n. 1).

17. Other closely associated texts include the War Scroll, Hodayot, and pesharim. Dimant ("Vocabulary," 349) notes that this group of texts was very quickly recognized as distinct and has received the designation "sectarian literature," as opposed to that literature which the community at Qumran copied but did not itself create.

18. Israel is further charged with despising the words of the prophets in CD VII, 17–18.
19. Motyer, *Your Father the Devil?* 146–50.
20. So also Callaway, "Hammer," 22. Of the Deuteronomistic History in particular, Kenton L. Sparks ("The Problem of Myth in Ancient Historiography," in *Rethinking the Foundations: Historiography in the Ancient World and in the Bible: Essays in Honour of John Van Seters*, ed. Steven L. McKenzie, Thomas Römer, and Hans Heinrich Schmid, BZAW 294 [Berlin: de Gruyter, 2000], 279) remarks: "The History presents Israel as a hopeless (or nearly hopeless) cause."
21. Callaway, "Hammer," 21.
22. Isa 64:6-7 furnishes another vivid example of this tendency in post-exilic literature. For an overview of the subject, see, among others, Rodney Alan Werline, *Penitential Prayer in Second Temple Judaism: The Development of a Religious Institution*, Early Judaism and Its Literature 13 (Atlanta: Scholars Press, 1998); Mark J. Boda, Daniel K. Falk, and Rodney A. Werline, eds., *Seeking the Favor of God*, vol. 1: *The Origins of Penitential Prayer in Second Temple Judaism*, Early Judaism and Its Literature 21 (Atlanta: SBL, 2006); idem, eds. *Seeking the Favor of God*, vol. 2: *The Development of Penitential Prayer in Second Temple Judaism*, Early Judaism and Its Literature 22 (Atlanta: SBL, 2007). A penitential piety also runs through a good number of the DSS, as shown by Mark A. Jason, *Repentance at Qumran: The Penitential Framework of Religious Experience in the Dead Sea Scrolls* (Minneapolis: Fortress, 2015).
23. The indictment of national apostasy varies in frequency and intensity in the prophetic corpus, and each book has its characteristic nomenclature. Indictments against the "house of Israel" occur frequently in Ezekiel (3:7; 6:11; 9:9; 12:9; 20:13-32; 22:18; 36:17-32) and are especially severe. "Men of Judah"/"men of Israel" (e.g., Jer 11:1-3; 18:11-12; 32:32) and "children of Israel"/"children of Judah" (Jer 7:30; 32:30-35) are mostly confined to the book of Jeremiah.
24. This, of course, includes pervasive allusions to the events at Sinai, which Eduard Käfer amply documents in *Die Rezeption der Sinaitradition im Evangelium nach Johannes*, WUNT 2/502 (Tübingen: Mohr Siebeck, 2019).
25. Adele Reinhartz, *The Word in the World: The Cosmological Tale in the Fourth Gospel*, SBLMS 45 (Atlanta: Scholars Press, 1992), 16.
26. So also, Wheaton, *Role of Jewish Feasts*, 16–17. Although some commentators (Rudolf Schnackenburg, *The Gospel according to St. John*, trans. Kevin Smyth, HThKNT [London: Burns & Oates, 1968], 269; Lindars, *The Gospel of John*, NCB [London: Marshall, Morgan & Scott, 1972], 94; Francis J. Moloney, *Gospel of John*, SP 4 [Collegeville, MN: Liturgical Press, 1998], 39, for example) give priority to associations with Jewish wisdom speculation, above all with Sir 24:8, most see in John 1:14 some allusion to the tabernacle and/or temple as the locus of God's presence among the Israelites. A notable exception is Bultmann (*Gospel of John*, 66) who, as is his *Tendenz*, makes little of the OT connections.
27. Noted especially by Hoskyns, *Fourth Gospel*, 148: "The phrase ["and we beheld his glory"] develops what is implied in the word *tabernacled* and demanded by the phrase *became flesh*." Also, Brown, *Gospel according to John*, 1:34; J. Ramsey Michaels, *The Gospel of John*, NICNT (Grand Rapids: Eerdmans, 2010), 79.

28. So, in detail, Käfer, *Rezeption der Sinaitradition*, 27–117; Anthony Tyrrell Hanson, "John 1:14-18 and Exodus 34," *NTS* 23 (1976): 90–101; also Wheaton, *Role of Jewish Feasts*, 16–18; Craig A. Evans, *Word and Glory: On the Exegetical and Theological Background of John's Prologue*, JSNTSup 89 (Sheffield: JSOT Press, 1993), 79–82. Although it is likely that not all commentators would describe Exod 33–34 as the "guiding imagery" of John 1:14-18, as Keener (*Gospel of John*, 405) does, nearly all find some allusion to this scene or to Exodus symbolism more broadly; similarly, Johannes Beutler, *Das Johannesevangelium: Kommentar* (Freiburg: Herder, 2013), 94.

29. At Exod 34:6 the LXX reads πολυέλεος καὶ ἀληθινός. Nonetheless, that the evangelist alludes to the passage is now close to a consensus position. So, Wheaton, *Role of Jewish Feasts*, 18; Wayne A. Meeks, *The Prophet-King: Moses Traditions and the Johannine Christology*, NovTSup 14 (Leiden: Brill, 1967), 288, n. 2; Reim, *Studien zum alttestamentlichen Hintergrund*, 140; Hanson, "John 1:14-18"; idem, *Prophetic Gospel*, 25, in addition to many commentators. Bultmann (*Gospel of John*, 74) is again an exception. He rejects any allusion to Exod 34:6, since he judges that the Johannine concepts of grace and truth are more indebted to Greek thought.

Although the Hebrew *ḥesed* and Greek *charis* have different semantic ranges, they are sufficiently close in meaning that writers like Paul and Philo often have *charis*, where the underlying Hebrew has *ḥesed* and the LXX has *eleos*. See, for example, James D. G. Dunn, *The Theology of Paul the Apostle* (Grand Rapids: Eerdmans, 1998), 321 (with respect to Paul) and E. E. Flack, "The Concept of Grace in Biblical Thought," in *Biblical Studies in Memory of H. C. Alleman*, ed. J. M. Myers, O. Reimherr, and H. N. Bream (Locust Valley, NY: J. J. Augustin, 1960), 139–45 (with respect to Philo). It could also be that the evangelist is not aiming for an exact quotation. It should be noted in that connection that in Exod 34:6, God also describes himself as gracious (*chanun*).

30. Similarly, Jerome H. Neyrey, "The Jacob Allusions in John 1:51," *CBQ* 44 (1982): 586–605. Justin comes back to this argument several times in *Dial.* 56–127.

31. So also Hanson, *Prophetic Gospel*, 21, 166; idem, *Jesus Christ in the Old Testament* (London: SPCK, 1965), 104–26; Charles Gieschen, "The Real Presence of the Son Before Christ: Revisiting an Old Approach to Old Testament Christology," *Concordia Theological Quarterly* 68 (2004): 105–26.

32. The background for the "I am" statement in John 8:58 may lie in the "I am he" statements of Deutero-Isaiah. See, for example, the discussion by Catrin Williams, *I Am He: The Interpretation of 'Anî Hû' in Jewish and Early Christian Literature*, WUNT 2/113 (Tübingen: Mohr Siebeck, 2000), 275–83. Jesus's pronouncement may also echo the revelation of God's name to Moses in Exod 3:14. In the LXX of Exodus, God reveals his name as the "one who is," but as noted above, the scriptural quotations in John do not agree completely with any of the major textual traditions known to us, so the wording of the LXX cannot be determinative of the allusion in John 8:58. In either case, Jesus's self-claim is extraordinary and strikes its hearers as blasphemy worthy of stoning.

33. Although this would not exclude seeing by the patriarch of the Messiah's future glory as well. See, for example, Catrin Williams, "Patriarchs and Prophets

Remembered: Framing Israel's Past in the Gospel of John," in *Abiding Words: The Use of Scripture in the Gospel of John*, ed. Alicia D. Myers and Bruce G. Schuchard, RBS 81 (Atlanta: SBL Press, 2015), 205.

34. With Nils Dahl, "The Johannine Church and History," in idem, *Jesus in the Memory of the Early Church* (Minneapolis: Augsburg, 1976), 100; Neyrey, "Jacob Allusions," 590; Hanson, *Prophetic Gospel*, 131; Steven A. Hunt, "And the Word Became Flesh—Again? Jesus and Abraham in John 8:31-59," in *Perspectives on Our Father Abraham: Essays in Honor of Marvin R. Wilson*, ed. Steven A. Hunt (Grand Rapids: Eerdmans, 2010), 81–109 at 96–101.

35. For a thorough analysis of the use of Isa 52–53 in John 12:12, see Daniel J. Brendsel, *"Isaiah Saw His Glory": The Use of Isaiah 52-53 in John*, BZNW 208 (Berlin: de Gruyter, 2014).

36. The German is *"über die Erde schreitende Gott"* from Käsemann's *Jesu letzter Wille nach Johannes 17* (Tübingen: Mohr Siebeck, 1966), 22. Ashton *(John and Christian Origins,* 157, n. 1*)* notes possible antecedents to Käsemann's famous phrase in the works of Wrede and Bultmann.

37. We see a prime example of this in Judges 13 when the angel of the LORD appears to Manoah's wife and then makes another visitation to the two of them together. It is only after the angel of the LORD, inextricably associated with the LORD himself, has ascended in the flames of their offering that they realize God had appeared to them. Manoah, coming to the recognition that they have encountered God, exclaims in fear: "We are doomed to die! . . . We have seen God." A similar story is told in Jdg 6 about Gideon. See also the scene in Gen 32:24-30, where Jacob wrestles with a man through the night before concluding that he has seen God face to face, and yet his life was spared. For a helpful analysis of the theophanies in the Pentateuch, see Nevada Levi Delapp, *Theophanic "Type-Scenes" in The Pentateuch: Visions of YHWH*, Library of Hebrew Bible/Old Testament 660 (London: Bloomsbury T&T Clark, 2018). Interestingly, many of the OT theophanies invoke categories of "seeing" or "vision," a theme which saturates the Fourth Gospel. Jesus famously tells the disciples in John 14:9: "Whoever has seen me has seen the Father. How can you say, 'Show us the Father'?"

38. Similarly, Gerber, *Scriptural Tale*, 305–26.

39. The background of Johannine signs in the exodus tradition is noted by Brown, *Gospel according to John*, 1:529; Evans, *Word and Glory*, 140; D. Moody Smith, *The Theology of the Gospel of John* (Cambridge: Cambridge University Press, 1995), 108; Andrew C. Brunson, *Psalm 118 in the Gospel of John: An Intertextual Study on the New Exodus Pattern in the Theology of John*, WUNT 2/158 (Tübingen: Mohr Siebeck, 2003), 162, among others.

40. Williams, "Patriarchs and Prophets," 190. The concepts of keying and framing have been developed by Barry Schwartz. See, among other studies, Barry Schwartz, "Memory as a Cultural System: Abraham Lincoln in World War II," *American Sociological Review* 61 (1996): 908–27; idem, "Frame Images: Towards a Semiotics of Collective Memory," *Semiotica* 121 (1998): 1–40; idem, *Abraham Lincoln and the Forge of National Memory* (Chicago: University of Chicago Press, 2000), 252; idem, "Where There's Smoke, There's Fire: Memory and History," in *Memory and Identity*

in Ancient Judaism and Early Christianity: A Conversation with Barry Schwartz, ed. Tom Thatcher, SemeiaSt 78 (Atlanta: SBL Press, 2014), 7–40. As Schwartz ("Where There's Smoke," 15) describes keying as an "aspect of typology," it is not surprising that we encounter this function of social memory in the Fourth Gospel. Among applications of social memory theory to the New Testament, see Alan Kirk and Tom Thatcher, eds., *Memory, Tradition, and Text: Uses of the Past in Early Christianity*, SemeiaSt 52 (Atlanta: SBL Press, 2005); Alan Kirk, *Memory and the Jesus Tradition* (London: Bloomsbury, 2018); Thomas R. Hatina, ed., *Biblical Interpretation in Early Christian Gospels*, 181–236.

41. On the role of these recitations in the shaping of Jewish collective memory in the Second Temple period, see Aubrey E. Buster, *Remembering the Story of Israel: Historical Summaries and Memory Formation in Second Temple Judaism* (Cambridge: Cambridge University Press, 2022). To be sure, the wilderness narratives also convey themes of God's provision and mercy toward his people. Buster thus states (ibid., 304): "The wilderness is remembered as a site of successful petition, pneumatic vitality, fateful sin, and divine provision."

42. This is almost universally noted by commentators. See also the studies of Susan Hylen, *Allusion and Meaning in John 6*, BZNW 137 (Berlin: de Gruyter, 2005), 149–52 and Sheridan, *Retelling Scripture: "The Jews" and the Scriptural Citations in John 1:19-12:15*, BibInt 110 (Leiden: Brill, 2012), 135–58; Käfer, *Rezeption der Sinaitradition*, 294. Bultmann (*Gospel of John*, 229) briefly considers the connection but does not lend it much weight.

43. *Gezerah shavah* was one of the rabbinic "rules" of exegesis (*middot*)—common methods of interpretation of biblical texts and legal precedents. These *middot* were gathered into several collections, associated with famous teachers. For an introduction to rabbinic exegesis and the collation of these *middot*, see H. L. Strack and Günter Stemberger, *Introduction to the Talmud and Midrash*, trans. and ed. Markus Bockmuehl, 2nd ed. (Minneapolis: Fortress, 1996), 15–30. Association or analogy by catchphrase presents itself in a variety of forms in ancient Jewish literature. On this, see Williams, "John, Judaism, and Searching the Scriptures," 83–94. Among the Dead Sea Scrolls, 4Q Florilegium furnishes a good example of how this general interpretive approach could be employed.

44. So also, Brown, *Gospel according to John*, 1:529; Evans, *Word and Glory*, 140; Brunson, *Psalm 118 in the Gospel of John*, 162. Daniel H. Fletcher, *Signs in the Wilderness: Intertextuality and the Testing of Nicodemus* (Eugene, OR: Wipf & Stock, 2014), 23, 83–84; Gerber, *Scriptural Tale*, 307, though only briefly.

45. Ex 16:3: ויאמרו אלהם בני ישׂראל מי־יתן מותנו ביד יהוה בארץ מצרים/καὶ εἶπαν πρὸς αὐτοὺς οἱ υἱοὶ Ισραηλ Ὄφελον ἀπεθάνομεν πληγέντες ὑπὸ κυρίου ἐν γῇ Αἰγύπτῳ; Num 14:2 ויאמרו אלהם כל־העדה לו מתנו בארץ מצרים או במדבר הזה לו מתנו/καὶ εἶπαν πρὸς αὐτοὺς πᾶσα ἡ συναγωγή Ὄφελον ἀπεθάνομεν ἐν γῇ Αἰγύπτῳ, ἢ ἐν τῇ ἐρήμῳ ταύτῃ εἰ ἀπεθάνομεν.

46. Ex 16:10: והנה כבוד יהוה נראה בענן/καὶ ἡ δόξα κυρίου ὤφθη ἐν νεφέλῃ; Num 14:10: וכבוד יהוה נראה באהל מועד/καὶ ἡ δόξα κυρίου ὤφθη ἐν νεφέλῃ ἐπὶ τῆς σκηνῆς τοῦ μαρτυρίου. The two passages are more closely aligned in the LXX with its inclusion of the cloud in Num 14:10.

47. As Fletcher (*Signs in the Wilderness*, 84, n. 74) observes, an allusion to Num 14:11 in John 12:37 fares well against the criteria that Richard B. Hays lays out in his influential *Echoes of Scripture in the Letters of Paul* (New Haven: Yale University Press, 1989), 29–32. In effect, what I have just been doing is implicitly applying Hays's criteria of availability, volume, and thematic coherence.

48. Brown, *Gospel according to John*, 1:485; also Evans, *Word and Glory*, 140; D. A. Carson, *The Gospel according to John* (Grand Rapids: Eerdmans, 1991), 447.

49. Evans, *Word and Glory*, 140: "It is apparent that the Fourth Evangelist's understanding of faith, or the lack of it, is significantly informed by traditions relating to Moses, especially in reference to God's mighty works and 'signs.'" So also, Marianne Maye Thompson, "Signs and Faith in the Fourth Gospel," *BBR* 1 (1991): 89–108.

50. This complex of themes is part and parcel of a larger motif of the "rejected prophet." On this motif in John 12:37-44, see Sandra Huebenthal, "Proclamation Rejected, Truth Confirmed: Reading John 12:37-44 in a Social Memory Theoretical Framework," in *Biblical Interpretation in Early Christian Gospels*, 183–200.

51. Similarly, Gerber (*Scriptural Tale*, 15) states: "If the fe [Fourth Evangelist] believed (as he did) that God had acted faithfully in Jesus to renew and save Israel, and if he was embroiled in a theological battle with fellow Jews (as the majority of Johannine scholars believe he was), then the fe [Fourth Evangelist] could implicitly witness against his Jewish interlocutors, and/or provoke them to faith, by framing his story of Jesus around the key events of Israel's story . . . . The resonant message would be: as God was faithful in the particulars of the past, my fellow Jews, and your ancestors were unfaithful, so God has been faithful again, *in the same particulars*, and *now, again*, you are being unfaithful."

52. Williams, "Patriarchs and Prophets," 192.

53. It is uncertain, however, to what extent the author of the Gospel of John knew the Book of Judges. This phenomenon in Judges would seem to attest to the influence of the Torah in the composition of the Deuteronomistic History or simply to a common Israelite tradition of historiographical convention.

54. It bears noting in this context that the evangelist turns to the desert wandering narratives in an effort to make sense of the lack of receptivity toward Jesus, much like in Rom 11 where Paul invokes the career of the prophet Elijah as precedent for Jewish opposition to God's revelation. Each thus tries to make what, for them was the theological conundrum of Israel's unbelief intelligible by keying present circumstances to the remembered past. This coheres with Alan Kirk's observation (*Memory and the Jesus Tradition*, 167) that this type of memorializing activity becomes especially pronounced in times of communal crisis. See also, Tom Thatcher, "Keys, Frames, and the Problem of the Past," in *Memory and* Identity, 2.

Conclusion

John and the Jews in Retrospect

Whence does the fourth evangelist write, not in terms of geography but in terms of social and ethnic self-identification? J. Louis Martyn, with many others in train, placed John and his community in a setting of social ferment and transition. Ethnic Jews who had come to believe in Jesus now found themselves cut off from the heart of Jewish communal life. As a threatened minority, they reciprocated the anger directed at them by renouncing their own Jewish identity and projecting this new state of relations back into the life of Jesus. I argued in ch. 1 that for all its explanatory power, this aspect of the synagogue-expulsion hypothesis, and religious-schism models more generally, stands in need of reassessment. The purported evidence for ethnically Jewish believers in Jesus relinquishing the name Ἰουδαῖοι is unreliable or ambiguous. The internal evidence of the Gospel also speaks against a renunciation of Jewish identity on the part of the evangelist. John exhibits what I have called a sectarian mentality, claiming Israel's heritage for Jesus and his followers and denying it to Jesus's opponents. According to the consensus reading, we must envision a group of ethnically Jewish believers in Jesus who asserted their continuity with Israel's past and their right to the name "Israel" but rejected the title "Jew" for themselves.

In chs. 2 and 3, I undertook a reevaluation of the evangelist's characterization of those named οἱ Ἰουδαῖοι. On the whole, the Johannine Jews are indeed portrayed as unreceptive of Jesus. They are very often Jesus's staunch opponents. Nevertheless, to reduce all Jews in the narrative to this role does not do justice to their diversity of response. Some of the Gospel's Jewish characters are sympathetic to Jesus. Among other groups of Jews there is division. A few individuals put their faith in Jesus. This dialectic of division, I endeavored to show in ch. 2, is not undone by the frequency of the phrase οἱ Ἰουδαῖοι nor its ostensible erasure of internal differentiation. When other

Jewish authors of roughly this period (above all, Josephus) speak of "Jews" or "the Jews," context indicates which group of Jews is acting at that point in the narrative. Sometimes the reference is to the customs or beliefs of the Jewish people, but often it is much narrower: the Jews of a particular time and place whose actions may or may not be representative of their people. The Fourth Gospel exhibits a similar pattern. The Jews of 11:36, for example, are specifically those Jews (or more accurately, some of them) who have come to visit Mary and Martha to mourn for Lazarus. We must always ask which particular subset of the Jews the evangelist has in mind as the referent of the term expands and contracts throughout the Gospel. Thus, a statement about the Jews in one part of the Gospel should not necessarily be transferred to those in another section. The name "Jew" has not become synonymous with someone who opposes Jesus. In this way, positive Jewish responses to Jesus can stand alongside the Gospel's pronounced theme of the rejection of Jesus by "his own."

Nor is this dialectic of faith and unbelief within the Jewish people collapsed through a process of alienation (ch. 3). That is, the fourth evangelist does not disassociate Jesus from the Jewish people or oppose Jewish identity and faith in Christ as mutually exclusive. Although John has assuredly reinterpreted Jewish custom and practice through a Christological lens and subordinated them to faith in Jesus, it is hard to extrapolate much about the religious life of the evangelist or those for whom he writes. Moreover, when Jesus, the disciples, or John the Baptist are said to perform some action in relation to the Jews, it is likely of little import, since even Caiaphas is said to have advised the Jews (18:14). Given that it is not only Jesus and his disciples who are set over against the Jews and that Jesus's status as a Jew is fundamental to the Gospel's Christology, it seems most reasonable to interpret the juxtaposition as a literary convention. John would have been familiar with this way of speaking from Israel's Scriptures, as the people of Israel and its leaders are often distinguished without implying that the latter are not Israelites themselves.

Chapters 2 and 3 are meant as a corrective to readings of the Gospel that universalize Jewish unbelief. Yet to say that John does not stereotype the Jews is not to neutralize the Gospel's criticism. Some rationale must be given for the evangelist's preference for the designation οἱ Ἰουδαῖοι over others that were available to him. My principal contribution to this question (ch. 5) is that the criticism of the Jews in the Fourth Gospel is modeled after the intramural criticism of the Israelites in Israel's Scriptures. John 1:1-18 and 12:37-50 frame the typology. Jesus manifests the glory of God, but just as the Israelites rebelled against God in the wilderness, so too Jesus's contemporaries refused to believe in spite of the signs which he performed. The evangelist writes as someone who still numbered himself among the Jewish people but who saw in the response to Jesus a recapitulation of Israel's past.

To a lesser extent, other factors may have contributed to the frequency of the ethnonym "the Jews" in the Fourth Gospel. In ch. 4, I entertained the possibility that John did not view greater Judea as monolithically Jewish. Jesus teaches and performs signs primarily among the Jews, but Samaritans and foreign visitors to Jerusalem also have minor roles to play in the Gospel. Consciousness of a multi-ethnic Palestine may help explain why the Gospel occasionally differentiates the Jews from some other group when this would otherwise seem superfluous. Moreover, despite the many unknowns about the Gospel's recipients, the explanation of Jewish customs intimates that at least some were Gentiles unfamiliar with aspects of Jewish life, culture, and ritual. If so, the evangelist may have suited his terminology for those less attuned to the various parties in mid-first-century Judea. Nevertheless, these potential influences on John's patterns in nomenclature stand in an ancillary position to the argument of ch. 5.

SITUATING THE EVANGELIST

I have sought throughout this study to let John be John: to understand the Gospel of John and its author on their own terms. However, in the course of historically contextualizing a text and its author(s), the question of analogues naturally arises. Are there figures or groups who inhabit a similar social and religious world or whose theological perspectives resemble that of the fourth evangelist? The analysis of Reinhartz, for example, puts the Gospel of John close in outlook to those church fathers who believed that God had rejected the Jewish people and replaced them with the Gentiles, who were now God's covenant people, the inheritors of all the blessings promised to the people of Israel.[1] She writes:

> That some of the Fathers read John as a history of God's turning from the synagogue to the church, from the Jews to the Gentiles, has no historical bearing on the real audience of the Fourth Gospel. Cyril, Augustine, and the other Fathers were writing centuries later than John, after the church had become a primarily gentile enterprise. Nevertheless, their reading of John suggests that the Gospel too may be advocating this same view of history as part of its rhetorical agenda.[2]

The weight of my argument, for its part, puts the fourth evangelist much closer in outlook to a figure like the apostle Paul than to the church fathers of the ensuing centuries. Both John and Paul present faith in Jesus as faithfulness to the God of Israel. They proclaim Jesus as the source of eternal life for a world that is passing away under the power of sin. They ascribe the gift of eternal life—the adoption as God's children—to those who believe, independent of the believer's ethnic affiliation. And Paul, like John, speaks of a divine hardening of the Jewish people (Rom 11:7, 25), a spiritual blindness that the prophets had foretold (v. 8).[3] Yet for all of the novelty in Paul's thought, he continued to identify as a Jew. And he persisted in the belief that God's faithfulness to Israel was unwavering, foreign (or noxious) as Paul's version of that enduring commitment may have seemed to his Jewish contemporaries. God had not rejected the Jewish people because his gifts and call are irrevocable (Rom 11:29). Would the evangelist have seen in Paul's theological ruminations on God's faithfulness to Israel religious convictions in harmony with his own? I suspect so.[4] We may say, at the very least, that the Scriptures in which John was immersed, in which he lived and breathed, and by which Paul likewise was nourished, speak not only of Israel's chronic unfaithfulness to the LORD but also of the LORD's steadfast commitment to his people. They speak of a God who chose one nation out of the many to be his treasured possession, a God who disciplined his people but who always promised to forgive and restore them.[5] With the depth of the evangelist's scriptural knowledge, he assuredly knew these stories and the prophetic assurances of a future for Israel just as he knew the stories of Israel's infidelity. Indeed, texts like Exod 33–34 and Num 14, to which the evangelist has keyed the story of Jesus's earthly career, also reaffirm God's covenantal faithfulness to Israel despite their fateful sins. They are stories of Israel's rebellion but also of God's unending mercy. The LORD, they remind the reader, is a compassionate and gracious God, slow to anger, abounding in love and faithfulness (Exod 34:5-7; Num 14:17-19). He does not abandon his people because he cannot deny his own character. We best understand the evangelist, I suggest, within this complex of traditions—a scripturally-formed believer in Jesus who saw himself, however others in antiquity appraised matters, as working from within the Jewish fold.

IMPLICATIONS AND REFLECTIONS

One of the appeals of Martyn's two-level reading is its specificity. He invites the reader to imagine life in John's city, to consider the day-to-day experiences of a small band of beleaguered Christians, to hear in the exalted cadences of Jesus the voice of a preacher in this community. My own account of the Gospel's historical setting remains more impressionistic: a Jewish author writing from somewhere in the Greek-speaking world for an audience about which we know relatively little, an author who interprets Jesus's earthly ministry and the hostility it aroused on the analogy of God's relationship with wayward Israel.

If, according to my reconstruction, the precise historical circumstances of the Gospel's composition fade partially from view, John's theological perspective—the asymmetry between God's revelation and the human response to it—becomes more prominent. The daily experience of the evangelist or the community of Johannine Christians is probably beyond recovery, but perhaps in the evangelist's attitude toward Jesus's Jewish contemporaries, we are able to retrieve something of the internal tension of an author and theologian on the margins: a self-conscious member of the Jewish people who believed that most of his own had gone astray. In that respect, the Fourth Gospel serves as a witness to the separation of Christianity and Judaism in a qualified sense. It could be said from the outside that two religions were forming or had already formed, but this is not how John casts it. This does not make the Fourth Gospel any less challenging to modern Jewish and Christian sensibilities. In our case, even if the evangelist felt an abiding attachment to the Jewish people and even if he would look aghast at what some have made of his words, as a Jewish believer in Jesus, he occupies what in the development of Judaism and Christianity quickly became a no man's land, caught between church and synagogue. And how we ought to categorize that social and religious stance has proven contentious and methodologically fraught. Would this make the Fourth Gospel a Jewish text? An anti-Jewish text? A text that stands within the Jewish tradition? A text that decisively breaks from the Jewish tradition? The answer will depend on how one construes the defining characteristics of Judaism or Jewish identity, the meaning we assign to each of our labels, and the importance we give to an individual's self-ascription. To make that judgment was not my task in this work.

That is not to say that the historical and philological arguments which I've presented contribute nothing to that ongoing conversation. In practice (if not always in theory), our ethical judgments about a text or other act of communication are usually not detached from our perception of their intent. For example, among the many abuses of the Bible that infested Nazi-era Germany, one of the most absurd came from the hand of Johannes Hempel, then professor of OT at Göttingen. While others were anxious to discard the OT as a corrupting influence on a pure, *völkisch* Christianity, Hempel saw its lasting value as "the most strongly anti-Semitic book of world literature."[6] The claim is absurd not because the Scriptures are optimistic about Israel's history as a people. As we have seen, sustained criticism of the Israelites is endemic to many of the OT writings. Hempel's statement is outlandish, rather, because it exteriorizes a critique that was meant for insiders. We reflexively see that he distorted the intent of the Jewish Scriptures. What the original authors meant and where they stood in relation to the people of Israel affects how we evaluate their polemic. Similarly, few would confuse the harangues of the Hebrew Scriptures against Israel and Judah and, say, the virulence masked as harsh mercy of Martin Luther's *On the Jews and Their Lies*. They are as far apart in intention as in time, and we judge them accordingly. The question of the evangelist's self-understanding, therefore, belongs to the broader conversation about the Gospel of John and anti-Judaism: What was John trying to do, how was the text received, and what does that mean for Jews and Christians today?

NOTES

1. As a careful historian, Reinhartz acknowledges the temporal distance between the Gospel of John and church fathers like Cyril of Alexandria and John Chrysostom. Yet, it is clear that she sees an affinity in their rhetorical programs with respect to the Jewish people.

2. Reinhartz, *Cast Out*, 150.

3. For an assessment of the relationship between John and Paul, see Jürgen Becker, "Das Verhältnis des johanneischen Kreises zum Paulinismus: Anregungen zur Belebung einer Diskussion," in *Paulus und Johannes: Exegetische Studien zur paulinischen und johanneischen Theologie und Literatur*, ed. Dieter Sänger and Ulrich Mell, WUNT 198 (Tübingen: Mohr Siebeck, 2006), 473–95; Stanley Porter, "Johannine and Pauline Christology," in *Johannine Christology*, ed. idem and Andrew W. Pitts, Johannine Studies 3 (Leiden: Brill, 2020), 11–30.

4. A more confident answer would require a study of its own. Nor is this to say that the fourth evangelist would have shared all the nuances of Paul's argument in Rom 9–11. It is to suggest, however, that John, like Paul, is best understood as an ethnic Jew who continued to esteem the Jews as his own people, with whose ancestors God had entered into an unbreakable covenant.

5. It is precisely that dynamic of judgment and restoration that underlies Paul's argumentation in Rom 9–11.

6. Johannes Hempel, *Das alte Testament und die völkische Idee* (Bonn: Gebr. Scheur, 1935), 8. From 1937 to 1945, Hempel directed the Institutum Judaicum in Berlin, a center for Protestant studies of Judaism. His career and work are surveyed by Susannah Heschel, *The Aryan Jesus: Christian Theologians and the Bible in Nazi Germany* (Princeton: Princeton University Press, 2008), 170–71. Cornelia Weber (*Altes Testament und völkische Frage: Der biblische Volksbegriff in der alttestamentlichen Wissenschaft der nationalsozialistischen Zeit, dargestellt am Beispiel von Johannes Hempel*, FAT 28 [Tübingen: Mohr Siebeck, 2000]) provides a more detailed account of Hempel's theology in relation to Nazi racial ideology.

Bibliography

Aberle, Moritz von. "Über die Zweck des Johannesevangeliums." *TQ* 42 (1861): 37–94.

Aland, Barbara, et al., eds. *Nestle-Aland Novum Testamentum Graece*. Edited by Holger Strutwolf and the Institute for New Testament Textual Research. 28th ed. Stuttgart: Deutsche Bibelgesellschaft, 2012.

Allen, David, and Steve Smith, eds. *Methodology in the Use of the Old Testament in the New: Context and Criteria*, LNTS 597. London: T&T Clark, 2020.

Anderson, Paul N., Felix Just, S.J., and Tom Thatcher, eds. *Critical Appraisals of Critical Views*. Vol. 1 of *John, Jesus, and History*. SymS 44. Atlanta: Society of Biblical Literature, 2007.

———, eds. *Aspects of Historicity in the Fourth Gospel*. Vol. 2 of *John, Jesus, and History*. ECL 2. Atlanta: Society of Biblical Literature, 2009.

———, eds. *Glimpses of Jesus through the Johannine Lens*. Vol. 3 of *John, Jesus, and History*. ECL 18. Atlanta: SBL Press, 2016.

Appelbaum, Alan. "'The Idumaeans' in Josephus' *The Jewish War*." *JSJ* 40 (2009): 1–22.

———. "On the Apostasy of Tiberius Julius Alexander." *JAJ* (2023): 47–76.

Ashton, John. "The Identity and Function of the Ἰουδαῖοι in the Fourth Gospel." *NovT* 27 (1985): 40–75.

———. *Understanding the Fourth Gospel*. Oxford: Oxford University Press, 1991.

———. *Understanding the Fourth Gospel*. 2nd ed. Oxford: Oxford University Press, 2007.

———. *The Gospel of John and Christian Origins*. Minneapolis: Fortress, 2014.

Augenstein, Jörg. "Jesus und das Gesetz im Johannesevangelium." *Kirche und Israel* 14 (1999): 161–79.

———. "'Euer Gesetz': Ein Pronomen und die johanneische Haltung zum Gesetz." *ZNW* 88 (1997): 311–13.

Aune, David E. *Revelation*. 3 vols. WBC 52A-52C. Dallas, TX: Word, 1997–1998.

Aviam, Mordechai. *Jews, Pagans and Christians in the Galilee: 25 Years of Archaeological Excavations and Surveys Hellenistic to Byzantine Periods*. Rochester, NY: University of Rochester Press, 2004.

Aviam, Mordechai, and Peter Richardson. "Appendix A: Josephus' Galilee in Archaeological Perspective." Pages 177–211 in *Life of Josephus: Translation and Commentary*. Vol. 9 of *Flavius Josephus: Translation and Commentary*. Edited by Steve Mason. Leiden: Brill, 2001.

Barclay, John M. G. "Paul among Diaspora Jews: Anomaly or Apostate?" *JSNT* 60 (1995): 89–120.

———. *Jews in the Mediterranean Diaspora: From Alexander to Trajan (323 BCE-117 CE)*. Berkeley: University of California Press, 1996.

———. "Who Was Considered an Apostate in the Jewish Diaspora?" Pages 80–98 in *Tolerance and Intolerance in Early Judaism and Christianity*. Edited by Graham N. Stanton and Guy G. Stroumsa. Cambridge: Cambridge University Press, 1998.

———. *Paul and the Gift*. Grand Rapids: Eerdmans, 2015.

Barrett, C. K. "The Old Testament in the Fourth Gospel." *JTS* 48 (1947): 155–69.

———. *A Commentary on the First Epistle to the Corinthians*. 2nd ed. BNTC. London: Black, 1971.

———. *The Gospel of John and Judaism*. Translated by D. M. Smith. Philadelphia: Fortress, 1975.

———. *The Gospel according to St. John*. 2nd ed. Philadelphia: Westminster, 1978.

Barton, Stephen C. "Can We Identify the Gospel Audiences?" Pages 173–94 in *The Gospels for All Christians: Rethinking the Gospel Audiences*. Edited by Richard Bauckham. Grand Rapids: Eerdmans, 1998.

Bassler, Jouette M. "The Galileans: A Neglected Factor in Johannine Community Research." *CBQ* 43 (1981): 243–57.

Bauckham, Richard. *The Theology of the Book of Revelation*. New Testament Theology. Cambridge: Cambridge University Press, 1993.

———, ed. *The Gospels for All Christians: Rethinking the Gospel Audiences*. Grand Rapids: Eerdmans, 1998.

———. "For Whom Were Gospels Written?" Pages 9–48 in *The Gospels for All Christians: Rethinking the Gospel Audiences*. Edited by Richard Bauckham. Grand Rapids: Eerdmans, 1998.

———. "The Audience of the Fourth Gospel." Pages 101–12 in *Jesus in Johannine Tradition*. Edited by Robert T. Fortna and Tom Thatcher. Louisville: Westminster John Knox, 2001.

———. *Jesus and the Eyewitnesses: The Gospels as Eyewitness Testimony*. Grand Rapids: Eerdmans, 2006.

———. "Historiographical Characteristics of the Gospel of John." *NTS* 53 (2007): 17–36.

———. *Jesus and the God of Israel: God Crucified and Other Studies on the New Testament's Christology of Divine Identity*. Grand Rapids: Eerdmans, 2008.

———. "Is There Patristic Counter-Evidence? A Response to Margaret Mitchell." Pages 68–110 in *The Audience of the Gospels: The Origin and Function of the*

Gospels in Early Christianity. Edited by Edward W. Klink III. LNTS 353. London: T&T Clark, 2010.
Bauckham, Richard, and Carl Mosser, eds. *The Gospel of John and Christian Theology*. Grand Rapids: Eerdmans, 2008.
Bauer, Elvira. *Trau keinem Fuchs auf grüner Heid und keinem Jud auf seinem Eid.* Nuremberg: Stürmer, 1936.
Bauer, Walter, et al. *Greek-English Lexicon of the New Testament and Other Early Christian Literature*. 3rd ed. Chicago: University of Chicago Press, 2000.
Baumbach, Günther. "Antijudaismus im neuen Testament: Fragestellung und Lösungsmöglichkeit." *Kairós* 25 (1983): 68–85.
Beale, G. K. *Handbook on the New Testament Use of the Old Testament: Exegesis and Interpretation*. Grand Rapids: Baker Academic, 2012.
Beale, G. K., and D. A. Carson, eds. *Commentary on the New Testament Use of the Old Testament*. Grand Rapids: Baker Academic, 2007.
Beasley-Murray, George R. *John*. 2nd ed. WBC 36. Nashville, TN: Thomas Nelson, 1999.
Becker, Jürgen. *Das Evangelium nach Johannes*. 2 vols. ÖTK 4. Gütersloh: Mohn, 1979.
———. *Paul, Apostle to the Gentiles*. Translated by O. C. Dean. Louisville: Westminster John Knox, 1993.
———. "Das Verhältnis des johanneischen Kreises zum Paulinismus: Anregungen zur Belebung einer Diskussion." Pages 473–95 in *Paulus und Johannes: Exegetische Studien zur paulinischen und johanneischen Theologie und Literatur.* Edited by Dieter Sänger and Ulrich Mell. WUNT 198. Tübingen: Mohr Siebeck, 2006.
Bekken, Per Jarle. *The Lawsuit Motif in John's Gospel from New Perspectives: Jesus Christ, Crucified Criminal and Emperor of the World*. NovTSup 158. Leiden: Brill, 2015.
Belser, Johannes. "Der Ausdruck οἱ Ἰουδαῖοι im Johannesevangelium." *Theologische Quartalschrift* 84 (1902): 168–222.
Bennema, Cornelis. "A Theory of Character in the Fourth Gospel with Reference to Ancient and Modern Literature." *BibInt* 17 (2009): 375–421.
———. "The Identity and Composition of οἱ Ἰουδαῖοι in the Gospel of John." *TynBul* 60 (2009): 239–63.
Bernier, Jonathan. *Aposynagōgos and the Historical Jesus in John: Rethinking the Historicity of the Johannine Expulsion Passages*. BibInt 122. Leiden: Brill, 2013.
Beutler, Johannes. "The Use of 'Scripture' in the Gospel of John." Pages 147–62 in *Exploring the Gospel of John: In Honor of D. Moody Smith*. Edited by R. Alan Culpepper and C. Clifton Black. Louisville: Westminster John Knox, 1996.
———. *Judaism and the Jews in the Gospel of John*. StudBib 30. Rome: Pontifical Biblical Institute, 2006.
———. *Das Johannesevangelium: Kommentar*. Freiburg: Herder, 2013.
Bieringer, Reimund, Didier Pollefeyt, and Frederique Vandecasteele-Vanneuville, eds. *Anti-Judaism and the Fourth Gospel*. Louisville: Westminster John Knox, 2001.

———. "Wrestling with Johannine Anti-Judaism: A Hermeneutical Framework for the Analysis of the Current Debate." Pages 3–37 in *Anti-Judaism and the Fourth Gospel*. Edited by Reimund Bieringer, Didier Pollefeyt, and Frederique Vandecasteele-Vanneuville. Louisville: Westminster John Knox, 2001.

Blumhofer, Christopher M. *The Gospel of John and the Future of Israel*. SNTSMS 177. Cambridge: Cambridge University Press, 2020.

Boda, Mark J., Daniel K. Falk, and Rodney A. Werline, eds. *Seeking the Favor of God*, vol. 1: *The Origins of Penitential Prayer in Second Temple Judaism*. Early Judaism and Its Literature 21. Atlanta: SBL, 2006.

———, eds. *Seeking the Favor of God*, vol. 2: *The Development of Penitential Prayer in Second Temple Judaism*. Early Judaism and Its Literature 22. Atlanta: SBL, 2007.

Boer, Martinus C. de. "L'Évangile de Jean et le christianisme juif (nazoréen)." Pages 179–204 in *Le déchirement: Juifs et chrétiens au premier siècle*. Edited by Daniel Marguerat. MdB 32. Geneva: Labor et Fides, 1996.

———. "The Nazoreans: Living at the Boundary of Judaism and Christianity." Pages 239–62 in *Tolerance and Intolerance in Early Judaism and Christianity*. Edited by Graham N. Stanton and Guy G. Stroumsa. Cambridge: Cambridge University Press, 1998.

———. "The Depiction of 'the Jews' in John's Gospel: Matters of Behavior and Identity." Pages 141–57 in *Anti-Judaism and the Fourth Gospel*. Edited by Reimund Bieringer, Didier Pollefeyt, and Frederique Vandecasteele-Vanneuville. Louisville: Westminster John Knox, 2001.

Boismard, M.-E. and A. Lamouille. *Un évangile pré-johannique*. 3 vols. EBib 17. Paris: Gabalda, 1993.

Borden, Sarah. *Edith Stein*. Outstanding Christian Thinkers. London: Continuum, 2003.

Borgen, Peder. *Bread from Heaven: An Exegetical Study of the Concept of Manna in the Gospel of John and the Writings of Philo*. NovTSup 10. Leiden: Brill, 1981.

———. *The Gospel of John: More Light from Philo, Paul, and Archaeology*. NovTSup 154. Leiden: Brill, 2014.

Boring, M. Eugene. "The Influence of Christian Prophecy on the Johannine Portrayal of the Paraclete and Jesus." *NTS* 25 (1978): 113–23.

Bornhäuser, Karl. *Das Johannesevangelium: Eine Missionsschrift für Israel*. BFCT 2/15. Gütersloh: Bertelsmann, 1928.

Bowman, John. "Samaritan Studies." *BJRL* 40 (1958): 298–327.

Boyarin, Daniel. "Justin Martyr Invents Judaism." *CH* 70 (2001): 427–61.

———. "The Ioudaioi in John and the Prehistory of 'Judaism.'" Pages 216–39 in *Pauline Conversations in Context: Essays in Honor of Calvin J. Roetzel*. Edited by Janice Capel Anderson, Philip Sellew, and Claudia Setzer. Sheffield: Sheffield Academic, 2002.

———. *Border Lines: The Partition of Judaeo-Christianity*. Philadelphia: University of Pennsylvania Press, 2004.

———. "The Christian Invention of Judaism: The Theodosian Empire and the Rabbinic Refusal of Religion." *Representations* 85 (2004): 21–57.

———. "Rethinking Jewish Christianity: An Argument for Dismantling a Dubious Category (to Which Is Appended a Correction of My Border Lines)." *JQR* 99 (2009): 7–36.

Bratcher, Robert G. "'The Jews' in the Gospel of John." *BT* 26 (1975): 401–9.

Broadhead, Edwin K. *Jewish Ways of Following Jesus: Redrawing the Religious Map of Antiquity*. WUNT 266. Tübingen: Mohr Siebeck, 2010.

Brodie, Thomas L. *The Quest for the Origin of John's Gospel: A Source-Oriented Approach*. New York: Oxford University Press, 1993.

Broszat, Martin, and Elke Fröhlich, eds. *Bayern in der NS-Zeit II: Herrschaft und Gesellschaft im Konflikt*. Munich: Oldenbourg, 1979.

Brown, Raymond E. *The Gospel according to John: Introduction, Translation, and Notes*. 2 vols. AB 29-29A. Garden City, NY: Doubleday, 1966–1972.

———. *The Community of the Beloved Disciple: The Life, Loves and Hates of an Individual Church in New Testament Times*. New York: Paulist, 1979.

Brumlik, Micha. "Johannes: Das judenfeindliche Evangelium." Pages 6–21 in *Teufelskinder oder Heilsbringer: Die Juden im Johannes-Evangelium*. Edited by Dietrich Neuhaus. 2nd ed. Arnoldshainer Texte 64. Frankfurt am Main: Haag & Herchen, 1993.

Bruneau, Philippe. "'Les Israélites de Délos' et la juiverie délienne." *BCH* 106 (1982): 465–504.

Brunson, Andrew C. *Psalm 118 in the Gospel of John: An Intertextual Study on the New Exodus Pattern in the Theology of John*. WUNT 2/158. Tübingen: Mohr Siebeck, 2003.

Buchanan, George Wesley. "The Samaritan Origin of the Gospel of John." Pages 149–74 in *Religions in Antiquity*. Edited by Jacob Neusner. Leiden: Brill, 1968.

Buell, Denise Kimber. *Why This New Race: Ethnic Reasoning in Early Christianity*. New York: Columbia University Press, 2005.

Bultmann, Rudolf. *Theology of the New Testament*. Translated by Kendrick Grobel. London: SCM, 1955.

———. *The Gospel of John: A Commentary*. Translated by G. R. Beasley-Murray. Philadelphia: Westminster, 1971.

Burkett, Delbert. *The Son of Man Debate: A History and Evaluation*. SNTSMS 107. Cambridge: Cambridge University Press, 2000.

Burney, C. F. *The Aramaic Origin of the Fourth Gospel*. Oxford: Clarendon, 1922.

Burridge, Richard A. "About People, by People, for People: Gospel Genre and Audiences." Pages 113–45 in *The Gospels for All Christians: Rethinking the Gospel Audiences*. Edited by Richard Bauckham. Grand Rapids: Eerdmans, 1998.

———. *What Are the Gospels? A Comparison with Graeco-Roman Biography*. 2nd ed. Grand Rapids: Eerdmans, 2004.

Buster, Aubrey E. *Remembering the Story of Israel: Historical Summaries and Memory Formation in Second Temple Judaism*. Cambridge: Cambridge University Press, 2022.

Byers, Andrew J. "Review of *Cast Out of the Covenant: Jews and Anti-Judaism in the Gospel of John*, by Adele Reinhartz." *RBL* (2020): 348–54.

———. *John and the Others: Jewish Relations, Christian Origins, and the Sectarian Hermeneutic*. Waco, TX: Baylor University Press, 2021.

Byrne, Brendan. *Romans*. SP 6. Collegeville, MN: Liturgical Press, 1996.

Callaway, Mary C. "A Hammer That Breaks Rock in Pieces: Prophetic Critique in the Hebrew Bible." Pages 21–38 in *Anti-Semitism and Early Christianity: Issues of Polemic and Faith*. Edited by Craig A. Evans and Donald A. Hagner. Minneapolis: Fortress, 1993.

Caron, Gérald. *Qui sont les Juifs de l'Évangile de Jean?* Recherches 35. Saint-Laurent, QC: Bellarmin, 1997.

Carroll, Kenneth L. "The Fourth Gospel and the Exclusion of Christians from the Synagogues." *BJRL* 40 (1957): 19–32.

Carson, D. A. *The Gospel according to John*. Grand Rapids: Eerdmans, 1991.

———. "Review of *Stilkritik und Verfasserfrage im Johannesevangelium*, by Eugen Ruckstuhl and Peter Dschulnigg." *JBL* 113 (1994): 151–52.

———. "John and the Johannine Epistles." Pages 245–64 in *It is Written: Scripture Citing Scripture: Essays in Honour of Barnabas Lindars*. Edited by D. A. Carson and H. G. M. Williamson. London: Cambridge University Press, 1998.

———. "Mystery and Fulfillment: Toward a More Comprehensive Paradigm of Paul's Understanding of the Old and the New." Pages 393–436 in *The Paradoxes of Paul*. Edited by D. A. Carson, Peter T. O'Brien, and Mark A. Seifrid. Vol. 2 of *Justification and Variegated Nomism*. WUNT 2/181. Tübingen: Mohr Siebeck, 2004.

Casey, Maurice. *From Jewish Prophet to Gentile God: The Origins and Development of New Testament Christology*. Louisville: Westminster John Knox, 1991.

Chancey, Mark A. *The Myth of a Gentile Galilee: The Population of Galilee and New Testament Studies*. SNTSMS 118. Cambridge: Cambridge University Press, 2002.

Charles, R. H. *A Critical and Exegetical Commentary on the Revelation of St. John*. ICC. Edinburgh: T&T Clark, 1920.

Charlesworth, James H. *Old Testament Pseudepigrapha*. 2 vols. New York: Doubleday, 1983–1985.

———. "The Historical Jesus in the Fourth Gospel: A Paradigm Shift." *JSHJ* 8 (2010): 3–46.

Chennattu, Rekha M. "Scripture." Pages 171–86 in *How John Works: Storytelling in the Fourth Gospel*. Edited by Douglas Estes and Ruth Sheridan. RBS 86. Atlanta: SBL Press, 2016.

Cirafesi, Wally V. "The Johannine Community Hypothesis (1968-Present): Past and Present Approaches and a New Way Forward." *CBR* 12 (2014): 173–93.

———. "The 'Johannine Community' in (More) Current Research: A Critical Appraisal of Recent Methods and Models." *Neot* 48 (2014): 341–64.

———. *John Within Judaism: Religion, Ethnicity, and the Shaping of Jesus-Oriented Jewishness in the Fourth Gospel*. AJEC 112. Leiden: Brill, 2021.

———. "Rethinking John and 'the Synagogue' in Light of Expulsion from Public Assemblies in Antiquity." *JBL* 142 (2023): 677–97.

Cohen, Shaye J. D. "Epigraphical Rabbis." *JQR* 72 (1981): 1–17.

———. *The Beginnings of Jewishness: Boundaries, Varieties, Uncertainties*. HCS 31. Berkeley: University of California Press, 1999.

Cohn-Sherbok, Dan. *Messianic Judaism*. London: Cassell, 2000.

Collins, Adela Yarboro. *Crisis and Catharsis: The Power of the Apocalypse*. Philadelphia: Westminster, 1984.

Cook, Michael J. "The Gospel of John and the Jews." *RevExp* 84 (1987): 259–71.

Counet, Patrick Chatelion. "No Anti-Judaism in the Fourth Gospel: A Deconstruction of Readings of John 8." Pages 197–225 in *One Text, A Thousand Methods: Studies in Memory of Sjef van Tilborg*. Edited by Patrick Chatelion Counet and Ulrich Berges. BibInt 71. Leiden: Brill, 2005.

Cranfield, C. E. B. *A Critical and Exegetical Commentary on the Epistle to the Romans*. 6th ed. 2 vols. ICC. London: T&T Clark, 1975–1979.

Crossley, James G., ed. *Judaism, Jewish Identities, and the Gospel Tradition: Essays in Honour of Maurice Casey*. London: Equinox, 2010.

Culpepper, R. Alan. *Anatomy of the Fourth Gospel: A Study in Literary Design*. FF. Philadelphia: Fortress, 1983.

———. "The Gospel of John and the Jews." *RevExp* 84 (1987): 273–88.

———. "The Gospel of John as a Threat to Jewish-Christian Relations." Pages 21–43 in *Overcoming Fear between Jews and Christians*. Edited by James H. Charlesworth, Frank X. Blisard, and Jerry L. Gorham. Shared Ground among Jews and Christians 3. New York: Crossroad, 1993.

———. "Anti-Judaism in the Fourth Gospel as a Theological Problem for Christian Interpreters." Pages 61–81 in *Anti-Judaism and the Fourth Gospel*. Edited by Reimund Bieringer, Didier Pollefeyt, and Frederique Vandecasteele-Vanneuville. Louisville: Westminster John Knox, 2001.

Culpepper, R. Alan, and Paul N. Anderson, eds. *John and Judaism: A Contested Relationship in Context*. RBS 87. Atlanta: SBL Press, 2017.

Cuming, Geoffrey J. "The Jews in the Fourth Gospel." *ExpTim* 60 (1949): 290–92.

Dahl, Nils. *Jesus in the Memory of the Early Church*. Minneapolis: Augsburg, 1976.

Darby, Michael R. *The Emergence of the Hebrew Christian Movement in Nineteenth-Century Britain*. SHR 128. Leiden: Brill, 2010.

Deines, Roland. "Galilee and the Historical Jesus in Recent Research." Pages 11–50 in *Life, Culture, and Society*. Vol. 1 of *Galilee in the Late Second Temple and Mishnaic Periods*. Edited by David A. Fiensy and James Riley Strange. Minneapolis: Fortress, 2014.

Delapp, Nevada Levi. *Theophanic "Type-Scenes" in the Pentateuch: Visions of YHWH*. Library of Hebrew Bible/Old Testament 660. London: Bloomsbury T&T Clark, 2018.

Dimant, Devorah. "The Vocabulary of Qumran Sectarian Texts." Pages 347–95 in *Qumran und die Archäologie: Texte und Kontexte*. Edited by Jörg Frey, Carsten Claussen, and Nadine Kessler. WUNT 278. Tübingen: Mohr Siebeck, 2011.

Dodd, C. H. *The Interpretation of the Fourth Gospel*. Cambridge: Cambridge University Press, 1953.

———. *The Epistle of Paul to the Romans*. MNTC 6. London: Hodder & Stoughton, 1960.

———. *Historical Tradition in the Fourth Gospel*. Cambridge: Cambridge University Press, 1963.
Dokka, Trond Skard. "Irony and Sectarianism in the Gospel of John." Pages 85–91 in *New Readings in John: Literary and Theological Perspectives*. Edited by Johannes Nissen and Sigfred Petersen. JSNTSup 182. Sheffield: Sheffield Academic, 1999.
Dunn, James D. G. *Romans*. 2 vols. WBC 38. Dallas, TX: Word, 1988.
———. "The Question of Anti-semitism in the New Testament Writings of the Period." Pages 177–211 in *Jews and Christians: The Parting of the Ways A.D. 70 to 135*. Edited by James D. G. Dunn. WUNT 66. Tübingen: Mohr Siebeck, 1992.
———. "Review of *From Jewish Prophet to Gentile God*, by Maurice Casey." *JTS* NS 44 (1993): 301–5.
———. "Who Did Paul Think He Was? A Study of Jewish-Christian Identity." *NTS* 45 (1999): 174–93.
———. "The Embarrassment of History: Reflections on the Problem of 'Anti-Judaism' in the Fourth Gospel." Pages 41–60 in *Anti-Judaism and the Fourth Gospel*. Edited by Reimund Bieringer, Didier Pollefeyt, and Frederique Vandecasteele-Vanneuville. Louisville: Westminster John Knox, 2001.
———. *The Partings of the Ways between Christianity and Judaism and Their Significance for the Character of Christianity*. 2nd ed. London: SCM, 2006.
Eisenbaum, Pamela. *Paul Was Not a Christian: The Original Message of a Misunderstood Apostle*. New York: HarperCollins, 2009.
Elliger, Karl, and Wilhelm Rudolph, eds. *Biblia Hebraica Stuttgartensia*. Stuttgart: Deutsche Bibelgesellschaft, 1983.
Elliott, John H. "Jesus the Israelite Was Neither a 'Jew' nor a 'Christian': On Correcting Misleading Nomenclature." *JSHJ* 5 (2007): 119–54.
Esler, Philip F. *Conflict and Identity in Romans: The Social Setting of Paul's Letter*. Minneapolis: Fortress, 2003.
———. "From *Ioudaioi* to Children of God: The Development of a Non-Ethnic Group Identity in the Gospel of John." Pages 118–24 in *In Other Words: Essays on Social Science Methods and the New Testament in Honor of Jerome H. Neyrey*. Edited by Anselm C. Hagedorn, Zeba A. Crook, and Eric Clark Stewart. Sheffield: Sheffield Phoenix, 2007.
———. "Judean Ethnic Identity in Josephus' *Against Apion*." Pages 73–91 in *A Wandering Galilean: Essays in Honour of Seán Freyne*. Edited by Zuleika Rodgers, Margaret Daly-Denton, and Anne Fitzpatrick-McKinley. JSJSup 132. Leiden: Brill, 2009.
Evans, Craig A. *Word and Glory: On the Exegetical and Theological Background of John's Prologue*. JSNTSup 89. Sheffield: JSOT Press, 1993.
Farrell, John, *The Varieties of Authorial Intention: Literary Theory Beyond the Intentional Fallacy*. Cham: Palgrave Macmillan, 2017.
Felsch, Dorit. *Die Feste im Johannesevangelium*. WUNT 2/308. Tübingen: Mohr Siebeck, 2011.
Felton, Tom, and Tom Thatcher. "Stylometry and the Signs Gospel." Pages 209–18 in *Jesus in Johannine Tradition*. Edited by Robert T. Fortna and Tom Thatcher. Louisville: Westminster John Knox, 2001.

Fischer, Diac. "Ueber den Ausdruck: οἱ Ἰουδαῖοι im Evangelium Johannis. Ein Beitrag zur Charakteristik desselben." *Tübinger Zeitschrift für Theologie* 2 (1840): 96–135.

Flack, E. E. "The Concept of Grace in Biblical Thought." Pages 137–54 in *Biblical Studies in Memory of H. C. Alleman*. Edited by J. M. Myers, O. Reimherr, and H. N. Bream. Locust Valley, NY: J. J. Augustin, 1960.

Flannery, Edward H. "Anti-Judaism and Anti-Semitism: A Necessary Distinction." *JES* 10 (1973): 581–88.

Fletcher, Daniel H. *Signs in the Wilderness: Intertextuality and the Testing of Nicodemus*. Eugene, OR: Wipf & Stock, 2014.

Fortna, Robert T. *The Gospel of Signs: A Reconstruction of the Narrative Source Underlying the Fourth Gospel*. SNTSMS 11. London: Cambridge University Press, 1970.

———. "Theological Use of Locale in the Fourth Gospel." *AThR* 3 (1974): 58–95.

———. *The Fourth Gospel and Its Predecessor: From Narrative Source to Present Gospel*. Philadelphia: Fortress, 1988.

Foster, Paul. "An Apostle Too Radical for the Radical Perspective on Paul." *ExpTim* 133 (2021): 1–11.

Frankfurter, David. "Jews or Not? Reconstructing the 'Other' in Rev 2:9 and 3:9." *HTR* 94 (2001): 403–25.

Freed, Edwin D. *Old Testament Quotations in the Gospel of John*. NovTSup 11. Leiden: Brill, 1965.

———. "Samaritan Influence in the Gospel of John." *CBQ* 30 (1968): 580–87.

Freedman, David Noel, ed. *Eerdmans Dictionary of the Bible*. Grand Rapids: Eerdmans, 2000.

Fredriksen, Paula. *Paul: The Pagans' Apostle*. New Haven: Yale University Press, 2017.

Frey, Jörg. "'Wie Mose die Schlange in der Wüste erhöht hat …': Zur frühjüdischen Deutung der 'ehernen Schlange' und ihrer christologischen Rezeption in Johannes 3,14f." Pages 153–205 in *Schriftauslegung im antiken Judentum und im Urchristentum*. Edited by Martin Hengel and Hermut Löhr. WUNT 73. Tübingen: Mohr Siebeck, 1994.

———. "Das Bild 'der Juden' im Johannesevangelium und die Geschichte der johanneischen Gemeinde." Pages 33–53 in *Israel und seine Heilstraditionen im Johannesevangelium: Festgabe für Johannes Beutler SJ zum 70. Geburtstag*. Edited by M. Labahn, K. Scholtissek, and A. Strotmann. Paderborn: Schöningh, 2004.

———. "Paul's Jewish Identity." Pages 285–321 in *Jewish Identity in the Greco-Roman World/Jüdische Identität in der griechisch-römischen Welt*. Edited by Jörg Frey, Daniel R. Schwartz, and Stephanie Gripentrog. AGJU 71. Leiden: Brill, 2007.

Fuglseth, Kåre Sigvald. *Johannine Sectarianism in Perspective: A Sociological, Historical, and Comparative Analysis of Temple and Social Relationships in the Gospel of John, Philo, and Qumran*. NovTSup 119. Leiden: Brill, 2005.

Gager, John. *Reinventing Paul*. Oxford: Oxford University Press, 2000.

Garroway, Joshua D. *Paul's Gentile-Jews: Neither Jew nor Gentile, but Both*. New York: Palgrave Macmillan, 2012.

Gaston, Lloyd. *Paul and the Torah*. Vancouver: University of British Columbia Press, 1987.

Gathercole, Simon J. *The Pre-existent Son: Recovering the Christologies of Matthew, Mark, and Luke*. Grand Rapids: Eerdmans, 2006.

Gerber, Edward H. *The Scriptural Tale in the Fourth Gospel: With Particular Reference to the Prologue and a Syncretic (Oral and Written) Poetics*. BibInt 147. Leiden: Brill, 2016.

Goodblatt, David. *Elements of Ancient Jewish Nationalism*. Cambridge: Cambridge University Press, 2006.

———. "Ancient Jewish Identity." *Ancient Jew Review*. https://www.ancientjewreview.com/read/2018/10/24/ancient-jewish-identity. Oct. 24, 2018.

Goode, Erich. *Deviant Behavior*. 12th ed. New York: Routledge, 2019.

Goodwin, Mark J. "Response to David Rensberger: Questions about a Jewish Johannine Community." Pages 158–71 in *Anti-Judaism and the Gospels*. Edited by W. R. Farmer. Harrisburg, PA: Trinity International, 1999.

Grabbe, Lester. L. "Ethnic Groups in Jerusalem." Pages 145–63 in *Jerusalem in Ancient History and Tradition*. Edited by Thomas L. Thompson. JSOTSup 381. London: T&T Clark, 2003.

Grässer, Erich. "Die antijüdische Polemik im Johannesevangelium." *NTS* 11 (1964): 74–90.

Griffith, Terry. "'The Jews Who Had Believed in Him' (John 8:31) and the Motif of Apostasy in the Gospel of John." Pages 183–92 in *The Gospel of John and Christian Theology*. Edited by Richard Bauckham and Carl Mosser. Grand Rapids: Eerdmans, 2008.

Hägerland, Tobias. "John's Gospel: A Two-Level Drama?" *JSNT* 25 (2003): 309–22.

Hakola, Raimo. *Identity Matters: John, the Jews and Jewishness*. NovTSup 118. Leiden: Brill, 2005.

Hamid-Khani, Saeed. *Revelation and Concealment of Christ: A Theological Inquiry into the Elusive Language of the Fourth Gospel*. WUNT 2/120. Tübingen: Mohr Siebeck, 2000.

Hanson, Anthony Tyrrell. "John 1:14-18 and Exodus 34." *NTS* 23 (1976): 90–101.

———. *The Prophetic Gospel: A Study of John and the Old Testament*. Edinburgh: T&T Clark, 1991.

Harvey, Graham. *The True Israel: Uses of the Names Jew, Hebrew and Israel in Ancient Jewish and Early Christian Literature*. AGJU 35. Leiden: Brill, 1996.

Hatina, Thomas R. *Biblical Interpretation in Early Christian Gospels*, vol. 4: *The Gospel of John*. LNTS 613. London: Bloomsbury, 2020.

Hayes, Christine. "Paul 'Within Judaism.'" *Ancient Jew Review*. https://www.ancientjewreview.com/read/responding-to-paul-within-judaism. Sept. 14, 2022.

Hays, Richard B. *Echoes of Scripture in the Letters of Paul*. New Haven: Yale University Press, 1989.

———. *Echoes of Scripture in the Gospels*. Waco, TX: Baylor University Press, 2006.

―――. *Reading Backwards: Figural Christology and the Fourfold Gospel Witness.* Waco, TX: Baylor University Press, 2014.

Hempel, Johannes. *Das alte Testament und die völkische Idee.* Bonn: Gebr. Scheur, 1935.

Hengel, Martin. *The Johannine Question.* Translated by John Bowden. London: SCM, 1989.

Herbstrith, Waltraud. *Edith Stein: A Biography.* San Francisco: Harper & Row, 1985.

Heschel, Susannah. *The Aryan Jesus: Christian Theologians and the Bible in Nazi Germany.* Princeton: Princeton University Press, 2008.

―――. "Historiography of Antisemitism versus Anti-Judaism: A Response to Robert Morgan." *JSNT* 33 (2011): 257–79.

Hickling, Colin J. A. "Attitudes to Judaism in the Fourth Gospel." Pages 347–54 in *L'Évangile de Jean: Sources, redaction, théologie.* Edited by Marinus de Jonge. BETL 44. Leuven: Leuven University Press, 1977.

Himmelfarb, Martha. *A Kingdom of Priests: Ancestry and Merit in Ancient Judaism.* Philadelphia: University of Pennsylvania Press, 2006.

Hoare, F. R. *The Original Order and Chapters of St. John's Gospel.* London: Burns, Oates & Washbourne, 1944.

Holmberg, Bengt. *Sociology and the New Testament: An Appraisal.* Minneapolis: Fortress, 1990.

Hornsey, Matthew J. "Ingroup Critics and Their Influence on Groups." Pages 74–91 in *Individuality and the Group: Advances in Social Identity.* Edited by Tom Postmes and Jolanda Jetten. London: Sage, 2006.

―――. "Kernel of Truth or Motivated Stereotype? Interpreting and Responding to Negative Generalizations about Your Group." Pages 317–38 in *Stereotype Dynamics: Language-Based Approaches to the Formation, Maintenance, and Transformation of Stereotypes.* Edited by Yoshihisa Kashima, Klaus Fiedler, and Peter Freytag. New York: Lawrence Erlbaum Associates, 2008.

Hornsey, Matthew J., and Armin Imani. "Criticizing Groups from the Inside and the Outside: An Identity Perspective on the Intergroup Sensitivity Effect." *Personality and Social Psychology Bulletin* 30 (2004): 365–83.

Hornsey, Matthew J., Tina Oppes, and Alicia Svensson. "It's OK if We Say It, But You Can't: Responses to Intergroup and Intragroup Criticism." *European Journal of Social Psychology* 32 (2002): 293–307.

Horsley, Richard A. "The Expansion of Hasmonean Rule in Idumea and Galilee: Toward a Historical Sociology." Pages 134–65 in *Second Temple Studies III: Studies in Politics, Class, and Material Culture.* Edited by Philip R. Davies and John M. Halligan. JSOTSup 340. Sheffield: Sheffield Academic, 2002.

Horst, Pieter W. van der. "Jews and Christians in Antioch at the End of the Fourth Century." Pages 228–38 in *Christian-Jewish Relations through the Centuries.* Edited by Stanley E. Porter and Brook W. R. Pearson. London: T&T Clark, 2004.

Hoskyns, Edwyn Clement. *The Fourth Gospel.* Edited by F. N. Davey. London: Faber and Faber, 1947.

Huebenthal, Sandra. "Proclamation Rejected, Truth Confirmed: Reading John 12:37-44 in a Social Memory Theoretical Framework." Pages 183–200 in *Biblical Interpretation in Early Christian Gospels*, vol. 4: *The Gospel of John*. LNTS 613. London: Bloomsbury, 2020.

Hunt, Steven A. "And the Word Became Flesh—Again? Jesus and Abraham in John 8:31-59." Pages 81–109 in *Perspectives on Our Father Abraham: Essays in Honor of Marvin R. Wilson*. Edited by Steven A. Hunt. Grand Rapids: Eerdmans, 2010.

Hutchinson, John, and Anthony D. Smith. *Ethnicity*. Oxford Readers. Oxford: Oxford University Press, 1996.

Hylen, Susan. *Allusion and Meaning in John 6*. BZNW 137. Berlin: de Gruyter, 2005.

———. *Imperfect Believers: Ambiguous Characters in the Gospel of John*. Louisville, KY: Westminster John Knox, 2009.

Isaac, Benjamin. *The Invention of Racism in Classical Antiquity*. Princeton: Princeton University Press, 2004.

Jackson-McCabe, Matt. *Jewish Christianity: The Making of the Christianity-Judaism Divide*. New Haven: Yale University Press, 2020.

Jacobs, Andrew S. *Remains of the Jews: The Holy Land and Christian Empire in Late Antiquity*. Stanford: Stanford University Press, 2004.

Jason, Mark A. *Repentance at Qumran: The Penitential Framework of Religious Experience in the Dead Sea Scrolls*. Minneapolis: Fortress, 2015.

Jeremias, Joachim. "Johanneische Literarkritik." *TBl* 20 (1941): 33–46.

Johnson, Brian D. "The Jewish Feasts and Questions of Historicity in John 5-12." Pages 117–30 in *Aspects of Historicity in the Fourth Gospel*. Vol. 2 of *John, Jesus, and History*. Edited by Paul N. Anderson, Felix Just, S.J., and Tom Thatcher. Atlanta: SBL Press, 2009.

Johnson, Luke T. "The New Testament's Anti-Jewish Slander and the Conventions of Ancient Polemic." *JBL* 108 (1989): 419–41.

Johnston, George. *The Spirit-Paraclete in the Gospel of John*. SNTSMS 12. Cambridge: Cambridge University Press, 1970.

Jones, F. Stanley. *An Ancient Jewish Christian Source on the History of Christianity: Pseudo-Clementine Recognitions 1.27-71*. Texts and Translations 37, Christian Apocrypha 2. Atlanta: Scholars Press, 1995.

———. "The Genre of the Book of Elchasai: A Primitive Church Order, Not an Apocalypse." Pages 87–104 in *Historische Wahrheit und theologische Wissenschaft: Gerd Lüdemann zum 50. Geburtstag*. Edited by Alf Özen. Frankfurt am Main: Lang, 1996.

Jonge, Henk Jan de. "'The Jews' in the Gospel of John." Pages 121–40 in *Anti-Judaism and the Fourth Gospel*. Edited by Reimund Bieringer, Didier Pollefeyt, and Frederique Vandecasteele-Vanneuville. Louisville: Westminster John Knox, 2001.

Juel, Donald. *Messianic Exegesis: Christological Interpretation of the Old Testament in Early Christianity*. Waco, TX: Baylor University Press, 2017.

Käfer, Eduard. *Die Rezeption der Sinaitradition im Evangelium nach Johannes*. WUNT 2/502. Tübingen: Mohr Siebeck, 2019.

Käsemann, Ernst. *Jesu letzter Wille nach Johannes 17*. Tübingen: Mohr Siebeck, 1966.

———. *The Testament of Jesus: A Study of the Gospel of John in Light of Chapter 17*. Translated by Gerhard Krodel. Philadelphia: Fortress, 1968.

Kasher, Aryeh. *Jews, Idumaeans, and Ancient Arabs: Relations of the Jews in Eretz-Israel with the Nations of the Frontier and the Desert during the Hellenistic and Roman Era (322 BCE – 70 CE)*. TSAJ 18. Tübingen: Mohr Siebeck, 1988.

Katz, Jacob. *Exclusiveness and Tolerance: Studies in Jewish-Gentile Relations in Medieval and Modern Times*. Scripta Judaica 3. London: Oxford University Press, 1961.

Keener, Craig S. *The Gospel of John: A Commentary*. 2 vols. Peabody, MA: Hendrickson, 2003.

Kierspel, Lars. *The Jews and the World in the Fourth Gospel: Parallelism, Function, and Context*. WUNT 2/220. Tübingen: Mohr Siebeck, 2006.

Kimelman, Reuven. "*Birkat Ha-Minim* and the Lack of Evidence for an Anti-Christian Jewish Prayer in Late Antiquity." Pages 226–44 in *Aspects of Judaism in the Greco-Roman Period*. Edited by E. P. Sanders, Albert I. Baumgarten, and Alan Mendelson. Vol. 2 of *Jewish and Christian Self-Definition*. Edited by E. P. Sanders. Philadelphia: Fortress, 1981.

Kinzig, Wolfram. "The Nazoraeans." Pages 463–87 in *Jewish Believers in Jesus: The Early Centuries*. Edited by Oskar Skarsaune and Reidar Hvalvik. Peabody, MA: Hendrickson, 2007.

Kirk, Alan. *Memory and the Jesus Tradition*. London: Bloomsbury, 2018.

Kirk, Alan, and Tom Thatcher, eds. *Memory, Tradition, and Text: Uses of the Past in Early Christianity*. SemeiaSt 52. Atlanta: SBL Press, 2005.

Kittel, Gerhard, and Gerhard Friedrich, eds. *Theological Dictionary of the New Testament*. Translated by G. W. Bromiley. 10 vols. Grand Rapids: Eerdmans, 1964–1976.

Klawans, Jonathan. "An Invented Revolution." *Marginalia*. http://marginalia.lareviewofbooks.org/invented-revolution-jonathan-klawans/. Aug. 26, 2014.

Klijn, A. F. J., and G. J. Reinink. *Patristic Evidence for Jewish-Christian Sects*. NovTSup 36. Leiden: Brill, 1973.

Klink, Edward W., III. *The Sheep of the Fold: The Audience and Origin of the Gospel of John*. SNTSMS 141. Cambridge: Cambridge University Press, 2007.

———, ed. *The Audience of the Gospels: The Origin and Function of the Gospels in Early Christianity*. LNTS 353. London: T&T Clark, 2010.

Knoppers, Gary N. *Jews and Samaritans: The Origins and History of Their Early Relations*. Oxford: Oxford University Press, 2013.

Koester, Helmut. *History, Culture, and Religion of the Hellenistic Age*. Vol. 1 of *Introduction to the New Testament*. 2nd ed. Berlin: de Gruyter, 1995.

Kohler, Kaufmann. "New Testament." *JE* 9:246-54, 1905.

Köstenberger, Andreas J. "John." Pages 415–512 in *Commentary on the New Testament Use of the Old Testament*. Edited by G. K. Beale and D. A. Carson. Grand Rapids: Baker Academic, 2007.

Kysar, Robert. "Anti-Semitism and the Gospel of John." Pages 113–27 in *Anti-Semitism and Early Christianity: Issues of Polemic and Faith*. Edited by Craig A. Evans and Donald A. Hagner. Minneapolis: Fortress, 1993.

Lagrange, Marie-Joseph. *Évangile selon Saint Jean*. Paris: Gabalda, 1925.

Lambrecht, Jan. "'Synagogues of Satan' (Rev. 2:9 and 3:9): Anti-Judaism in the Book of Revelation." Pages 279–92 in *Anti-Judaism and the Fourth Gospel*. Edited by Reimund Bieringer, Didier Pollefeyt, and Frederique Vandecasteele-Vanneuville. Louisville: Westminster John Knox, 2001.

Langer, Ruth. *Cursing the Christians? A History of the Birkat Haminim*. Oxford: Oxford University Press, 2012.

Lea, Thomas D. "Response to David Rensberger." Pages 172–75 in *Anti-Judaism and the Gospels*. Edited by W. R. Farmer. Harrisburg, PA: Trinity International, 1999.

Leibig, Janis E. "John and 'the Jews': Theological Antisemitism in the Fourth Gospel." *JES* 20 (1983): 212–16.

Lentz, August, ed. *Grammatici Graeci*. 4 vols. Leipzig: Teubner, 1867–1910.

Levine, Amy-Jill. *The Misunderstood Jew: The Church and the Scandal of the Jewish Jesus*. San Francisco: HarperOne, 2006.

Liddell, Henry George, Robert Scott, and Henry Stuart Jones. *A Greek-English Lexicon*. 9th ed. Oxford: Clarendon, 1996.

Lieu, Judith. "'The Parting of the Ways': Theological Construct or Historical Reality?" *JSNT* 56 (1994): 101–19.

———. *Image and Reality: The Jews in the World of the Christians in the Second Century*. Edinburgh: T&T Clark, 1996.

———. *Christian Identity in the Jewish and Graeco-Roman World*. Oxford: Oxford University Press, 2004.

———. *Marcion and the Making of a Heretic: God and Scripture in the Second Century*. Cambridge: Cambridge University Press, 2015.

Lieu, Judith, and Martinus C. de Boer, eds. *The Oxford Handbook of Johannine Studies*. Oxford: Oxford University Press, 2018.

Lightfoot, R. H. *Locality and Doctrine in the Gospels*. London: Hodder & Stoughton, 1938.

Lindars, Barnabas. *Behind the Fourth Gospel*. Studies in Creative Criticism 3. London: SPCK, 1971.

———. *The Gospel of John*. NCB. London: Marshall, Morgan & Scott, 1972.

Lowe, Malcom. "Who Were the Ἰουδαῖοι?" *NovT* 18 (1976): 101–30.

Luomanen, Petri. *Recovering Jewish-Christian Sects and Gospels*. Supplements to Vigiliae Christianae 110. Leiden: Brill, 2012.

Lütgert, Wilhelm. "Die Juden im Johannesevangelium." Pages 147–54 in *Neutestamentliche Studien: Georg Heinrici zu seinem 70. Geburtstag dargebracht von Fachgenossen, Freunden und Schülern*. Leipzig: J. C. Hinrichs, 1914.

Malina, Bruce, and Richard L. Rohrbaugh. *Social-Science Commentary on the Gospel of John*. Minneapolis: Fortress, 1998.

Marrow, Stanley B. "Κόσμος in John." *CBQ* 64 (2002): 90–102.

Martyn, J. Louis. "The Salvation-History Perspective in the Fourth Gospel." PhD diss., Yale, 1957.

———. "A Gentile Mission that Replaced an Earlier Jewish Mission?" Pages 124–44 in *Exploring the Gospel of John: In Honor of D. Moody Smith*. Edited by R. Alan Culpepper and C. Clifton Black. Louisville: Westminster John Knox, 1996.

———. *History and Theology in the Fourth Gospel*. 3rd ed. NTL. Louisville: Westminster John Knox, 2003.

———. "Glimpses into the History of the Johannine Community: From its Origins through the Period of Its Life in Which the Fourth Gospel Was Composed." Pages 145–67 in idem, *History and Theology in the Fourth Gospel*. 3rd ed. NTL. Louisville: Westminster John Knox, 2003.

———. "The Johannine Community among Jewish and Other Early Christian Communities." Pages 183–90 in *What We Have Heard from the Beginning: The Past, Present, and Future of Johannine Studies*. Edited by Tom Thatcher. Waco, TX: Baylor University Press, 2007.

Mason, Steve. *Flavius Josephus on the Pharisees: A Compositional-Critical Study*. StPB 39. Leiden: Brill, 1991.

———. *Life of Josephus: Translation and Commentary*. Vol. 9 of *Flavius Josephus: Translation and Commentary*. Edited by Steve Mason. Leiden: Brill, 2001.

———. "Jews, Judaeans, Judaizing, Judaism: Problems of Categorization in Ancient History." *JSJ* 38 (2007): 457–512.

———. *Judean War 2*. Vol. 1b of *Flavius Josephus: Translation and Commentary*. Edited by Steve Mason. Leiden: Brill, 2008.

———. "Ancient Jews or Judeans? Different Questions, Different Answers." *Marginalia*. http://marginalia.lareviewofbooks.org/ancient-jews-judeans-different-questions-different-answers-steve-mason/. Aug. 26, 2014.

———. "Josephus's *Judean War*." Pages 13–35 in *A Companion to Josephus*. Edited by Honora Howell Chapman and Zuleika Rodgers. Chichester: Wiley-Blackwell, 2016.

———. *A History of the Jewish War: A.D. 66-74*. Cambridge: Cambridge University Press, 2016.

———. *Orientation to the History of Roman Judaea*. Eugene, OR: Cascade, 2016.

———. "Paul Without Judaism: Historical Method over Perspective." Pages 9–40 in *Paul and Matthew among Jews and Gentiles: Essays in Honour of Terrence L. Donaldson*. Edited by Ronald Charles. LNTS 628. London: Bloomsbury, 2021.

McCready, Wayne O., and Adele Reinhartz, eds. *Common Judaism: Explorations in Second-Temple Judaism*. Minneapolis: Fortress, 2008.

McKay, K. L. "On the Perfect and Other Aspects in New Testament Greek." *NovT* 23 (1981): 289–329.

Meeks, Wayne A. *The Prophet-King: Moses Traditions and the Johannine Christology*. NovTSup 14. Leiden: Brill, 1967.

———. "The Man from Heaven in Johannine Sectarianism." *JBL* 91 (1972): 44–72.

———. "Galilee and Judea in the Fourth Gospel." *JBL* 85 (1966): 159–69.

———. "Am I a Jew?—Johannine Christianity and Judaism." Pages 163–86 in *Christianity, Judaism and Other Greco-Roman Cults: Studies for Morton Smith at Sixty*. Part 4: *Judaism after 70: Other Greco-Roman Cults*. Edited by J. Neusner. SJLA 12. Leiden: Brill, 1975.

———. "Breaking Away: Three New Testament Pictures of Christianity's Separation from the Jewish Communities." Pages 93–115 in *"To See Ourselves as Others See*

Us": *Christians, Jews, "Others" in Late Antiquity*. Edited by J. Neusner and E. S. Frerichs. Chico, CA: Scholars Press, 1985.

Menken, Maarten J. J. *Old Testament Quotations in the Fourth Gospel: Studies in Textual Form*. CBET 15. Kampen: Kok Pharos, 1996.

———. "Observations on the Significance of the Old Testament in the Fourth Gospel." *Neot* 33 (1999): 125–43.

Menoud, Philippe-H. *L'Évangile de Jean d'après les recherches récentes*. 2nd ed. CahT 3. Neuchatel: Delachaux & Niestlé, 1947.

Merenlahti, Petri, and Raimo Hakola. "Reconceiving Narrative Criticism." Pages 13–48 in *Characterization in the Gospels: Reconceiving Narrative Criticism*. Edited by David Rhoads and Kari Syreeni. JSNTSup 184. Sheffield: Sheffield Academic, 1999.

Meyer, Ben F. *Critical Realism and the New Testament*. Allison Park, PA: Pickwick, 1989.

Michaels, J. Ramsey. *The Gospel of John*. NICNT. Grand Rapids: Eerdmans, 2010.

Milik, J. T. "Textes hébreux et araméens." Pages 67–205 in *Les grottes de Murabba'ât*, vol 1. Edited by P. Benoit, J. T. Milik, and R. de Vaux. DJD 2. Oxford: Clarendon, 1961.

Miller, David M. "Ethnicity, Religion and the Meaning of *Ioudaios* in Ancient 'Judaism.'" *CBR* 12 (2014): 216–65.

Moll, Sebastian. *The Arch-Heretic Marcion*. WUNT 250. Tübingen: Mohr Siebeck, 2010.

Moloney, Francis J. *The Gospel of John*. SP 4. Collegeville, MN: Liturgical Press, 1998.

———. *Love in the Gospel of John: An Exegetical, Theological, and Literary Study*. Grand Rapids: Baker Academic, 2013.

Montanaro, Andrew. "The Use of Memory in the Old Testament Quotations in John's Gospel." *NovT* 59 (2017): 147–70.

Moo, Douglas. *The Epistle to the Romans*. NICNT. Grand Rapids: Eerdmans, 1996.

Mor, Menachem, and Friedrich V. Reiterer, eds. *Samaritans: Past and Present: Current Studies*. SJ 53. Berlin: de Gruyter, 2010.

Morgan, Robert. "Susannah Heschel's Aryan Grundmann." *JSNT* 32 (2010): 431–94.

Mosser, Carl. "The Earliest Patristic Interpretations of Psalm 82, Jewish Antecedents, and the Origin of Christian Deification." *JTS* NS 56 (2005): 30–74.

Motyer, Stephen. *Your Father the Devil? A New Approach to John and "the Jews."* Paternoster Biblical and Theological Monographs. Carlisle: Paternoster, 1997.

———. "The Fourth Gospel and the Salvation of Israel: An Appeal for a New Start." Pages 83–100 in *Anti-Judaism and the Fourth Gospel*. Edited by Reimund Bieringer, Didier Pollefeyt, and Frederique Vandecasteele-Vanneuville. Louisville: Westminster John Knox, 2001.

———. "Bridging the Gap: How Might the Fourth Gospel Help Us Cope with the Legacy of Christianity's Exclusive Claim over against Judaism." Pages 143–67 in *The Gospel of John and Christian Theology*. Edited by Richard Bauckham and Carl Mosser. Grand Rapids: Eerdmans, 2008.

Moyise, Steve. *The Old Testament in the New: An Introduction.* London: T&T Clark, 2001.
Myers, E. A. *The Ituraeans and the Roman Near East: Reassessing the Sources.* Cambridge: Cambridge University Press, 2010.
Nanos, Mark D. "The Myth of the 'Law-Free' Paul Standing between Christians and Jews." *Studies in Christian-Jewish Relations* 4 (2009): 1–21.
———. *Reading Paul within Judaism.* Eugene, OR: Cascade, 2017.
———. *Reading Corinthians and Philippians within Judaism.* Eugene, OR: Cascade, 2017.
Nanos, Mark D., and Magnus Zetterholm, eds. *Paul within Judaism: Restoring the First-Century Context to the Apostle.* Minneapolis: Fortress, 2015.
Neusner, Jacob. "Defining Judaism." Pages 3–19 in *The Blackwell Companion to Judaism.* Edited by Jacob Neusner and Alan Avery-Peck. Oxford: Blackwell, 2000.
Neyrey, Jerome H. "The Jacob Allusions in John 1:51." *CBQ* 44 (1982): 586–605.
Nissen, Johannes, and Sigfred Pedersen, eds. *New Readings in John: Literary and Theological Perspectives.* JSNTSup 182. Sheffield: Sheffield Academic, 1999.
North, Wendy E. S. "'The Jews' in John's Gospel: Observations and Inferences." Pages 207–26 in *Judaism, Jewish Identities and the Gospel Tradition: Essays in Honour of Maurice Casey.* Edited by James G. Crossley. London: Equinox, 2010.
Numada, Jonathan. *John and Anti-Judaism: Reading the Gospel in Light of Greco-Roman Culture.* McMaster Biblical Studies Series 7. Eugene, OR: Pickwick, 2021.
Nyman, Ludvig. "New Perspectives on the Old Covenant: 2 Corinthians 3 and *Paul within Judaism.*" *Neot* 54 (2020): 351–71.
Obermann, Andreas. *Die christologische Erfüllung der Schrift im Johannesevangelium: Eine Untersuchung zur johanneischen Hermeneutik anhand der Schriftzitate.* WUNT 2/83. Tübingen: Mohr Siebeck, 1996.
Odeberg, Hugo. *The Fourth Gospel: Interpreted in Its Relation to Contemporaneous Religious Currents in Palestine and the Hellenistic-Oriental World.* Uppsala: Almqvist & Wiksells, 1929.
O'Neill, J. C. "The Jews in the Fourth Gospel." *IBS* 18 (1996): 58–74.
Overman, Andrew J. *Matthew's Gospel and Formative Judaism: The Social World of the Matthean Community.* Minneapolis: Fortress, 1990.
Painter, John. "The Church and Israel in the Gospel of John: A Response." *NTS* 25 (1978): 103–12.
Pancaro, Severino. "'People of God' in John's Gospel." *NTS* 16 (1970): 114–29.
———. *The Law in the Fourth Gospel: The Torah and the Gospel, Moses and Jesus, Judaism and Christianity according to John.* NovTSup 42. Leiden: Brill, 1975.
Parkes, James. *The Conflict of the Church and the Synagogue: A Study in the Origins of Antisemitism.* London: Soncino Press, 1934.
Pedersen, Sigfred. "Anti-Judaism in John's Gospel: John 8." Pages 172–93 in *New Readings in John: Literary and Theological Perspectives.* Edited by Johannes Nissen and Sigfred Petersen. JSNTSup 182. Sheffield: Sheffield Academic, 1999.
Penwell, Stewart. *Jesus the Samaritan: Ethnic Labeling in the Gospel of John.* BibInt 170. Leiden: Brill, 2019.

Perrin, Robin D. "Cognitive Deviance: Unconventional Beliefs." Pages 401–21 in *The Handbook of Deviance*. Edited by Erich Goode. Malden, MA: Wiley Blackwell, 2015.

Peterson, Dwight N. *The Origins of Mark: The Markan Community in Current Debate*. BibInt 48. Leiden: Brill, 2000.

Pew Research Center. "A Portrait of Jewish Americans." http://www.pewforum.org/files/2013/10/jewish-american-full-report-for-web.pdf.

———. "Israel's Religiously Divided Society." http://www.pewforum.org/files/2016/03/Israel-Survey-Full-Report.pdf.

Pippin, Tina. "'For Fear of the Jews': Lying and Truth-Telling in Translating the Gospel of John." *Semeia* 76 (1996): 81–97.

Pitre, Brant, Michael P. Barber, and John A. Kincaid. *Paul A New Covenant Jew: Rethinking Pauline Theology*. Grand Rapids: Eerdmans, 2019.

Popkes, Enno Edzard. *Die Theologie der Liebe Gottes in den johanneischen Schriften: Zur Semantik der Liebe und zum Motivkreis des Dualismus*. WUNT 2/197. Tübingen: Mohr Siebeck, 2005.

Porsch, Felix. "'Ihr habt den Teufel zum Vater' (Joh 8,44): Antijudaismus im Johannesevangelium?" *BK* 44 (1989): 50–57.

Porter, Christopher A. *Johannine Social Identity Formation After the Fall of the Jerusalem Temple: Negotiating Identity in Crisis*. BibInt 194. Leiden: Brill, 2022.

Porter, Stanley E. *John, His Gospel, and Jesus: In Pursuit of the Johannine Voice*. Grand Rapids: Eerdmans, 2015.

Porter, Stanley E., and Andrew W. Pitts, eds. *Johannine Christology*. Johannine Studies 3. Leiden: Brill, 2020.

Pourkier, Aline. *L'hérésiologie chez Épiphane de Salamine*. Christianisme antique 4. Paris: Beauchesne, 1992.

Pratscher, Wilhelm. "Die Juden im Johannesevangelium." *BL* 59 (1986): 177–85.

Pritz, Ray A. *Nazarene Jewish Christianity: From the End of the New Testament Period until Its Disappearance in the Fourth Century*. Jerusalem: Magnes, 1988.

Pummer, Reinhard. *The Samaritans in Flavius Josephus*. TSAJ 129. Tübingen: Mohr Siebeck, 2009.

———. *The Samaritans: A Profile*. Grand Rapids: Eerdmans, 2016.

Rahlfs, Alfred, and Robert Hanhart, eds. *Septuaginta: Editio altera*. Stuttgart: Deutsche Bibelgesellschaft, 2006.

Rajak, Tessa. *Josephus, The Historian and His Society*. 2nd ed. London: Duckworth, 2002.

Rappaport, Uriel. "Les Iduméens en Égypte." *RevPhil* 43 (1969): 73–82.

Reed, Annette Yoshiko. *Jewish-Christianity and the History of Judaism*. TSAJ 171. Tübingen: Mohr Siebeck, 2018.

Reed, Jonathan L. *Archaeology and the Galilean Jesus: A Re-examination of the Evidence*. Harrisburg, PA: Trinity International, 2000.

Reim, Günter. *Studien zum altestamentlichen Hintergrund des Johannesevangeliums*. SNTSMS 22. Cambridge: Cambridge University Press, 1974.

———. "Joh. 8,44—Gotteskinder/Teufelskinder: Wie antijudaistisch ist 'die wohl antijudaistischste Äusserung des NT'?" *NTS* 30 (1984): 619–24.

Reinhartz, Adele. *The Word in the World: The Cosmological Tale in the Fourth Gospel*. SBLMS 45. Atlanta: Scholars Press, 1992.

———. "The Johannine Community and Its Jewish Neighbors: A Reappraisal." Pages 111–38 in *Literary and Social Readings of the Fourth Gospel*. Edited by Fernando F. Segovia. Vol. 2 of *What is John?* SymS 7. Atlanta: Scholars Press, 1998.

———. *Befriending the Beloved Disciple: A Jewish Reading of the Gospel of John*. New York: Continuum, 2001.

———. "'Jews' and Jews in the Fourth Gospel." Pages 213–27 in *Anti-Judaism and the Fourth Gospel*. Edited by Reimund Bieringer, Didier Pollefeyt, and Frederique Vandecasteele-Vanneuville. Louisville: Westminster John Knox, 2001.

———. "The Gospel according to John." Pages 152–96 in *The Jewish Annotated New Testament*. Edited by Amy-Jill Levine and Marc Zvi Brettler. Oxford: Oxford University Press, 2011.

———. "Forging a New Identity: Johannine Rhetoric and the Audience of the Fourth Gospel." Pages 123–34 in *Paul, John, and Apocalyptic Eschatology: Studies in Honour of Martinus C. de Boer*. Edited by Jan Krans et al. NovTSup 149. Leiden: Brill, 2013.

———. "The Vanishing Jews of Antiquity." *Marginalia*. http://marginalia.lareviewofbooks.org /vanishing-jews-antiquity-adele-reinhartz/. June 24, 2014.

———. *Cast Out of the Covenant: Jews and Anti-Judaism in the Gospel of John*. Lanham, MD: Lexington Books/Fortress Academic, 2018.

Reiss, Yonah. "Halakhic Views toward Different Jews." Pages 243–58 in *The Relationship of Orthodox Jews with Believing Jews of Other Religious Ideologies and Non-Believing Jews*. Edited by Adam Mintz. Orthodox Forum. New York: Ktav, 2010.

Rensberger, David. *Johannine Faith and Liberating Community*. Philadelphia: Westminster, 1988.

———. "Anti-Judaism and the Gospel of John." Pages 120–75 in *Anti-Judaism and the Gospels*. Edited by W. R. Farmer. Harrisburg, PA: Trinity International, 1999.

Rissi, Mathias. "Das Judenproblem im Lichte der Johannesapokalypse." *TZ* 13 (1957): 241–59.

———. "Die 'Juden' im Johannesevangelium." Pages 2099–141 in *Aufstieg und Niedergang der römischen Welt: Geschichte und Kultur Roms im Spiegel der neueren Forschung*. Part 2, *Principat*, 26.3. Edited by Hildegard Temporini and Wolfgang Haase. New York: de Gruyter, 1996.

Robinson, J. A. T. "The Destination and Purpose of St. John's Gospel." *NTS* 6 (1960): 117–31.

Roetzel, Calvin J. *Paul: A Jew on the Margins*. Louisville, Westminster John Knox, 2003.

———. "*Ioudaioi* and Paul." Pages 3–15 in *The New Testament and Early Christian Literature in Greco-Roman Context: Studies in Honor of David E. Aune*. Edited by John Fotopoulos. NovTSup 122. Leiden: Brill, 2006.

Rogers, Jeffrey S. "Texts of Terror and the Essence of Scripture: Encountering the Jesus of John 8: A Sermon on John 8:31-59." *RevExp* 103 (2006): 205–12.

Ruckstuhl, Eugen. *Die literarische Einheit des Johannesevangeliums: Der gegenwärtige Stand der einschlägigen Forschungen*. Studia Friburgensia 2/3. Freiburg: Paulusverlag, 1951.

Ruckstuhl, Eugen, and Peter Dschulnigg. *Stilkritik und Verfasserfrage im Johannesevangelium*. NTOA 17. Göttingen: Vandenhoeck & Ruprecht, 1991.

Rudolf. David J. *A Jew to the Jews: Jewish Contours of Pauline Flexibility in 1 Corinthians 9:19-23*. WUNT 2/304. Tübingen: Mohr Siebeck, 2011.

Rudolf, David J., and Joel Willitts, eds. *Introduction to Messianic Judaism: Its Ecclesial Context and Biblical Foundations*. Grand Rapids: Zondervan, 2013.

Ruether, Rosemary Radford. *Faith and Fratricide: The Theological Roots of Anti-Semitism*. New York: Seabury, 1974.

Runia, David T. *Philo and the Church Fathers: A Collection of Papers*. Supplements to Vigiliae Christianae 32. Leiden: Brill, 1995.

Safrai, Samuel. "Relations between the Diaspora and the Land of Israel." Pages 184–215 in *The Jewish People in the First Century: Historical Geography, Political History, Social, Cultural and Religious Life and Institutions*. Edited by S. Safrai and M. Stern in co-operation with D. Flusser and W.C. van Unnik. Leiden: Brill, 1974.

Saldarini, Anthony J. *Matthew's Christian-Jewish Community*. CSHJ. Chicago: University of Chicago Press, 1994.

Sanders, E. P. *Paul, the Law, and the Jewish People*. Philadelphia: Fortress, 1983.

———. *Judaism: Practice and Belief, 63 BCE-66 CE*. Philadelphia: Trinity International, 1992.

Sanders, Jack T. *The Jews in Luke-Acts*. Philadelphia: Fortress, 1987.

———. "The Jewish People in Luke-Acts." Pages 51–75 in *Luke-Acts and the Jewish People: Eight Critical Perspectives*. Edited by Joseph B. Tyson. Minneapolis: Augsburg, 1988.

Schäfer, Peter. "Die sogenannte Synode von Jabne: Zur Trennung von Juden und Christen im ersten/zweiten Jh. N. Chr." *Judaica* 31 (1975): 54–64, 116–24.

Schiffman, Lawrence H. *Who Was a Jew? Rabbinic and Halakhic Perspectives on the Jewish Christian Schism*. Hoboken, NJ: Ktav, 1985.

Schlatter, Adolf. *Die Sprache und Heimat des vierten Evangelisten*. BFCT 4. Gütersloh: Bertelsmann, 1902.

Schnackenburg, Rudolf. *The Gospel according to John*. Translated by Kevin Smyth. 3 vols. HThKNT 4. New York: Seabury, 1968–1982.

Schnelle, Udo. "Die Juden im Johannesevangelium." Pages 217–30 in *Gedenkt an das Wort: Festschrift für Werner Vogler zum 65. Geburtstag*. Edited by Christoph Kähler, Martina Böhm, and Christfried Böttrich. Leipzig: Evangelische Verlagsanstalt, 1999.

Schram, Terry Leonard. "The Use of *Ioudaios* in the Fourth Gospel: An Application of Some Linguistic Insights to a New Testament Problem." Th.D. diss., University of Utrecht, 1973.

Schwartz, Barry. "Memory as a Cultural System: Abraham Lincoln in World War II." *American Sociological Review* 61 (1996): 908–27.

———. "Frame Images: Towards a Semiotics of Collective Memory." *Semiotica* 121 (1998): 1–40.

———. *Abraham Lincoln and the Forge of National Memory*. Chicago: University of Chicago Press, 2000.

———. "Where There's Smoke, There's Fire: Memory and History." Pages 7–40 in *Memory and Identity in Ancient Judaism and Early Christianity: A Conversation with Barry Schwartz*. Edited by Tom Thatcher. SemeiaSt 78. Atlanta: SBL Press, 2014.

Schwartz, Daniel R. "'Judaean' or 'Jew'? How Should We Translate *Ioudaios* in Josephus." Pages 3–37 in *Jewish Identity in the Greco-Roman World/Jüdische Identität in der griechisch-römischen Welt*. Edited by Jörg Frey, Daniel R. Schwartz, and Stephanie Gripentrog. AGJU 71. Leiden: Brill, 2007.

———. *Judeans and Jews: Four Faces of Dichotomy in Ancient Jewish History*. Toronto: University of Toronto Press, 2014.

Schwartz, Eduard. "Aporien im vierten Evangelium." *Nachrichten von der königlichen Gesellschaft der Wissenschaften zu Göttingen* 63 (1907): 342–72; 64 (1908): 115–48, 149–88, 497–650.

Schwartz, Seth. "Conversion to Judaism in the Second Temple Period: A Functionalist Approach." Pages 223–36 in *Studies in Josephus and the Varieties of Ancient Judaism: Louis H. Feldman Jubilee*. Edited by Shaye J. D. Cohen and Joshua J. Schwartz. Ancient Judaism and Early Christianity 67. Leiden: Brill, 2007.

———. "How Many Judaisms Were There? A Critique of Neusner and Smith on Definition and Mason and Boyarin on Categorization." *Journal of Ancient Judaism* (2011): 208–38.

Schweizer, Eduard. *Ego eimi: Die religionsgeschichtliche Herkunft und theologische Bedeutung der johanneischen Bildreden, zugleich ein Beitrag zur Quellenfrage des vierten Evangeliums*. FRLANT 2/38. Göttingen: Vandenhoeck & Ruprecht, 1939.

Sechrest, Love L. *A Former Jew: Paul and the Dialectics of Race*. LNTS 410. London: T&T Clark, 2009.

Segal, Alan F. *Two Powers in Heaven: Early Rabbinic Reports about Christianity and Gnosticism*. SJLA 25. Leiden: Brill, 1977.

———. *Paul the Convert: The Apostolate and Apostasy of Saul the Pharisee*. New Haven: Yale University Press, 1990.

Sheridan, Ruth. *Retelling Scripture: "The Jews" and the Scriptural Citations in John 1:19–12:15*. BibInt 110. Leiden: Brill, 2012.

———. "Issues in the Translation of οἱ Ἰουδαῖοι in the Fourth Gospel." *JBL* 132 (2013): 671–95.

Simpson, John A., and Edmund S. C. Weiner, eds. *The Oxford English Dictionary*. 2nd ed. 20 vols. Oxford: Clarendon, 1989.

Skarsaune, Oskar. "Jewish Believers in Jesus in Antiquity—Problems of Definition, Method, and Sources." Pages 3–21 in *Jewish Believers in Jesus: The Early Centuries*. Edited by Oskar Skarsaune and Reidar Hvalvik. Peabody, MA: Hendrickson, 2007.

Skarsaune, Oskar, and Reidar Hvalvik, eds. *Jewish Believers in Jesus: The Early Centuries*. Peabody, MA: Hendrickson, 2007.

Smith, D. Moody. *The Composition and Order of the Fourth Gospel: Bultmann's Literary Theory*. Yale Publications in Religion 10. New Haven: Yale University Press, 1965.

———. "Judaism and the Gospel of John." Pages 76–96 in *Jews and Christians: Exploring the Past, Present, and Future*. Edited by James H. Charlesworth, Frank X. Blisard, and Jeffrey S. Siker. Shared Ground among Jews and Christians 1. New York: Crossroad, 1990.

———. *The Theology of the Gospel of John*. Cambridge: Cambridge University Press, 1995.

———. "The Contribution of J. Louis Martyn to the Understanding of the Gospel of John." Pages 1–23 in J. Louis Martyn, *History and Theology in the Fourth Gospel*. 3rd ed. NTL. Louisville: Westminster John Knox, 2003.

Smith, Jonathan Z. "Birth Upside Down or Right Side Up?" *HR* 9 (1970): 281–303.

———. "Native Cults in the Hellenistic Period." *HR* 11 (1971): 236–49.

Smith, Joshua Paul. *Luke Was Not a Christian: Reading the Third Gospel and Acts Within Judaism*. BibInt 218. Leiden: Brill, 2024.

Söding Thomas. "'Was kann aus Nazareth schon Gutes kommen?' (Joh 1.46): Die Bedeutung des Judeseins Jesu im Johannesevangelium." *NTS* 46 (2000): 21–41.

Sparks, Kenton L. "The Problem of Myth in Ancient Historiography." Pages 269–80 in *Rethinking the Foundations: Historiography in the Ancient World and in the Bible: Essays in Honour of John Van Seters*. Edited by Steven L. McKenzie, Thomas Römer, and Hans Heinrich Schmid. BZAW 294. Berlin: de Gruyter, 2000.

Spilsbury, Paul. *The Image of the Jew in Flavius Josephus' Paraphrase of the Bible*. TSAJ 69. Tübingen: Mohr Siebeck, 1998.

Stark, Rodney, and William Sims Bainbridge. *The Future of Religion: Secularization, Revival, and Cult Formation*. Berkeley: University of California Press, 1985.

Staples, Jason A. *The Idea of Israel in Second Temple Judaism: A New Theory of People, Exile, and Israelite Identity*. Cambridge: Cambridge University Press, 2021.

Stern, Sacha. *Jewish Identity in Early Rabbinic Writings*. AGJU 23. Leiden: Brill, 1994.

Stibbe, Mark. *The Gospel of John as Literature: An Anthology of Twentieth-Century Perspectives*. NTTS 17. Leiden: Brill, 1993.

———. *John's Gospel*. New Testament Readings. London: Routledge, 1994.

Strack, H. L., and Günter Stemberger. *Introduction to the Talmud and Midrash*. Translated and edited by Markus Bockmuehl. 2nd ed. Minneapolis: Fortress, 1996.

Sutton, Robbie M., Tracey J. Elder, and Karen M. Douglas. "Reactions to Internal and External Criticism of Outgroups: Social Convention in the Intergroup Sensitivity Effect." *Personality and Social Psychology Bulletin* 32 (2006): 563–75.

Swetnam, James. "The Meaning of πεπιστευκότας in John 8.31." *Bib* 61 (1980): 106–9.

Swoboda, Sören. *Tod und Sterben im Krieg bei Josephus: Die Intention von* Bellum *und* Antiquitates *im Kontext griechisch-römischer Historiographie*. TSAJ 158. Tübingen: Mohr Siebeck, 2014.

Tenney, M. C. "The Old Testament and the Fourth Gospel." *BSac* 120 (1963): 300–308.

Thackeray, Henry St. John, et al., trans. *Josephus*. 10 vols. LCL. Cambridge: Harvard University Press, 1926–1965.

Thatcher, Tom, ed. *Memory and Identity in Ancient Judaism and Early Christianity: A Conversation with Barry Schwartz*. SemeiaSt 78. Atlanta: SBL Press, 2014.

———. "Keys, Frames, and the Problem of the Past." Pages 1–6 in *Memory and Identity in Ancient Judaism and Early Christianity: A Conversation with Barry Schwartz*. Edited by Tom Thatcher. SemeiaSt 78. Atlanta: SBL Press, 2014.

Thiel, Nathan. "'Israel' and 'Jew' as Markers of Jewish Identity in Antiquity: The Problems of Insider/Outsider Classification." *JSJ* 45 (2014): 80–99.

———. "The Use of the Term 'Galileans' in the Writings of Flavius Josephus Revisited." *JQR* 110 (2020): 221–44.

Thiessen, Matthew. *Contesting Conversion: Genealogy, Circumcision, and Identity in Ancient Judaism and Christianity*. Oxford: Oxford University Press, 2011.

———. *A Jewish Paul: The Messiah's Herald to the Gentiles*. Grand Rapids: Baker, 2023.

Thompson, Marianne Meye. "Signs and Faith in the Fourth Gospel." *BBR* 1 (1991): 89–108.

———. *The God of the Gospel of John*. Grand Rapids: Eerdmans, 2001.

Thyen, Hartwig. "'Das Heil kommt von den Juden.'" Pages 163–84 in *Kirche: Festschrift für Günther Bornkamm zum 75. Geburtstag*. Edited by Dieter Lührmann and Georg Strecker. Tübingen: Mohr Siebeck, 1980.

———. "Über die johanneischen Gebrauch von Ἰουδαῖος und Ἰουδαῖοι." Pages 651–62 in idem, *Studien zum Corpus Iohanneum*. WUNT 214. Tübingen: Mohr Siebeck, 2007.

Tilborg, Sjef van. "Jezus temidden van de joden van het Loofhuttenfeest in Johannes 8." Pages 53–66 in *Jaarboek 2001—Theologie en Exegese*. Edited by H. J. M. Schoot. Utrecht: Thomas Instituut Utrecht, 2002.

Tolmie, François D. "The Ἰουδαῖοι in the Fourth Gospel: A Narratological Perspective." Pages 377–97 in *Theology and Christology in the Fourth Gospel*. Edited by Gilbert van Belle, Jan G. van der Watt, and Petrus Maritz. BETL 184. Leuven: Leuven University Press, 2005.

Tomson, Peter J. *Paul and the Jewish Law: Halakha in the Letters of the Apostle to the Gentiles*. CRINTS Sec. 3, Jewish Traditions in Early Christian Literature 1. Assen: Van Gorcum; Minneapolis: Fortress, 1990.

———. "'Jews' in the Gospel of John as Compared with the Palestinian Talmud, the Synoptics, and Some New Testament Apocrypha." Pages 176–212 in *Anti-Judaism and the Fourth Gospel*. Edited by Reimund Bieringer, Didier Pollefeyt, and Frederique Vandecasteele-Vanneuville. Louisville: Westminster John Knox, 2001.

Townsend, John T. "The Gospel of John and the Jews: The Story of a Religious Divorce." Pages 72–97 in *Antisemitism and the Foundations of Christianity*. Edited by Alan T. Davies. New York: Paulist, 1979.

Trible, Phyllis. *Texts of Terror: Literary-Feminist Readings of Biblical Narratives*. OBT 13. Philadelphia: Fortress, 1984.

Tyson, Joseph B. "Jews and Judaism in Luke-Acts: Reading as a Godfearer." *NTS* 41 (1995): 19–38.

Unnik, W. C. van. "The Purpose of St. John's Gospel." *SE I*. Berlin: Akademie, 1959.
Van Belle, Gilbert. *Les parenthèses dans l'Évangile de Jean*. SNTA 11. Leuven: Leuven University Press, 1985.
Van Maaren, John. "Review of *John Within Judaism*, by Wally Cirafesi." *RBL* (2023): 362–65.
Verkuyten, Maykel. *The Social Psychology of Ethnic Identity*. European Monographs in Social Psychology. Hove: Psychology Press, 2005.
Volf, Miroslav. "Johannine Dualism and Contemporary Pluralism." Pages 19–50 in *The Gospel of John and Christian Theology*. Edited by Richard Bauckham and Carl Mosser. Grand Rapids: Eerdmans, 2008.
Von Wahlde, Urban. C. "The Terms for Religious Authorities in the Fourth Gospel: A Key to Literary-Strata?" *JBL* 98 (1979): 231–53.
———. "Archaeology and John's Gospel." Pages 523–86 in *Jesus and Archaeology*. Edited by James H. Charlesworth. Grand Rapids: Eerdmans, 2006.
———. "The Pool(s) of Bethesda and the Healing in John 5: A Reappraisal of Research and of the Johannine Text." *RB* 116 (2009): 111–36.
———. "The Puzzling Pool of Bethesda: Where Jesus Cured the Crippled Man." *BAR* 27 (2011): 40–47.
———. "The Gospel of John and Archaeology." Pages 101–20 in *The Oxford Handbook of Johannine Studies*. Edited by Judith M. Lieu and Martinus C. de Boer. Oxford: Oxford University Press, 2018.
Vouga, François. *Le cadre historique et l'intention théologique de Jean*. Paris: Beauchesne, 1977.
Watt, Jan van der. "'Is Jesus the King of Israel?': Reflections on the Jewish Nature of the Gospel of John." Pages 39–56 in *John and Judaism: A Contested Relationship in Context*. Edited by R. Alan Culpepper and Paul N. Anderson. RBS 87. Atlanta: SBL Press, 2017.
Watt, Jan van der, and Jacobus Kok. "Violence in a Gospel of Love." Pages 163–83 in *Coping with Violence in the New Testament*. Edited by Pieter de Villiers and Jan Willem van Henten. Studies in Theology and Religion 16. Leiden: Brill, 2012.
Weber, Cornelia. *Altes Testament und völkische Frage: Der biblische Volksbegriff in der alttestamentlichen Wissenschaft der nationalsozialistischen Zeit, dargestellt am Beispiel von Johannes Hempel*. FAT 28. Tübingen: Mohr Siebeck, 2000.
Weizsäcker, Carl. *Untersuchungen über die evangelische Geschichte: Ihre Quellen und den Gang ihrer Entwicklung*. 2nd ed. Tübingen: Mohr Siebeck, 1901.
Wengst, Klaus. *Bedrängte Gemeinde und verherrlichter Christus: Ein Versuch über das Johannesevangelium*. 3rd ed. Munich: Kaiser, 1990.
Werline, Rodney Alan. *Penitential Prayer in Second Temple Judaism: The Development of a Religious Institution*. Early Judaism and Its Literature 13. Atlanta: Scholars Press, 1998.
Westcott, Brooke Foss. *The Gospel according to St. John*. London: Murray, 1908.
Westerholm, Stephen. *Perspectives Old and New on Paul: The "Lutheran" Paul and His Critics*. Grand Rapids: Eerdmans, 2004.
Wheaton, Gerry. *The Role of Jewish Feasts in John's Gospel*, SNTSMS 162. Cambridge: Cambridge Univeristy Press, 2015.

Williams, Catrin H. *I Am He: The Interpretation of 'Anî Hû' in Jewish and Early Christian Literature*. WUNT 2/113. Tübingen: Mohr Siebeck, 2000.

———. "Patriarchs and Prophets Remembered: Framing Israel's Past in the Gospel of John." Pages 187–212 in *Abiding Words: The Use of Scripture in the Gospel of John*. Edited by Alicia D. Myers and Bruce G. Schuchard. RBS 81. Atlanta: SBL Press, 2015.

———. "John, Judaism, and 'Searching the Scriptures.'" Pages 77–100 in *John and Judaism: A Contested Relationship in Context*. Edited by R. Alan Culpepper and Paul N. Anderson. RBS 87. Atlanta: SBL Press, 2017.

Williams, Frank, trans. *The Panarion of Epiphanius of Salamis: Book I (Sects 1-46)*. 2nd ed. NHS 63. Leiden: Brill, 2009.

Wilson, Stephen G. *Leaving the Fold: Apostates and Defectors in Antiquity*. Minneapolis: Fortress, 2004.

Windisch, Hans. "John's Narrative Style." Pages 25–64 in *The Gospel of John as Literature: An Anthology of Twentieth-Century Perspectives*. Edited by Mark W. G. Stibbe. NTTS 17. Leiden: Brill, 1993.

Windsor, Lionel J. *Paul and the Vocation of Israel: How Paul's Jewish Identity Informs his Apostolic Ministry, with Special Reference to Romans*. BZNW 205. Berlin: de Gruyter, 2014.

Wrede, Wilhelm. *Charakter und Tendenz des Johannesevangeliums*. Tübingen: Mohr Siebeck, 1903.

———. *Paul*. Translated by Edward Lummis. London: Philip Green, 1907.

Yee, Gale A. *Jewish Feasts and the Gospel of John*. Zacchaeus Studies: New Testament. Wilmington, DE: Glazier, 1989.

Zetterholm, Karin Hedner and Anders Runesson, eds. *Within Judaism? Interpretive Trajectories in Judaism, Christianity, and Islam from the First to the Twenty-First Century*. Lanham, MD: Lexington Books/Fortress Academic, 2023.

Zimmermann, Ruben. "'The Jews': Unreliable Figures or Unreliable Narration?" Pages 71–109 in *Character Studies in the Fourth Gospel: Narrative Approaches to Seventy Figures in John*. Edited by Steven A. Hunt, D. Francois Tolmie, and Ruben Zimmermann. Grand Rapids: Eerdmans, 2016.

Index

Abraham: ancestor of the Jewish people, 34, 36, 42, 75; children of, 30, 44, 47; witness to Jesus, 45, 127, 135; as "your father" in relation to the Jewish people, 91–92
anti-Judaism/anti-Semitism, 1–3, 11–12, 17–18n18, 155
apostasy/apostates, 34, 38–40; national apostasy of Israel, 141; theme in the Gospel of John, 73–74
audience of Gospel, 115–18
authorial intention, 5–6

Birkat Haminim, 26, 32
Bultmann, Rudolf, 15–16n2, 64–65, 85–86

Caiaphas, 72, 94–96
chief priests, 45, 72, 74, 85; in Josephus, 68–69
children of God, 42, 73; nested hierarchy vs. transethnic identity, 86–87, 100n8
Christianity: break with Judaism, 27–28, 33–35, 109, 155; as counterpart to Judaism in the church fathers, 35–37
church fathers, 7, 35–37, 40–41, 134, 153–54; Epiphanius, 36–37, 40–41, 44; Ignatius of Antioch, 36–37; Irenaeus, 40, 117; Jerome, 36–37, 40; Justin Martyr, 37, 134; Tertullian, 36, 89, 117
collective memory theory, 136–37
covenant, 43–45, 131–33, 154; annulled, 6–7, 36, 153; restriction to Jews, 31

darkness, metaphor, 4, 76
Dead Sea Scrolls, 1–2, 28, 127
desert wandering narratives, 133–39
Deuteronomistic History/Deuteronomist, 131–33
devil: as father of those named "the Jews," 1, 4, 7, 70–74; and Judas, 73
disciples: Jewish identity, 96–99; Nathanael, 26, 46–47, 97; Peter, 42, 96–97, 117
dualism, 65–66, 76

ethnicity: connection with custom/practice, 37–40; Jewish self-understanding as an *ethnos*, 34–35; in relation to the "Jew" vs. "Judean" debate, 12–14

fourth evangelist: as creative author, 7–8; ethnic identity, 7–9; self-understanding, 5–7, 153–54

Galileans, 114–15
glory, 129–30, 134–39

God: faithfulness to covenant, 154; judgment of, 2–3, 73; love for enemies, 2–4; revealed by the Son, 93–94
Greeks: in the Gospel, 98–99; mercenaries allied with Alexander, 68; taxonomic order with Jews, 13, 75

hatred, 1–4
Hebrew prophets, 6, 44–45, 127–39, 154
historical criticism, 10
Holy Spirit, 76, 91–92, 141

Idumeans, 12, 111–13
implied author, 21–22nn45–46
intra-group criticism, 3, 17n13
intra-Jewish polemic, 27–31
irony, 30–31, 110–11
Isaiah: polemic, 127, 130–31; vision of God, 135–37
Israelites, 92, 96, 128–33, 139–41

Jerusalem, 15, 30, 68–69, 72–75, 98, 112–15
Jesus: as a deceiver, 38–39; identity as a Jew, 45–47, 96; uniqueness, 91–93
Jewish Christians, 48–49n8; Nazoraeans, 36, 40–41
Jewish festivals, 74, 115–16; evangelist's knowledge of, 9, 115
Jews: alleged stereotyping of, 64–66, 69, 75–76; fear of, 86, 98–99; meaning of term in antiquity, 13, 34–35; messianic Jews, 33–34; response to Jesus, 64–66, 75–76; translation of Greek term, 11–15
Johannine community, 4, 9–11, 26–33, 39, 45–48, 91–94
Josephus, 66–70, 74, 95–97, 112–14
Judaism, 2–3, 6–7, 13–15, 27–29, 35–37, 55n68
"within Judaism" movement, 103n28; John within Judaism, 6–7, 29, 155; Paul within Judaism, 90–91

law of Moses. *See* Torah
Lazarus, 70–71, 87, 152
love, 2–3, 76, 91

Marcion, 89
Martyn, J. L., 9, 25–27, 32, 40, 46, 151–55
Mary and Martha, 70–72
Moses, 88–89, 92–96, 129–34; encounter with God on Sinai, 134–40; as witness to Jesus, 44–47

narrative criticism, 8, 22n46, 79n18

Palestine, demographics of, 111–15
"parting of the ways" metaphor, 6–7, 47–48, 109–10
Paul, 153–54; as an accused apostate, 90; identity as a Jew, 42–44; portrayal in Acts, 95; question of Torah observance, 90–91
Pharisees, 71–72
Philo, 66–67, 74
Pilate, Pontius, 45, 83n50

Qumran, 142n5, 144n17

rabbis, 39–40
rebirth, metaphors for, 86–87
Reinhartz, Adele, 6–7, 27, 65, 86, 97, 153–54
religion, 33–35, 47; conversion in antiquity, 33–34; and Jewish identity, 14–15; sociology of, 2–4
religious schism model, 33–35, 45–48
remnant, 29, 38, 47, 141–42, 153–55

Sabbath, 89–90, 93
salvation, 3, 45–46, 63, 74
Samaritans, 70–71, 75, 88, 111–16
scripture, 6–10, 89, 129–30, 133, 141–42; as witness to Jesus, 44–45
sectarianism, 2–3, 110; Johannine sectarian mentality, 44–45, 47–48
self-ascription, 6, 155

sense and referent, 63, 66–69, 75
signs, 134–35, 138–39; book of, 129, 138, 141
social memory theory. *See* collective memory theory
source criticism, 7–8, 63–64
Stein, Edith, 33–34
supersessionism, 88–89, 100n8, 101n17, 153
synagogue expulsion, 9–10, 25–28, 47–48, 89; passages in the Gospel, 71–72
Synoptic Gospels: christology of, 99; terms for Jewish groups, 64, 109

temple, 88, 112–13; and Jewish identity, 12–13; loss of, 27–28
theophany, 134–36
third race, 41–44
Torah, 88–94; as central to Jewish identity, 37–39; in the church fathers, 36–37; Paul's relationship to, 90–91; as "your law," 86, 88, 91–92
two-level reading strategy, 26–27, 39, 154–55; and the audience of the Gospel, 116; criticism of, 32–33

the world, 1–4, 64–65, 76, 85–87, 116, 137

About the Author

Nathan Thiel, PhD (Marquette University, 2016), is an independent scholar who resides in Seymour, Wisconsin. His main areas of research are ancient Near Eastern and Mediterranean history and culture, with a focus on Second Temple Judaism and early Christianity. He is the author of articles on matters ranging from textual criticism of the Johannine epistles to Jewish identity formation in antiquity.